A FISHERMAN IN THE SADDLE

A FISHERMAN IN THE SADDLE

JULIAN ROUP

Copyright © 2021 Julian Roup.

ISBN 978-1-913762-92-6

First published in 2003 by Jacana Media.

A catalogue record for this book is available from the British Library.

No part of this publication may be reproduced, stored in a retrieval system, or transmitted in any form or by any means, electronic, mechanical, photocopying, recording, or otherwise, without written permission of the publisher.

All rights reserved including the right of reproduction in whole or in part in any form. The moral right of the author has been asserted.

EST. 2019
BLKDOG

www.blkdogpublishing.com

Also by Julian Roup:

Life in a Time of Plague:
A Coronavirus Lockdown Diary

Life in a Time of Plague is the story of Britain under the first 75 days of its unprecedented Covid-19 lockdown, seen from the author's rural East Sussex valley home in England.

From the refuge of a seemingly idyllic rural idyll, the book monitors in bleak and forensic detail the failure of the Government to protect Britain, and its woeful response at every stage of the pandemic.

The author's age and medical issues colour this diary with a dark humour, as his age group is most at risk. He is determined to make his 70th birthday at least, despite the thousands of deaths in Britain to date.

It is a quiet slow appreciation of the bright green spring and summer of 2020 in the English countryside, set against the horrors faced by frontline workers. However, what is most surprising is that amid the death, heartache and economic carnage, there is also a silver lining, a chance to simply stop and stare, and rethink our lives.

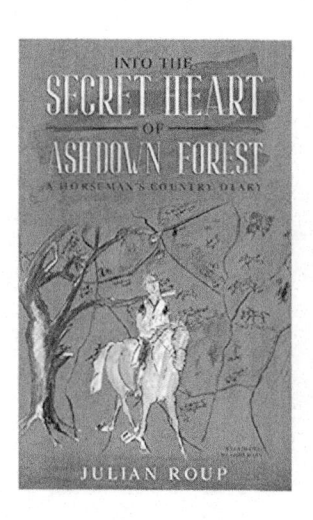

Into the Secret Heart of Ashdown Forest:
A Horseman's Country Diary

Into the Secret Heart of Ashdown Forest is a love letter after a forty-year affair. Wry, funny, moving and vivid, this memoir chronicles the life of the author and the ten square miles of country he calls his Kingdom. This book is as good as a brisk walk in the woods on an autumn day.

Written with love and passion, it is a hymn to landscape and freedom. It is a close and deep observation of the writer's adopted country, the fabled Ashdown Forest in East Sussex, England, (the home of Winnie the Pooh), where he has lived and ridden for the past forty years.

His gift is the ability to take you deep into the landscapes that make this place resonate in his heart: its streams, woods, heathlands. You meet its literary residents, A.A, Milne, Sir Arthur Conan Doyle, Ezra Pound and W.B. Yeats. You get beneath its skin among the networks of fungi that allow the trees to speak. You taste its foods, meet its locals, both the living and the ghosts, and see its huge importance during the plague year 2020-21 through the pandemic lockdowns.

Praise for *Life in a Time of Plague*

"It is a wonderful account of the time of coronavirus; I especially like the reverie at the end with its sense of time regained in that Proustian way. Julian Roup has a great gift for evocation and description."
Bernard O'Donoghue, Whitbread Prize winning Irish poet, Oxford don, author of *Seamus Heaney and the Language of Poetry*.

"Witty, incisive, irreverent, iconoclastic."
George Plumptre, CEO National Garden Scheme, author of *The English Country House Garden* and *Royal Gardens of Europe*.

"Journalist Julian Roup tells the story of his corner of rural Britain under the first 75 days of lockdown. His beautiful writing captures the way the world slowed down amid the strangeness of the new reality. The book is a snapshot of the details that make up the fabric of history – thinking back on memories of friends passed, observations on humanity and the natural world in his East Sussex valley, and of course his lovely horse Callum. Riders will appreciate how horses – in both reality and in our imagination – serve as an escape."
Horse & Hound.

Praise for *A Fisherman in the Saddle*

"This is story telling charged with raw emotion and always a deep appreciation for the sheer beauty and the enduring magic of nature which transcends politics, implosion of families, emigration. Horses, the author says, became 'my nation, my friends, my identity, my medicine. When I am in the saddle I'm home."
Robyn Cohen, *The Cape Times*.

"Every now and then a gem of a new book lands on my desk: sometimes but rarely a diamond. This is one. I laughed. I

cried. I was deeply moved. This is among the best books I have ever read about fishing, horses, growing up, the pain of maturity, leaving one's homeland and the things that make up the richness of life."
Dave Bristow, *Getaway Magazine*.

"The ability of horses to help and heal is boundless. In A Fisherman in the Saddle, Julian Roup explains how he feels about horses. 'The feeling of elation, of freedom, of excitement was indescribable. It was like being given wings and the gift of flight. I was hooked for life.' I know the feeling, and I hope many others discover it for themselves."
Octavia Pollock, *Country Life*.

Praise for *Boerejood*

"Brilliant, just terrific, really very, very good. Engaged, intelligent, personal, fast moving and funny."
Graham Watts, *Financial Times*, London.

"A delicate exploration of a society 10 years after the end of apartheid and the onset of majority rule. Roup has no nostalgia for the old regime, but immense sadness for the embattlement of the Afrikaans language and culture."
John Lloyd, Editor, *FT Weekend Magazine*.

To my father, Leon Roup, who made it all possible;

To Pascoe Grenfell who taught me to cast and so much more;

To Jay and Guy Louw who encouraged me to reel in the words;

To Herman, my brother, the best company, straight, on the rocks;

And to Henry Vel, Martin Tshila and Piet Sedgwick who gave more than asked.

Acknowledgements

There are the ponies and horses to thank, of course. Without them, there would be no book. I have loved you all.

There are all those people and places that made my years of fishing such a rich mine of memories. A special thanks to my father, Leon Roup, for putting a fishing rod in my hand; Pascoe Grenfell, for his wisdom, guidance and humour, and my brother, Herman Roup, who helped to make fishing magic. To Elise Louw, my mother, for whom no thanks will ever repay the many gifts she gave me. "Liza, agteros is in die kraal."

There is Maggie Davey of Jacana, my publisher who first recognised that there might be something here. For a first-time author that is a gift beyond price. To Nicky, at BlkDog, who has given me the chance to give the book new life with this second edition.

To Jane Murray Brown, on whose Irish connections and knowledge I drew shamelessly. To Tracey Hawthorne, who so kindly pointed me in the direction of Maggie Davey. To Guy Louw, my brother-in-law, who provided a first edit for factual accuracy and whose enthusiasm drove me on, a great debt is owed. Any mistakes remaining are mine! To my sister, Jay Louw, who suggested the direction for the book, and then offered great encouragement, thank you.

And finally, to Janice Warman, wife, lover, friend, and my first and best editor, thank you for your constant encouragement and specifically your work on this book.

Julian Roup
East Sussex
July 2021

Foreword

A *Fisherman in the Saddle* is a meditation on joy; it is a return to those things that have given me the greatest pleasure in life – horses and fishing. Both have been lifesavers in their time, like medicine in their effect.

I have always said that riding is cheaper than seeing a shrink and I mean it. I find contemplation or meditation on their own difficult things to do, but when they come as a by-product of riding or fishing it works for me.

I left South Africa for political reasons in 1980 with my wife, Janice Warman, who shared my viewpoint. We never thought that we would live to see a free South Africa under majority rule. But 14 years after our departure we watched joyously with millions of others as Nelson Mandela walked free.

Yet there is a sadness that remains. They say that you can take the boy out of Africa but you cannot take Africa out of the boy. That is certainly true of me, and so a part of me is forever in Africa and I see with a bi-focal vision, half in Africa half in Europe. This book also considers this issue; the emotional cost of emigration.

The book was born out of the death of a horse, Sebastian and the arrival of Chancer, who replaced him. I was 49 at the time. I was deeply troubled by the death of Sebastian. It was the first and I hope the last time that I have to have a horse put down. But the habit of a lifetime is not given up that easily and after a few months I went in search of a new horse and Chancer's arrival gave me such a shot in the arm that I started writing about all the horses that have enriched my life.

Since then there have been other horses about whom I have written in other books – 'Life in a Time of Plague' and into the Secret Heart of Ashdown Forest'.

A Fisherman in the Saddle follows no plan or pattern, other than that of my life. It is a series of lucky dips, with I trust some prizes worth having. If you have loved the outdoors and found solace under the sky, then this book is for you. And if you have loved horses and landscape, or the sea and fishing, then you will find a bonus here.

In some strange way this book wrote itself. It was as if some dam had burst and all the stories of my horses, my friends, came rushing out. And once I had written the last one Janine and Guy Louw, my sister and brother-in-law, suggested that I match the horse stories with my other great love, sea-fishing. So I had the pleasure of mentally revisiting all those places and people and fishing expeditions that have meant so much to me.

In this new re-published edition of the book by my British publisher, BLKDOG Publishing there are three new fishing stories in Seawitched that are the three chapters before the final one.

Writing this book has been great fun, and has given me a lot of pleasure, I hope its pages bring you pleasure too.

A Fisherman in the Saddle

SEAWITCHED: PART ONE

Julian Roup

Julian's children Dominic and Imogen, 2005

Prologue

Cape Town is a city at the edge of tides. It is a marginal place, lying as it does where three great worlds collide – Africa to the north, the Indian Ocean to the east, and the Atlantic to the west. What a place to grow up a fisherman!

It is cosmopolitan, yet it lies at the edge of the world. This beautiful city is washed by powerful currents and survives by clinging crab-like to its mountain buttress. A place that is all edges, it is inhabited by folk living interesting lives.

The Cape's first inhabitants, known as *strandlopers*, lived off the tides' rich pickings, leaving as their monuments heaps of empty seashells, the only sign of their passing. The Hottentots, another Khoi people, were pastoralists, herding their fat-tailed sheep along these shores. They too are gone, though their genes live on in the present inhabitants.

Over centuries, this thinly populated place was inhabited by other peoples living precariously, pushed out to the edge of the known world by circumstance, ambition, persecution, wanderlust, Dutch and German merchant adventurers, French Huguenots, Malays, East European Jews, younger sons and remittance men, the black sheep of their families. There were also those who looked for land, new beginnings, new challenges and wider horizons. They made a mixed society of people who liked space and enjoyed crossing frontiers.

To the north, black tribes pushed south, also looking

for new country, eager to escape the black Napoleon, Shaka Zulu. The white and black tides met in the northern reaches of the Cape and the sound of that meeting has yet to die down. Its turbulence washes people back and forth across the land and everywhere they cling on, waiting for calm.

But however harsh the environment, there are those who adapt and thrive. In the turmoil of the Cape, both ashore and at sea, there are winners, creatures who are energised by the very clash of waves and the extra oxygen that action generates. They seem driven by an awareness of ebb and flow, of the certainty of change, the liquid pendulum of time.

To survive at the sea's margins requires special adaptation, a crab-like tenacity, a tough shell, an opportunistic lifestyle and, above all, adaptability. I like to think that I learned much from observing life in this place where I first opened my eyes.

I grew up at the tip of Africa, on shores washed by the South Atlantic and Indian Oceans and saw that my society was very much like the sea; just as unpredictable, it rose and fell, was storm tossed and calm by turns. Those who would survive had to be tenacious or be swept away. Those who gave in had one sure end; their empty husks were washed up, lying above the tide-wrack for beachcombers to muse over, among the white sand, sea grass and flies.

I took heart from the creatures of the sea's edge, the small tough things of the tide pools, periwinkles, mussels, limpets, coral worms and the small rockfish, dancing to the music of change on each tide. They were pushed first one way and then the other, managing in their small worlds fringed with green, brown and gold seaweeds to live a life vibrant with energy.

They were beautiful too, I thought, especially the starfish, the exotic tasselled anemones, the spiky purple and green sea urchins. All had a place and a function in the society of the sea. To play their part they had but to live and die, breed and perish, eat and be eaten. Finally, they lay as part of some dazzling beach, reflecting light beneath the southern sky. I admired their beauty and their ability to live with grace within the harsh rules that governed their lives.

This life of the seashore was seemingly indestructible. After storms, the filthy sea-froth, khaki brown, piled six feet high, a shaking, shivering, salt blancmange, staining all that lay beneath it the same dreary colour, until sun and rain had once more cleansed the pools and a multiplicity of colour and life lay exposed in silent, swaying beauty.

In the changeless tide pools, haunt of crayfish, octopus, eels and crabs, life continued despite the unremitting harshness. There was a clearly defined food chain with seagulls, cormorants, seals and sharks patrolling these seas above and below water, harvesting an unending crop. At high tide, the bigger fish also took their toll. The creatures of these pools were truly the quick and the dead. It did not depress me; it was simply how the world was.

On land, it was no different; there too a chain of life was evident, there too were predators and prey, as well as beauty.

Growing up in the Cape was a gift that has lasted a lifetime. It is a cross as well, for wherever you wander from the Cape; you never find its like again. But fishing connects you. When I cast a line in the sea, I find I am back, once more. Once again, I feel the old excitement, the old expectation in the pull and sway of the sea, this wonder that connects places and which makes up most of our world, this blue planet – home of fishermen.

Julian's father, Leon, on his horse in the early 1930s

LEARNING THE BUSINESS

Like any skill worth having, fishing presents a boy with a fantastic amount of learning; luckily, it also provides the best motivation in the world – catching fish. The hunting instinct cannot be dead within us if you can get an eight-year-old boy to keep at it, learning to make trace, learning to cast, learning to untangle crows'-nests in his reel, while around him adults and others more proficient than himself are catching fish.

A proper fishing apprenticeship is one of the toughest things for a boy to handle. If he succeeds, he masters not only the necessary skills to catch fish, but a set of rules that will serve him well in life. It teaches him, amongst other things, to manage on his own, to observe with care how others do things, to become co-ordinated enough to cast well, patience to outwait fish, the self-control needed to untangle a snarled-up reel amid good fishing – it's always amid good fishing – the self-control that stops him whining when he is tired, cold, wet and has just lost the biggest fish he's ever hooked, the need to respect others' space, to limit his talking, to avoid bragging, to lie a little but not a lot, and to observe nature. He learns, too, the need to keep at it, the harder working the fisherman, the more he catches. And he learns something about luck. No less an authority than Napoleon was known for asking about a general, 'Is he lucky?' Luck helps – a lot.

If a boy learns these things – and most fishing types were boys once, or girls – he or she is doing well, and the catching of fish is just a great bonus on top of everything else. I was no exception to this rule, though whining and lying and bragging are qualities that took the longest to master – now and then I still slip up on these.

My apprenticeship began, as do the best ones, beside my father. He was a keen fisherman who would slip away most weekends for a spot of surf-angling on the beaches near our home in Cape Town. He'd head for Swartklip, Strandfontein or Betty's Bay. Later, he would build a house at Cape Infanta at the mouth of the Breede River and a shack at Hamerkop on the Bredasdorp coast.

He did me three great kindnesses as a father: he bought me a pony, he took me along on his fishing trips and he introduced me to Pascoe Grenfell, his fishing pal. Pascoe would regularly interrupt his own fishing to give me advice and help on casting and would untangle my over-winds. As a result, he won my everlasting respect and love. Pascoe Grenfell was my first hero. An Anglo-Irishman, short, stocky, with reddish hair and a very pale skin, which burned easily in the sun, he was a former Wing Commander in the RAF and had flown Spitfires during the Battle of Britain. What more could a boy ask for? He wore hairy ex-army surplus khaki with a red bandana at his neck, a cream Panama hat with the brim turned down all the way round and he smoked Mills cigarettes which came in yellow tins – ideal for storing fish-hooks.

Time and again he would show me how to swing hook, line and sinker in an easy, effortless-seeming cast that took the line way out beyond the breaking surf into deep water. He would offer constructive criticism and praise in equal measure. He would help me untangle crows' nests beyond my abilities, and he would do it all with a quiet, understated humour.

He had style, a great sense of humour, and a temper, which I never saw, but which in later years I heard the odd tale about. In his seventieth year, he knocked a man down for some reason or other, a good one, I'm sure. And I recall the glee I felt on hearing from my father about Pascoe's treatment of a driver who stole a parking space he considered his. Stupidly, the man left his keys in the ignition, perhaps intending to run into a shop and directly out again. But by the time he returned, he had four flat tyres and his keys were down a storm water drain, while Pascoe, the perfect innocent, stood idly by, whistling a favourite tune – 'If You Knew Suzie!'

He enjoyed mangling the odd Afrikaans word which took his fancy. He'd say, 'I must just stop at the *winkel*,' pronouncing the word with a 'w' instead of correctly with a 'v'. It tickled me greatly that he was popping into an English shellfish, a winkle, rather than a shop, to buy something.

He had a sort of twitchy relationship with Ferdie Bergh, the huge old former rugby Springbok who also owned a house at Infanta and who had arranged the Hamerkop deal, where he too had a cottage. Hamerkop – that fisherman's paradise – swarmed with life. One of its particular pleasures for my father and Pascoe were the numbers of wild oysters, which crowded its rocks. I never took to oysters, but they would snack on them right from the rocks. The problem was that Ferdie, who had after all 'discovered' Hamerkop, felt proprietorial about what was now a shared joint enterprise – ten miles of pristine coastline, cut off from the rest of the world by a mountain range and a hellish seaward approach of jumbled rock and collapsed cliff at either end.

It was rare to find any of the other three cottages occupied, and I suppose each family with a stake in the place felt it was their private fiefdom. Ferdie certainly did. One of his 'rulings' was that the oysters were to be conserved – a good and sensible thought. But to Pascoe – not a great fan of rules – the fact that the rule had been decreed by Ferdie was enough to guarantee its flouting.

On one particular trip, he and my father had their cook, ghillie, and general factotum, an affable and shrewd Xhosa man named Martin Tshila, whip up an oyster feast for them. They ate dozens, each with thinly sliced brown bread, lemon and a dash of paprika or Worcestershire sauce. The rattle of the empty shells in the bins by their feet went on long into the night. I must have fallen asleep in the one-room shack which held three beds, a couch, a dining table, and one or two armchairs, all lit by mellow gas lamps that illuminated the dried *blaasoppie* fish, rotating slowly from a line to the ceiling, a fetish which was apparently capable of predicting the weather – how, I never fathomed.

The next morning, both men appeared a little off-colour and were slow to get going. I headed down the beach for Monument Rock on my own with a rod, bait and the raring enthusiasm of a youth set free in the palace of his dreams. At lunchtime, I returned to find Ferdie Bergh ensconced with a whisky in hand promising Dad and Pascoe the oyster feast to end all oyster feasts that night! His promised generosity seemed to fall on less than grateful ears as the two midnight feasters made cheesy grins and said they looked forward to it.

Ferdie's feast was quite a production. He had had his hired help scour the rocks and balanced precariously on our dining table was a rock-shelled castle of seafood, surrounded by buttresses of bread and lemon and condiments. The buckets, empty once more, stood ready by three chairs, awaiting the action.

It was at that point that my father discovered that he had developed a tummy bug and much as it frustrated him, he feared that oysters would be the end of him. Damn! To Pascoe's everlasting credit he braced up to that table and made a trencherman's assault on the walls and turrets of that seemingly impregnable redoubt. He ate for England. The next day, Pascoe was not on best form; in fact he cried off fishing for a day or two and sat nursing himself, sipping concoctions of his own devising.

Ferdie could not resist a dig. 'Hey, Pascoe, not feeling so good, hey? Don't they teach you how to eat in England?' Pascoe kept *shtum*; a statue of Buddha would have looked livelier.

My father rather patted himself on the back for avoiding this martyrdom by food. But whenever there was an issue of precedence in the future between Pascoe and my father, the former would remind the latter that he had saved their bacon and would take his due. The whole thing amused them greatly and became a kind of benchmark for guile, cunning, and sheer gut-wrenching stomach.

Pascoe was one of those people who seem to live a charmed life, constructing from it the raw material for the amusement of others. He told a story which I'm still not sure about. He had married Joan, an identical twin, and said that he was fairly sure it was Joan. Whether this was true, or the idea simply took his fancy, I still don't know. But at the age of eight it struck me as nothing short of calamitous.

Anyway, he was the one who taught me most about fishing. He was the one who would wade into the water to gaff my fish and he would be the one whose 'Bad luck, old boy!' would appease my aching heart when I lost one. It does a lot for a boy, being treated as an equal by a war hero. I have a picture of myself with him and Joan on the green baize notice board above my desk. He is aged 80 in the photo and is dying. He sits there in blue pyjamas and a maroon gown with red and yellow piping round the cuffs and lapels. His reading glasses are in his clasped hands, his thick neck and bullish shoulders are still there and his blue eyes still have that look of absolute bloody mischief that so entranced me. I miss him a lot.

Like all true heroes, he saved my life once. My father kept a light 10-foot glass-fibre dingy at Infanta for the occasional spot of river fishing. We used it seldom, preferring the superb rock angling. However, one sunny morning we hauled the boat out of the garage and towed it down to a launch site on the river, well upstream from the treacherous river-mouth sandbar.

What is it about boat fishing? When it's good, everything in life seems like a rehearsal for the moment when you are finally, rod in hand, there. You are then truly in the moment, the sun, the pewter water, the company of other fishermen, the gentle sway of the boat, that promising river/sea smell and the feeling that finally you are in water deep enough to harbour anything, water beyond your best casting length and then some.

And then it gets even better as the fish start to come in. You don't want a lot of fish. Two men and a boy in a 10-foot boat is much too crowded for frenzied fishing, but a nice steady number of up-to-size fish with a good spread of varieties is simply the best thing. Even then, it is capable of getting better. One of you gets into something truly big, kob, he says, and you reel your line in to give him space to play the fish, ducking as the line sweeps over and round, sometimes under the boat and away again. A good boat fight is like watching a slowed-down version of orchestral conducting. Fewer head nods, perhaps.

We fished like that on this day, anchoring off the hotel on the far side of the river for lunch. We noted that the wind had picked up and that the tide was ebbing strongly, the combination kicking up a sizeable chop. A mile downstream, you could see the breakers on the bar baring their teeth. A dark cloud moved in from the sea and we felt the first drops of rain, which promised a deluge shortly. Seabirds were flying inland.

At that point, we noticed that the anchor had started to drag; we were heading down past the hotel, fast. We packed up quickly and hauled up the anchor. I was in the prow, Pascoe amidships, and Dad by the three-horsepower Seagull engine. He pulled the ripcord of the starter; nothing happened. He pulled at it again and again. Now we were getting dangerously close to the bar approach, the current had us and the chop was sending water into the boat, the rain was lashing down so that Dad's glasses were totally fogged up and streaming. At that point, both men told me to put the single life preserver over my head and tie it on. Dad tried again. Nothing.

At that point, Pascoe changed places with Dad. We drifted helplessly, broadside on to the waves, ever closer to the bar and certain death. I was not a strong swimmer and, in that turmoil, knew I wouldn't stand a chance. A great sadness descended on me.

I'm not sure exactly what Pascoe was doing at this

point, if he was letting the flooded engine clear on its own or drying the plugs, but then he ripped once more, and the engine spluttered into life. In that mad tide-race, the little engine barely held its own. We stayed put for what seemed like ages, and then slowly, agonisingly, we began to inch clear, heading upstream at a long diagonal for the south shore where Martin Tshila danced and gesticulated. It was a damned close-run thing. Back at the house, I tasted whisky for the first time.

In quieter moments, Pascoe told me that as a boy he would fish for trout and salmon near his home at Ard na sidhe – The High Place of the Fairies – in the lee of the McGillicuddy's Reeks in southern Ireland. What magic those names conjured up for me. Many, many years later, I visited his childhood home, now an expensive hotel frequented by wealthy Germans. It was a bit of a pilgrimage. The strange thing is that Pascoe died on that very day, the day that I walked in his youthful footsteps for the first and last time.

Even now, if I am hassled or losing it, I can hear his voice. 'Steady on old lad, steady, the Buffs!' I can see his cast, a work of art for such a short man, taking his line out and out and out. I can see the rod in the crook of his left arm as he lights a cigarette. How these things stay with you.

He was gallant, and he taught me something else along with the fishing lore; he taught me just enough about England and Ireland to make them seem the perfect places, his places, though he had not been back since the end of the war. Perhaps it is no great surprise that I live there now. In a way, they are the biggest fish I ever landed.

Julian Roup

Julian surf casting at Newhaven, Sussex, 2019

Boyhood by the Sea

The house was called 'Just Ashore' and it was well named; at high tide, the waves would wash against the 10-foot high retaining wall that fronted the rocky beach. One could stand on the deck above it as though on a ship and cast a line into the turbulent, creamy waves crashing over the great craggy rocks that were a feature of this beach village, Bloubergstrand, ten miles from Cape Town. Right in front of the house itself there was a double tidal pool, fed by two breaks in the rocks through which the South Atlantic tides of Table Bay pushed and surged with impatient waves. This is where I first met the sea on first name terms and where my lifelong love of it was born.

The horizon to the north was open, with just one or two guano-spattered rock islands half a mile offshore. Due west and five miles out to sea, directly in front of our deck, was the prison of Robben Island with its lighthouse; to the south, the great flat-topped sphinx of Table Mountain. The east lay behind the house and the rising sun would blaze through its roadside windows and deep into the green sea, which, when still, allowed the light to penetrate, illuminating it like a jewel. It was a privileged place to be a boy. Blues, sea greens, surf-white, silver moon-glitter, gold and crimson sunsets painted the backdrop to my life.

I was born in 1950 and spent my early summers in our holiday house by the sea. I grew up with a community of sea creatures as neighbours. I suppose I must have seemed rather un-neighbourly, as I spent much of my time trying to catch them. But as they were doing pretty much the same thing themselves, devouring their neighbours, it did not seem that bad.

I learned the geography of those sea-rocks intimately. I knew, by the age of ten, each and every inch of them, the flat ledges on which it was comfortable to sit or lie while fishing or dreaming; the good places to find bait, coral worm, black mussel, redbait, periwinkles, and crayfish. The coral worm colonies, grey-tunnelled mounds between the rocks, washed twice a day by the rising tides, would crunch under the soles of my tackies, the tennis shoes I wore. The blue-green, muscled, steel-headed coral worm was dynamite bait – fish could not resist it. Then there was redbait, succulent fleshy lumps found in leathery, nippled pouches at the most dangerous of the sea-facing rock ledges. Cutting redbait was exciting at best and dangerous at worst; people drowned cutting redbait. The redbait colonies were a laugh though, spouting thin arcs of seawater indecently from their nipples.

The rock pools and gullies provided innumerable crevices and secret hiding places beneath the water for small slippery rockfish, crabs and crayfish, some of which grew to a massive size. It took a brave boy to stick his hand deep into these sea crevices, for instead of crayfish antennae one would, from time to time, touch a small octopus, a suckerfish or a sea eel, whose vile purple-blue colour convinced me it was electric. My younger brother, Herman, was far braver than me in this respect and he would soon overtake my crayfishing exploits, using flippers and snorkel to get himself eye to eye with this quarry.

My father was a dedicated surf-angler, and he kitted us out from the earliest age with the gear necessary to take on the local fish species. We began with klipvis and haarders. The first had to be caught singly by hook, while the other could be gathered in their dozens in a homemade net, an old towel serving the purpose more often than not. They were whitebait, but it would take me many years to recognise them

A Fisherman in the Saddle

as such on a plate in southern Europe.

The memory of those days is imprinted in my flesh. I can still feel the sun-warmed rock beneath my thighs, and the moles on my back stand testimony to the fact that all I wore for months on end was a bathing costume. I can feel the sun and the wind on my skin, feel my eyes crinkle against the glare, feel the ice-cold sea in which my feet dangled, tickled and caressed by swirling seaweed. I was at one with this world, totally focused on the sea and its creatures.

'Watch the sea, watch your back, keep an eye on it always.' The warning had been drilled into us. My sister and brother and I grew up with a healthy respect for the sea. We had stood by enough drowned children to know with cold certainty the deadly seriousness of the warning. Despite this, the sea caught us out from time to time, the seventh wave now and then giving us a salutary fright. The sea took few locals, usually it was the children of upcountry visitors to whom the sea seemed a wet funfair of unbridled delight, and not the death trap that it could so easily be.

A dead child on a sunny beach is a shocking thing, once seen never forgotten. They may not know it, but their deaths kept me safe. I watched the sea with great respect and learned to know its every mood.

One day, the sea rose and entered the house. The afternoon suddenly became dark with vast, grey clouds racing up to engulf Table Mountain, lightning slashed and thunder boomed. The lights in the house flickered and died. It was exciting at first but as the wind picked up and the sea began to menace the house, it was less so. My parents sent me with a maid to buy candles from the one shop in the village. We lit these and made a fire in the fireplace, something unheard of. The sea in front of the house seemed to climb over itself to claw at us. It felt as though we must be swept away. My father ordered sandbags to be filled and placed against the seaward-facing glass doors. And still the sea rose. There is something uncanny and very frightening in seeing waves bear down on you from above head height, crashing into the living room rather than onto the beach. Through the night the wind screamed, while the sea tore and thrashed and savaged us.

The house stood firm. With the morning light, we saw that the only real damage was to the carpets in the rooms at the front of the house. Around the house lay what looked like the remains of a giant's feast – filthy froth of the past night's passion, and all manner of flotsam and jetsam washed up onto the sea-road and beyond. At one point, the sea had encircled the house, wave-wet tentacles tugging at its foundations. But the house stood firm.

Seeing what the Atlantic was capable of made us truly respect and fear it a little, watching it with new eyes. Not only would it take sacrificial victims, too ignorant or unlucky to know better, it was capable of coming in search of you, right in the safety of your home. It was a salutary lesson for a beachcombing boy.

Let me describe the near boundaries of this world. To the front and left of the house was a rock the size of a small aircraft carrier, about ten feet above the water and fairly flat. Like all the rocks in the vicinity, it was a deep maroon colour – a mix between raw and cooked liver with chunks of cream-and-white marl here and there. To the front and right of the house was an even larger equivalent. Both of these rocks made good fishing platforms but were surrounded by water at high tide, so a watch had to be kept to avoid being marooned. Between these two monsters lay half a dozen jumbled rocks each the size of a small house, none practical as fishing posts as they were always surrounded by water and heaving beds of kelp, long black-brown tubes which we called sea-bamboo.

My earliest fishing exploits were with a simple handline, a reel of nylon, a lead sinker and a small hook. Using a freshly crushed periwinkle from the rocks for bait, I caught the red-brown or green-grey paisley patterned rockfish whose outsize mouths could accommodate a surprisingly large hook and bait. On fine nylon and hauling by hand, they gave a child a tremendous thrill. Most were no bigger than four inches long, but occasionally I would haul in a whopper at around six inches. Most I threw back but occasionally I'd put them into a freshly filled rock pool within the rock I was

A Fisherman in the Saddle

sitting on – a sort of holding tank as big as a small swimming pool.

The water was so crystal clear that at low tide one could glimpse the fish lying on the gravelly or sandy bottom and could place the bait right in front of them. There would be a feeding flurry as others dashed out of the kelp. A quick jerk and another fish would rocket heavenward.

People who have never fished describe it as boring. I was never bored. Even when things were quiet with nothing biting, there was so much to see; the constant movement of the water, the incoming waves, the swirling kelp. All of this bore messages about the change in the tide, the state of the wind and the currents. Now and then, a cormorant would land on one of the nearby offshore rocks to dry its wings in the sun and wind. Just beyond the first line of breaking surf, schools of porpoises would parade past up the coast, the curve of their dorsal fins rising and falling in unison. Occasionally, one would leap clear, or a pair would surf down the face of a wave.

Ashore, there was interest too. There was a fairly steady parade of people walking the water's edge, picking up and inspecting smooth pieces of wood, sea-glass, seashells or dry cast-off crab and crayfish shells. Now and then one of them would come over for a chat, asking how the fishing was. Above were the ceaselessly patrolling seagulls, with beady eyes and raucous cries, keeping a close lookout for your bait or catch. Out in the bay there was the movement of ships – tankers, cargo boats, passenger liners and yachts coming and going from the harbour in Cape Town.

Enveloping me was the overwhelming smell of the sea, rich in iodine. Now and then, the tantalising smell of barbecue would be carried on the breeze – usually the farmer's sausage, *boerewors,* and chops. This was a community of big eaters, farmers who came down after their wheat and fruit harvest to holiday in their cottages by the sea, and they did themselves proud. Each family would have its own secret marinade and methods for preparing barbecues. Wood was important, some swearing by the local Port Jackson, while the more discerning would only use old vine stumps and cut-offs.

Living by the sea, you become attuned to its moods, its phases and its sounds. A shift in any of these quickly gets your attention, as your life depends on noticing such changes. The colour of the sea would darken instantly as clouds came and went or the wind rose and fell. What in one minute had been a picture of calm, a blue lake with spangles reflecting the sun, would suddenly be a green-grey soup with waves seeking you out on your perch. Alertness was all. Familiarity taught you comfort with this reality, but, like a lion tamer with an old partner, one part of your mind was always watchful.

Almost as powerful a presence as the sea was the wind, for this could be a very windy place. Here, the wind could blow for days on end. It generally meant an end to fishing. High wind is death to fishing, as it bows your line into a great arc and the ability to feel a fish bite instantly is lost, and so your sensitive attachment to every movement affecting your tackle is blunted. Casting, too, is hampered by wind, with the distance limited or the direction diverted. And the wind's tugging like a fretful child tires you, shifting the focus back on yourself, away from the sea and fishing. But, when the wind stopped, this sea world was reborn, the fresh quiet filled with boundless opportunities.

One of these was crayfishing. Crayfish were so numerous that at low tide you could see them among the kelp about their business if you knew where to sit. With an incoming tide, larger crayfish would appear, making for the safety and choice feeding spots under the coral worm mounds. Now and then, when expecting guests from up country for whom crayfish was a great treat, my mother would ask my brother and me to bring her a dozen or so. It was usually the work of moments. They would be popped into a huge cauldron of boiling seawater and cooked in minutes. Later, they would be served cold with mayonnaise or hot with butter.

Now and then, the sea would throw up something special. I remember waking up one morning to find a large black seal perched in front of a neighbour's house. It must have been injured in a fight for it had a number of lacerations on its body. A small group of people kept watch nearby – but not too close. Its watchful stance and wicked teeth kept us well clear of its space. Later in the day it lolloped back to the sea and slipped away. Years later, seeing the first astronauts on the moon I was reminded of that seal, a distant traveller that had briefly graced my world.

For a shy boy with few friends, the sea is a marvellous playmate. You could never be bored, as it provided endless things to do. If fishing palled, you could collect a particular type of flat, knobbled seaweed that could be turned into pointed piping bags by slipping a finger in between two layers and opening them out, and then by making a tiny hole at one end, hey presto, you had a seaweed water-pistol.

There were shark's eggs to find, always empty, but you lived in hope. There was an endless array of things to make with seashells, glue and paint. There were smooth, round, flat, sun-warmed stones to skip on water or to bombard a stick with. There was the inspection round to make of the many small tidal pools on the rocks, perfect worlds with sea anemones, sea urchins, crabs and fish, replenished by each tide.

There was the bright yellow Indian canoe to launch on the tidal pool, watching the sea creatures and like them learning to ride the sea. There were the secret private places where the smooth maroon rocks provided hollows – a perfect fit for your bottom – an ideal place to sit and read or dream. There was a choice of small coves and large beaches. There were curves of crushed shell, pure white sand beaches, pebbly beaches and beaches piled high with throwing stones.

This was my patch. Small wonder, then, that I grew up loving the sea and fishing. If I think of the future years, the miles to drive, the fishing paraphernalia, the rigmarole of getting to particular and admittedly awkward fishing places, the need to open, air, provision, staff, and run fishing shacks, and the vehicles that took you there, the need for special and particular types of bait requiring cooling or freezing and all that this entails, it's a wonder that fishing maintained its hold on me.

But there is such a thing as sea fever – one can be sea-witched. The feeling that comes on you at first sight of the sea, the heightened senses, the quickened pulse, feeling the water for temperature, checking of tide tables, shaking out of rods from canvas covers, selecting the best tackle for the day, the rod, the reel, the back-up rod and reels, the selection of nylon line with a choice of breaking strain, the boxes of equipment, elasticised cotton for securing bait, the spare hooks, and sinkers, and lures for spinning, the knives, the bait boards, the swivels, the hand-cleaning clothes, the sunscreen, the caps and hats, the food and drink; the windcheaters and the raingear. The sunglasses. It is a never-ending list.

As a boy, I walked out of the house, picked up my handline and went fishing. It was all so simple then. I'd climb my favourite rock, bait up and send my line and my hopes into the magical wishing well of the sea. As the fish came up, I'd hold them high for the inspection and applause of my mother or father sitting on the deck just yards away. Fishing had me hooked.

Not just the fishing

Considering the amount of time you actually have a line in the water, it's amazing the hold fishing can have on you. The thing is, fishing has a great deal to do with ritual, though you would search long and hard to find a fisherman who would admit to that. But the good ones, the truly passionate ones, the real aficionados, the cognoscenti of fishing, would know exactly what it is you refer to.

My blooding into the fraternity of fishermen began when I was about seven or eight, I suppose, a boy already a bit lost at SACS Junior School, where Mr Hunter, the head, made much of rugby and cricket achievements. Sometimes I think that if educationalists stuck to education, instead of sport, there would be many more great sportsmen about. There is something about teachers – never the most popular figures in the world – acting as recruiting sergeants for team sports that has something about it of army drill sargeants, doing head counts. Know what I mean? Teachers and I did not get on well.

With this going on in the background, an invitation to join my father and his fishing mate for a day out was more than a little exciting. Pascoe Grenfell was, after all, a Battle of Britain Spitfire pilot. I was kitted out with a light rod and reel, a fishing saddle with the belt wound round my waist twice and still hanging down to my knees, on my head a version of the Foreign Legion desert cap with a flap down my neck, suntan oil, a jersey, and a windcheater.

It's at this point, with the basics sorted, that you start looking for luck, whatever your age, for signs, and signals, reading into things perhaps more than they deserve, looking for pointers, bribing the oracle. If fishing is a little bit like gambling, and it *is* a bit like that, it's hardly surprising that fishermen all have their fetishes, their beliefs, their superstitions. You make a deal with yourself – two red Volkswagens mean I've got a good chance today. None show. Okay, let's make that two in the next ten miles – and so on. Why do we do that? I'm not sure, but we do. I know I did.

Generally, at around seven, Pascoe would arrive and we would pile into Dad's turquoise Land Rover, Pascoe at the wheel. We'd head out through Lansdowne, and Philippi and then out into the sand-dune country that is now Mitchell's Plain and Khayelitsha, stopping briefly to engage four-wheel drive and sometimes to deflate tyres a mite, if the conditions merited it. Then slowly, rocking from side to side, we would head along the single-track sand paths for Swartklip, climbing and descending dunes and brushing through overgrown Port Jackson bush. I recall the heat of the differential between my legs as the Land Rover got down to work. We would pause at Piccadilly Circus, so named because from this point there were eight ways to choose from. We would head for one of three spots – Broken Road, Seagull Cliff or Pens 'n Pootjies. Usually, it was Seagull Cliff.

For me, there was a real sense of safari about all this *bundu-bashing*, driving through the Port Jackson bush that heightened expectation to a fever pitch. Soon I could smell the sea and its effect was to tighten the muscles of my stomach. We would inch down to a spot on the cliffs above Seagull Cliff at Swartklip, which commanded views of the whole of False Bay, Strandfontein and Muizenberg to your right with the back of the Table Mountain range beyond and The Strand and Gordon's Bay below the Hottentot Mountains to your left, the two mountain ranges hemming it all in neatly. There was no coastal road as there is today, just a rough sand track with places where sand-driving expertise was needed to avoid getting stuck. Those who came here came with one purpose in mind – fishing.

Dad and Pascoe would debate the wind, the colour of the sea, the state of the tide, the presence or lack of other fishermen, while I itched to get out and get going. Finally, we loaded the gear onto our backs and with rods and gaffs in hand, carefully descended the slippery sand paths 300 feet down to the beach. Once there, the cliffs reared up above you and you knew the serious stuff was about to begin.

It would start with the two men walking to the water's edge to feel its temperature; warm was good for kob, cold meant a thin day. We'd get reels on rods, make trace, bait up and get the first cast out. Usually, Pascoe or my father would help me with all this preparatory stuff and, if I was in luck, the first cast too.

Then there was that wonderful moment towards which you had been working. There were three lines in the water, including yours, which you watched with hawk-like concentration. Anything was possible. A wave would come in with a whoosh, run up the beach and then return seaward, making its strange gurgling noise as the shell, stones and debris churned in the backwash. And then silence. Profound silence, just for a moment, and then the next wave swept in and the process was repeated. If you were standing barefoot, as invariably I was, the sand would be sucked from under your feet by the retreating water, and you would gradually sink up to your ankles and beyond until extricating yourself.

There would be that first small knock on your line as your bait registered interest. You'd tense up a little, lift the tip of the rod to improve your feel, tighten the line, eliminating any sag, and wait. Suddenly there would be a series of knocks as a larger fish harried the bait, and you struck. With luck you'd be in, and the fight was on. Happiness was a tangible thing in those days, not some existential consideration. If you could have made tangible the emotion, it would have formed dunes to match those around you, such was the power of the feeling. And people ask why I fish!

Lead sinkers would play an unusually large role in my

fishing experience. Each of us would make his own mark on a fish's tail – the ones we kept – after landing and dispatching it, to 'brand' the fish as his. At the end of the day, there would a general weigh-in to see who had caught the heaviest fish. It was not unheard of to find back home, when cleaning one of my father's fish, that for some strange reason it appeared to have eaten one or two sinkers, taking the lead rather than the bait! It took me a while to work this out, so perhaps my much-maligned teachers may have been right about me after all.

One day when the fishing was slow, I reeled in my line, neatly stacked my rod against the cliff face and went to play in the sand. It was fun to hollow out of the relatively soft sand cliff small holes, like the ones the seagulls made for their nests at the cliff's high point. As I sat there in a daydream, I looked around and the thought came to me, out of nowhere, that this would not last, that I would not be a boy forever, and that, inconceivable as it seemed to me then, I might one day no longer visit this beloved beach.

I got up and went to the bag of lead sinkers and took out a handful, five or six of the large heavy ones we used. I placed them carefully in the back of a deep hole, dug at my shoulder height, and as deep as my arm. Then carefully I replaced the sand and patted it back so that one could not see where the hole was. I thought to myself that now I had buried treasure here, there would always be something of me on this beach, and that like all good pirates, one day I would come back and reclaim my own.

Almost half a century has passed since I buried something of myself on that Cape beach, and as I sit under grey English skies and recall those far off days, I'm glad my cache of sinkers is still there, as it must be, anchoring me to my roots.

KABELJOU PIET AND HENRY VEL

Some of the best things about fishing are not fish, but people. Two of the most amazing characters I met while fishing in the waters of the Cape were Henry Vel and Piet Sedgwick. From them I learned many things, some connected to fishing, and some not. Henry came back from the dead and Piet, though dead, still lives. These are powerful things to learn as a boy. From these two brown men, Henry and Piet, ghillies on my father's fishing trips, I learned irreverence for life, because life is not something one should take too seriously; it is too precarious and precious for that. It's best to walk softly and smile through life, they taught me. They also taught me an acceptance of myself that made their cause my own.

Henry would sit next to me while I fished under a full moon and we'd talk. I'd be clutching a sea-taut fishing rod and he'd be holding an illicit whisky. He liked a drop, did Henry, and he liked to talk. Like an old man by the fire, he'd talk, and he had a tale or two.

As we sat on the low rock bank at the mouth of the Breede River, 180 miles from Cape Town on the Indian Ocean coast, he'd talk as I waited for the great *kabeljou*, the giant fish that grew up to 200 pounds in weight. These mighty fish came in on full moon nights in summer to hoover up the shrimp and prawn that made the river mudflats their home.

I would be warmly dressed, because that close to the water it got cold past midnight. I'd be in double socks and Wellington boots, jeans and two jerseys, under a waterproof jacket. Belted round my waist was a battered fishing saddle holding the butt of my 10-foot glass fibre rod on which I had a Penn 49 reel, with 250 yards of 45-pound breaking strain line. At the other end, lying just above the riverbed, where the current would move my bait, was a sizeable hook and a great wad of chokka – fresh, absolutely fresh, cuttlefish squid.

The waiting was terrible and wonderful, like waiting in a church for your bride who is late. It was a good but tense sort of waiting. Henry's stories reminded me to breathe while I waited. They lent a human perspective to a night that might otherwise have seemed too loaded with meanings. The sea, the moonlight, the hunter's expectation, the rivalry with other fishermen risking the danger of crossed lines, the great swathe of southern night sky – it might all have seemed too damned much for a boy. Henry made it manageable, like a good trainer helping a boxer in the midst of a bloody fight. I'd have an ear and an eye for Henry and the others on the ocean, lapping at my feet.

This was a special place, one of the most special in the world. In the middle of this mile-wide river estuary a frill of waves marked the bar, that death-trap to ships, one of which gave the place its name, Cape Infanta, for the *Infanta Dom Enrique* which had capsized here three centuries before. But those ill-fated Portuguese were recent arrivals. Beyond the entrance bar were silver-white sand dunes on the far shore, which was our birthplace as hominids. A classmate, later a Professor of Anthropology, would find traces of man's presence in sea caves beyond the dunes that marked this place as man's original home. His find at Blombos cave, pushed the known presence of man here back a few more million years. Where I sat and fished, man had fished for millennia.

While we waited for the elusive kob, Henry would tell me his story. He'd worked for years as a stoker on coastal

A Fisherman in the Saddle

tramps. A thin brown man, he did not look capable of such gruelling work, but he'd worked the ships' furnaces for years. His black, oiled hair had a kink in it and he wore thick glasses in rickety, much-mended tortoiseshell frames. He'd served with the South African Forces during the Second World War in the Western Desert as a truck driver. This is how he came to be sitting by me. He had worked for my father as a bread van driver. Now he helped on fishing trips and back home in Cape Town, he worked at odd jobs in the factory.

His driving days had ended one day when he was knocked clear through a brick wall at the factory as he washed down a truck. A van boy messing around in the cab had released the handbrake. The truck rolled down the washing incline and caught Henry square in the back, pushing him through a foot thick wall. He should have died. By all accounts, he came close.

Chuckling, he said he could remember the nurses at Victoria Hospital speaking about him, thinking he was dead. Sitting there by me on the rocks, he told me that he'd been able to see his body from above and wondered why he could not make his arm stretch out and pinch the prettier nurse's bottom, and he cackled. He was a bit of a devil. With every bone in his body broken, he was still thinking of pinching. It took him a year to recover, but he was never quite the same man. Like a well-repaired vase, you couldn't see the cracks, but you knew they were there. His surname, Vel, means skin in Afrikaans, and it suited him; he was all skin and bones.

He was odd in other ways too. After a few drinks, he was quite capable of taunting the white fishermen. He'd tease them about the WW2 Battle of Tobruk, and the capture of thousands of South African soldiers by the Germans. He'd laugh so hard at this that he would sometimes fall off his stool. Another ghillie said to me once, 'You see, coming back from the dead just makes you reckless!'

My line flicked into life with a sudden rat-a-tat series of bites and I quickly gathered in the slack, trying hard to identify the source of the activity. But usually it was just barbel, getting a free feed. I looked out to check the direction of my line and its relation to those of my father and the other fishermen on the rock. It did not do to get one's line crossed or tangled here, there was too much at stake. There had been instances of lines cut and some anger if a fish was being played and your line was anywhere near the action. When a fisherman yelled 'I'm in!' it was both good manners and a shrewd move to bring your line in rapidly. Casting was just as crucial. Weighing the heavy sinker and bait one would aim for clear water directly ahead, having once more noted the position of other fishermen's lines. I had an added concern; at seventeen, I was the youngest person there and did not want to disgrace my father.

The other great character I met as a teenage fisherman at Cape Infanta was Piet Sedgwick. A small, wizened man, he was an Infanta institution, and perhaps its rugged spirit. In Piet's veins ran the blood of Strandlopers and Hottentots, the people found on these coasts by the first white settlers. He knew everything there was to know about this coast. He knew where to find bloodworm, prawns, mussels, and which pools the octopus like best. His surname wasn't anything like Sedgwick, but what it was he did not know or care. He called himself Sedgwick because he had worked for that family for so many years that he thought of himself as a Sedgwick. The fact that they owned one of the leading liquor businesses in South Africa might have had something to do with it too.

It was an appropriate surname for him, for his love affair with liquor went back a long way. It was perhaps part of the reason he looked like a pickled walnut. It is perhaps also the reason why Cape Infanta has a drunken ghost.

Only four and a half foot tall, slightly built, with short, patchy, peppercorn hair, Piet was the lowest of the low socially, in this caste- and colour-addicted society. He managed the distinction of the disreputable with some flair. He was an original.

The fact of the matter was that many of the fishermen who had weekend and holiday cottages at Infanta rather envied him his life, his closeness to the river for one thing. He

A Fisherman in the Saddle

lived in a stone cottage half sunk into a meadow, edged with Port Jackson trees and sprouting sour fig succulents, the fruit of which his wife turned into jam. The place might have been rural Ireland, were it not for the blazing sun and the succulents. He had a dog that followed him everywhere and which had more dignity than its master.

But Piet got a good reception wherever he went. Acting as the local newsagent, he carried the week's doings from door to door, along with the bait – or more accurately, promises of bait. He would bring news of who had caught what, where and how. He'd have tales of seasick fisherman out in the bay or a missed opportunity at The Bank, the famous rock ledge at the river mouth, our favourite fishing site. He seemed to accept what he was given – food and drink – more out of politeness than anything else. Drunk and lying in a ditch, Piet knew his value.

Despite his size, Piet's capacity for drink was legendary. He'd be sober as a judge for weeks, then go on an absolute bender. A fisherman, more than usually generous after a good catch on Piet's bait, would slip him five rand and that would be that. Piet would 'borrow' a boat and row across the river to the hotel off-licence, buying cheap brandy or bottles of syrupy sweet wine made from Muscatel grapes. The row back always took longer than the first crossing. Once beached, he'd career home with his diminished cargo.

At the cottage, he'd get a hero's welcome from Anna, who was not one of those disapproving wives. Far from it, she'd match old Piet swig for swig. Sitting outside with their backs against the whitewashed wall, they'd sip away and be happy. Happy, that was, until one got aggressive. Piet was the mildest of men, always smiling, doing a little jig, cap in hand, to amuse the white bosses, patience itself on the fishing rock when sober; but once he'd had a few, he became a different person, capable of just about anything.

Of course, Anna didn't do too badly herself. For one thing, she had all her teeth, unlike so many coloured girls who go to the city and learn sophistication (and have the front ones pulled out!). Depending, then, on who got angry first, a fight would break out and sometimes Piet came off best, sometimes Anna. It was equality in marriage, of a kind.

The fishermen knew Piet's foibles but forgave him for the luck they said he brought when he joined them on the fishing rocks. They say it still when he appears. It was more than luck though; Piet knew fish and he loved fishing with a passion. Each fish landed was a joy to Piet and he would do a little dance of delight as each fish was heaved ashore.

The fishermen believed there was a mystique about bait. Having the best kind, the firm white flesh of the local chokka, was an investment and a kind of insurance. It was proof of caring and they hoped the god of fishing would approve. Piet brought the best bait.

The surrounding area was one of rugged stony, brown hills with sparse vegetation, home to sheep farmers. Here little coloured children earned cents picking up the stones that littered the barbed-wired fields. They lived, as did Piet, in square box-like hovels whitewashed with lime, exact unconscious copies of the Bethlehem architecture that Christ knew. Their parents worked as farm labourers and servants, with income paid in a little cash but mainly in food, accommodation and drink. Piet's thirst was partly inherited.

At weekends there were fights and quite often someone was stabbed – perhaps fatally. Then, cursing, the farmer would load the body into his pick-up truck and trailing a plume of dust and impatience, drive into Swellendam, the nearest town. Once there, depending on his cargo's condition, his destination would be the hospital or the morgue.

This was a hard place, where the echoes of frontier life were louder than the distant promise of city pleasures. It was an alien world to visitors and that was its charm. And the fishing was good. Echoing the harsh, brutal life on its banks, game fish as well as small fry – bream, blacktail, elf, barbel and haarders – swarmed to the river's riches, eating or being eaten. The river too had its pecking order and the big sea scavenging shark visited regularly, following the game fish.

The night that Piet became an Infanta legend was one of a full moon. The river looked like mercury cut by the jag-

A Fisherman in the Saddle

ged silver moonpath, as it spilled its cargo of topsoil deep into the midnight black Indian Ocean. The fishermen stood in line abreast, dark hulks, their lines stabbing the sea thirty or forty yards out in the current that was turning with the incoming tide. Piet swaggered onto the rock and as usual took up position behind the men, cadging a drink here and there as they turned from the water to re-bait or to check their trace lines for signs of wear.

What happened that night is engraved on my heart, although it was more than fifty years ago. I had never yet landed one of the great kabeljou. Always it was someone else, my father or his fishing mate, Pascoe Grenfell, or one of the others on the rock, never me. I had learned how hard it is to be gracious about the success of others, when you want it so much yourself. This night would be different.

Henry Vel was smoking beside me, chatting away. Piet was just to the rear, getting a shot of Bells whisky from Dad, when a horse kicked me in the stomach. It is amazing how much information the brain can process in a split second. I dropped the tip of the rod low, reeled in furiously and struck back for all I was worth, setting the hook hard into the jaw of what felt like a runaway steam train. My line screamed out and I shouted 'IN! I'M IN!' I'm sure the sound did not have the laconic by-the-way tone of the old hands. But kindly, pleased and excited for me, they reeled in their lines, giving me sea-space to play this monster. It was the first strike of the evening and they knew there would now be others.

Torches were doused to avoid frightening the fish away from the rock where gaffs waited. A small knot of men, my father among them, gathered by me, giving quiet advice. 'Give him time. Let him run. He'll tire. Don't worry, you've got him well hooked. Just be patient, don't hurry him.'

My arms were shaking with nerves and strain as the huge fish surged into the current, using the incoming tide's strength on its flank to help it take line. I gasped for air, struggling to hold that great rod, as it bent double and dipped and bobbed to every movement of my adversary. The fear of losing this great fish was big within me. It is a terrible fear.

I let the fish run. It was fresh and full of fight and swam out and away, moving now against the tide, swimming strongly out to sea. A new fear gripped me; did I have enough line on the reel, was it free of nicks, would the trace hold? Abruptly the line went slack. A sickening feeling struck me. The fish had escaped. My right hand blurred as I fought to bring in the slack. The fish was still there! It had just changed tactics. Tired of the pain of the hook, it tried a new ploy, coming back toward the source of the restraint, giving itself freedom as well as line to snag on the riverbed rocks.

I took the full strain of the fish again and then in the moonlight saw and then heard a splash as the fish breached fifty yards out. 'Big fish! Hold him, boy, that's a decent fish you've got there.' For the first time I felt what it was to be a man among men, even though they called me boy. There was real respect and a little envy in their voices. More slowly now my line went out, the fish was tiring. Someone said, 'Now start pumping – he's had half an hour.' I could not believe that I had been playing the fish for thirty minutes – it seemed both like seconds and days. Strange. I could no longer feel my arms.

Piet, always more volatile than anyone else, said urgently, 'Pump boss, pump.' I dropped the tip of the rod a fraction and hauled back, the fish gave and I began the agonising process of hauling him in. Out of the corner of my eye I saw a massive gaff hook appear in the hands of my father. He dropped it low to avoid spooking the fish and waited. 'Keep it up my boy, you're doing well!' God, those words and his tone were sweet to me, and they also sent a new fear, the fear of letting my father down by losing the fish, now that we almost had it. 'Please, please, please God,' I prayed, 'let me catch this fish.'

The fish was now only thirty feet out and rolling on the surface, copper and silver in the moonlight. I reeled and hauled for all I was worth. The fish still struggled but more feebly now, and it moved towards us. My father lunged with the gaff but missed and the great fish, sensing this new danger in the water, unbelievably, began taking line off my reel again.

Something then snapped in Piet. Shouting, 'Hold him, boss,' he jumped, fully clothed, into the black night-live river. It was a mad thing to do. Sharks big enough to bite a man in half cruised these waters. Hardly able to swim, Piet dog-paddled out to the straining fish. Reaching it, he threw an arm across its back and, hugging the fish to himself, swam it back to the rock. My father got the hook set under its jaw and hauled it out onto the rock.

There was a stunned silence among the fishermen. I heard the fish grunting and my own breath rasping in my throat. Someone reached down and helped Piet out of the water. The silence seemed to last minutes. The sea is not lightly insulted. Piet's leap seemed a kind of sacrilege. I was both glad to have the fish safely ashore and perturbed about the unexpected help I'd received.

Piet's teeth flashed in the moonlight. 'It's a big one, boss. We landed him!' The laughter then erupted and rang out over the water. This was one that had not got away. This was a story! The fishermen slapped Piet's wet back, forcing whisky on him. 'Well done, lad.' It was my father and Pascoe. 'Played like a professional.' Happiness descended on me then the like of which I would rarely experience again. Truly, it was the happiest night of my life.

The kob weighed 102 pounds. It was a female, heavy with roe. Years later I would regret that, but on this night, no such thoughts concerned me. The fish was gutted and scaled after being photographed with me by its side. It fed many people, fried, curried or steamed. My father ate the head, his favourite, and gave me the two, white, flint-like bones from its centre, which I now wear, set in gold, as cufflinks.

A few years later I sat once more under the moonlight at Infanta, rod in hand. A neighbouring angler offered cigarettes and he asked:

'Aren't you the bloke whose fish Piet Sedgwick landed?' I said yes, and we laughed.

'Isn't it a pity he drowned? He was a bloody good ghillie.'

I was stunned. 'Drowned?' I asked.

'Yes, just a few weeks ago. Silly bugger went over to the hotel, to the off-licence for booze, and drank too much coming back. He never made it. The tide was going out and it took the boat, old Cilliers' dingy. It must have overturned at the sandbar. They never found Piet. Funny – Piet dying at the bar. I'll bet he never thought he'd be drinking salt water when the end came!'

Silence fell on the rock. I watched the moon's path, the distant dunes and felt the sea thrumming on the line, the salt sea that had finally slaked Piet's thirst forever.

They no longer call him Piet Sedgwick. At last, he has found a name of his own. 'Kabeljou Piet' is what they call him now, when talk turns to fishing. There are some who say he'll be back with the secret of where the kob go in winter. Others say he's back already; that on moonlit nights when the kob come, shouldering aside the outgoing tide, he sits near the fishing boxes in the shadows, waiting for someone to offer him a drink. I don't believe it really, but who knows?

They were special men, Piet and Henry, and here's the funny thing; looking back on that night, and so many others like it, it's not the fish that I remember, though I loved catching them, it is Piet and Henry whom I remember best.

Shark!

The shark is well named. The very sound of the name, the shushing it starts with, as if to warn one to beware, to be silent, to take cover, and the hard 'k' at the end, like a bite. There is an unwritten but ever-present exclamation mark behind the word, like the pilot fish that swim in attendance to these great predators of the sea.

I grew up with sharks and they fill me with horror. In this case, familiarity does not breed contempt; rather I feel the greatest respect and fear. My first encounter with a shark was on a school outing to Robben Island, aboard the tugboat ferry, the *John X. Merriman*, in the late 1950s, before the place became famous for housing Nelson Mandela. The memory of the visit itself is vague, but I recall the unease I felt on my first sight of a big shark.

I had been invited on the outing by a second cousin of my mother's, a teacher at a Sea Point School, not mine, who was coaching me in mathematics, a subject that would always defeat me. I made a new friend on the trip, a boy called Roy who stood with me at the boat's rail, watching the sea. As we chatted away, we were amazed, thrilled and aghast, all at once, to see a gigantic shark at least 20 foot long, ease up to the boat, and rolling on one side, give us the once over with its cold pearl eye. It chilled the blood.

Sharks are attracted to the Cape by the thousands of seals inhabiting every rocky island off the coast and the seals are there because of the richness of the fish stocks. The sharks seldom attack humans, but once in a while there is a memorable savaging, or even a death. Clifton, Cape Town's most popular beach, where the young and the beautiful parade amid a scented haze of hormones and suntan cream, saw one such attack. Three lads filled with high spirits had swum out fairly deep and were horsing around when what could only have been a Great White took one of them in a single great lunge. He was never seen again. It must have been a long, long swim back to the beach for his friends.

As I grew up, I learned much more about sharks. We caught the occasional one on our fishing expeditions for the great kabeljou. Most of the sharks we caught we killed and left for the seagulls. But there was a summer when our garden was overrun (or should that be undermined) by moles. After trying every kind of deterrent, from smoke bombs to jagged broken bottles, and a vicious sprung trap with steel tines that was supposed to harpoon any mole silly enough to come near, someone told my father that shark guts would drive the moles away. He was right, and you couldn't blame the moles for skedaddling. The smell was horrendous.

I'm not sure where the sharks came from. I was around eight at the time, but I was fascinated to watch three six-footers hung by their tails to be gutted. The first knife went in at the anal vent and cut a line to the bottom jaw, our gardener leaning hard on the super-sharp flensing knife. The guts rolled out, grey, yellow and white, and with them came an oily, yellow, clinging, rotten, gorge-raising stink the like of which I have never ever smelled since. It was vile and I vomited on the spot. I did not stick around to see the second or third shark gutted, and the moles took off to pastures new. We never again suffered from moles, and who can blame them; our garden must have carried the taint of shark guts below ground for years, I imagine.

In my teens, I spent treasured weekends with my father and Pascoe at the Cape Infanta fishing shack, where we went to catch kabeljou at the famous Bank, the rock ledge at the river's mouth, where I had caught my first big kob with the

A Fisherman in the Saddle

help of Piet Sedgewick. What made this particular spot interesting, besides the kabeljou, was the number of big sharks in the water. Marine biologists and ichthyologists tell us that shark like the murky water of river estuaries, and the Breede River estuary was no exception. It was not that unusual for a fisherman playing a kob for half an hour or more to lose it to a shark. Making this all so very interesting was the fact that the fatal grab would often take place less than 30 yards from where you were standing in thigh deep water, as the tide came in, pushing you eventually off the low rock ledge and up onto the beach behind it.

The kabeljou we landed here were often well over 100 pounds. Now and then, a disgusted fisherman would haul in a 30-pound kabeljou head, the rest having been taken by a shark in one clean bite – a gulp of anything from 50 to 150 pounds. That is a big shark.

Watching this in the moonlight – we invariably fished at night under a full moon – all one would see would be the gleaming body of the exhausted kabeljou rolling on the surface, its thrashings sending out 'come-get-me' messages to every shark in the area; there would be a swirl, and that unmistakable dorsal fin, and most of the kabeljou would be gone, leaving the fisherman cursing.

One afternoon after lunch, my brother and I were walking along the rocky coast near the fishing shack when we spotted a large dolphin that had beached itself on the low flat rock ledges that are covered by about six foot of water at high tide. When we got to it, we saw that it was still alive, and though quite badly lacerated, nothing looked particularly deep. We ran back home to get hessian sacks to soak in seawater and cover the dolphin, to keep it wet and out of the sun. We hoped that by the time the tide started coming in, it might have recovered sufficiently to swim off the rocks and back out to sea.

We wet the sacks in nearby rock pools and covered the dolphin, touching its smooth rubbery skin with wonder. Its large eyes observed us benignly. We kept vigil by it until the tide started to push in over the rock shelf, reaching across the

100 feet from the river to the beach quite quickly. Soon there was six inches of water on the seaward side of the dolphin, and it was moved gently from side to side by the little lapping wavelets.

About then something caught our eyes and we looked out at the dorsal fins of two or three shark, I forget the exact number, just a few yards away, moving around in no more than two foot of water. A slightly larger wave brought in enough water to allow one of the sharks, bolder or hungrier than the others, to reach the dolphin's side. We were so amazed that it was only when the shark half-wriggled alongside the dolphin, more out of the water than in, that we woke up sufficiently to act. Picking up stones we hurled them at the shark and it veered off. But within minutes the water was covering the dolphin's back and the sharks were back, tearing hungry gobbets out of the dolphin's side. I'm not sure when the dolphin died but it did not take long before its eyes glazed over, as blood from gaping wounds on its seaward side leaked into the water.

At that point, our focus moved to the sharks and we decided to run for tackle to try and catch one of them. We came back with a short stout boat rod, no more than six feet long and a huge Policansky reel. We rigged up a steel trace with the biggest hook we could find – the length of a man's hand – and cutting off a piece of the dead dolphin, virtually placed it in the mouth of the next shark to come alongside, an eight-footer. We were standing by now in a couple of feet of water on the beachside of the dolphin, while sharks appeared in relays to bite and savage hunks just on the other side.

My brother held the rod and struck hard, the line screaming off the reel as the shark made for deep water. Herman walked himself backwards out of the water and up onto the beach to get some height and to find a place to sit with his feet braced against a boulder. That shark kept a steady pressure on the rod as it continued to take line off the reel. I held a boat gaff on the off-chance that he'd manage to land the shark. There was to be no such luck. That shark stripped the reel and just before it pulled the rod and reel out my brother's hands, he cut the line, saving the tackle, and avoiding a bollocking from our father.

By now, it was dusk and the sharks had turned the dolphin into a red and white mess that bobbed in the surf. Soon there was nothing and the last shark fin vanished. We went home, to get ready for a night on the Bank, fishing for kob.

You watch something like that, and it stays with you. You may forget the detail; certainly, the memory is not as clear as it was. But the horror of it is still there, the slithery, frenetic activity of those shark working in water that was often just as deep as themselves, coming in on their sides, mouths opening and the wriggling, and the rolling to tear off hunks, the blood in the boiling, churning water. That stuff stays.

A few years later I found someone else who shared my passion for fishing, a girlfriend who would become my wife, and we too shared a close encounter with a shark.

Our shared land at Hamerkop was virgin coast and it teemed with that king of Cape rock fishing, the galjoen, a round-muscled metal-blue grey bruiser that looks like a grown-up version of the Amazonian piranha, with an appetite to match, an angry, high-tempered fighter, a decent one weighing in at five pounds. There were also red roman, blacktail, mussel-cracker, steenbras and kabeljou amongst others, and – of course – shark.

This was a special place. It took a great deal of getting to, as do all the best fishing places, and that for a boy was half its charm. We would drive for three hours from Cape Town to a metal barn Dad had erected at the foot of the coastal range, which separates the farming area from the sea. At the barn, we would transfer everything from the cars to two Willy's Jeeps stored inside, vintage vehicles from the Second World War that had somehow or other made their way to Cape Town. Then, with the cars safely stashed under cover in the barn, we'd begin the tortuous ride over the mountain on what passed for a track, a tooth-rattling, shock-absorber destroying Calvary, taken in low four-wheel drive at much slower than walking pace, as we climbed. Here and there was a piece of flattish concrete, laid down to help make headway possible. For the rest, we were climbing, rock by rock.

The mountain was covered in the indigenous *fynbos*, with many proteas and pincushions. There were dung beetles industriously at work; snakes, baboons and the odd leopard, living in enormous caves we kept well clear of. Cresting the mountain after half an hour of tenacious climbing, you'd get your first view of the sea and then begin the descent to the wooden shack, just back from the dune line, trucked in years ago in pieces and erected on site. In front of it, a small thread-like stream formed a froggy boundary from which a leg-testing dune rose, and then the beach, about a mile in length, with inviting rock formations at either end. Each fishing spot had a name, as is the way with fishermen; The Pier, *Baaitjies se Ban*k, Monument Rock, Dorothy's Hole, *Lynkrans*. We almost never fished the beach, always the rocks – that was where the action was.

One weekend, I managed to slip away to Hamerkop alone with Jan, or almost. My brother had said he might fly down to a farm airstrip with his girlfriend. We left one of the Jeeps in the barn for them, opened the shack and aired it, unpacked and went down for a first walk on the beach. We knew we had the place to ourselves – miles of coast, with the nearest permanent neighbours ten miles away. It was magical. We stripped off our clothes and walked along the water's edge, enjoying our complete nakedness. Suddenly a light aircraft swooped low over the hill and at what seemed like head height buzzed us, roaring off up the beach and away over the coast range to the right. Bloody brothers!

One morning, we sat watching the crystal clear sea – in 'glassy' condition as fishermen call it – lit by the sun. Each lazy wave lifted and held for long moments, untroubled by wind, and one could look right into the wave as though through a window. After a while, a particular wave rose and we caught our breath; outlined in clear detail, a truly massive shark swam at its centre, the size of a small submarine. How many people had ever seen its sinister shape, we wondered? Perhaps we were the first.

A Fisherman in the Saddle

The good depth of sea brought large fish close in here, as well as the massive Southern Right whales, which came to this coast to calve. We would sit fascinated as they stood on their heads waving flukes in the sun, the distance of two casts off the rocks. We thought they were rubbing barnacles off themselves, but it might just have been fun.

That evening, Jan and I lit a fire on the beach, using wood washed up by the sea, which burned with blue and green flames. Using heavy tackle and steel trace, we fished for large kob or shark. We did not have long to wait. Jan barely held onto her rod as a shark struck and lazily began to strip line off the reel. We 'walked' the fish along the beach till we could reach the start of the rocks from which I thought we'd have a better chance of bringing it to gaff, avoiding the obvious danger of wading out into the surf to hook it.

After a long hard fight, she brought the fish to the water in front of us. In the torchlight it seemed larger than most shark we'd seen with the exception of the morning's sighting, which was in a league of its own. The heavy rod was bent almost double and Jan at around 115 pounds was barely able to hold on. I stood behind her hanging onto the belt of her fishing saddle while trying to keep the torch on the shark which thrashed just two feet below us in the surging water, and also hold onto the gaff. In the commotion, the front of the torch swung open and all the batteries exited into the sea. We, and the shark, were now in total darkness. We were perched precariously on slippery wet rocks with a sea swell running and one very angry shark in close proximity. We agreed to give the shark best, and cut the line.

We knew enough about shark not to be foolhardy. Jan's closest friend had lost a brother, who went skin diving in False Bay on his own and never returned. The theory was that a shark took him.

I had also heard the ultimate 'one that got away' shark story from a couple of tough up-country farmers who owned a ski-boat in Cape Town. Once a year they would come down to the Cape for the shark fishing. The newspaper for which I was working at the time as a student reporter, *The*

Cape Times, had hired their boat to ferry me and a photographer out to the start of the Cape to Rio Yacht Race. It was not an easy brief. Trying to get last-minute comments from skippers jockeying for position at the start of a trans-Atlantic yacht race leaves one feeling akin to a cockroach, but with a vastly increased vocabulary of saltwater curses.

On the way back to the harbour, we talked fishing, after I'd written up my meagre notes –those that were fit to print. These blunt fishing farmers told me that they had caught some big shark, but had now given up. When I asked them why, they told me this story.

Each day's fishing would begin with a trip to the abattoir, where they'd fill a 44-gallon drum with oxblood. This would be wrestled onto the boat and once at sea with the troll lines out, they would 'chum', dripping blood over the side. It seldom failed. They showed me pictures of themselves dockside with some monsters strung up on pulleys, 12 foot and more, a good number of them Great Whites.

One day, as they paused for lunch, they had an uninvited guest come calling. A Great White hurled itself out of the water onto their 18-foot ski-boat, almost capsizing it and only by the grace of God missing them. As the fish thrashed on the boat they jumped overboard, clinging in fear to the side, in shock and not sure what would happen next. After what felt like hours, the shark managed to free itself and fell back into the sea. At this point the friends climbed back in, fairly sharpish. They discovered on their return to harbour that this behaviour was not that unusual. Shark at the Cape feed on seal and a big shark will think nothing of using a swell to lift it onto a rock on which a seal is lying and knock it into the water for instant consumption. That was the end of the shark fishing.

No, sharks are not nice. Currently they are benefiting from some biological revisionism. The people behind it should put their money where their mouths are and go swim with a Great White – outside of a cage. Truly, our great mammalian ancestor who decided to leave the sea for the land was onto a good thing.

Muscle-Cracker

In my father's study in Cape Town there were two mussel-crackers mounted on wooden plaques hanging on the wall amid crossed fishing rods. One fish was considerably bigger than the other. Dad's is the smaller one, my younger brother lays claim to the second, larger fish, but it's all much more complicated than that.

The bigger fish is a handsome 17-pound brute with large scales like English 50p coins, and teeth that would not be out of place as crocodile molars. It's a nice specimen. And each time I see it, I smile. For that fish is mine too, in a way.

This story hinges on the fact that when you have three men in one house all mad keen on fishing, you have a certain amount of inevitable rivalry. It says a lot for my father's love for my brother that he was prepared to hang the bigger fish up in the same room, a sort of permanent nose-thumbing at his measly eleven-pound specimen. But there it hung. And when guests inevitably asked who caught the bigger one, there would be a moment's silence before Dad answerered. There was a father's pride in the statement that his younger son caught it, but there is also a fisherman's pride in the rider – 'though he had a little help in landing it.' It's all a bit of a juggling act.

There they hung, those two musselcrackers, mute testimony to the difficulty of defining truth, like the scales of justice, the two protagonists are dead and blind, but they weighed the truth in that small cosy room with infinite pains.

My father caught his fish fair and square, was thrilled by its size and had it stuffed and mounted. It took pride of place in his study. And then the three of us went fishing at Hamerkop, on the Bredasdorp coast, where we would catch galjoen at a great rate, throwing back any undersized fish. Nevertheless, even with a self-imposed limit of just three rods, and a limit on fish size, we would catch enough to feed the whole extended family network. It has taken some time for the galjoen to repopulate the coast north and south of Hamerkop and it took a Government Decree and an Act of Parliament to wrest it away from Dad. He never forgave them. Others may have had more right to criticise the Nationalists and bigger axes to grind, but most would have to stand back when it comes to my father's vehemence on the subject of the Nationalist Government that proposed turning his fishing paradise into a missile impact zone and then declared it 'De Hoop Nature Reserve'! So those fish emerged from what would later become a war between my father, who was trying to hang onto his fishing fiefdom, and the Government, who decided otherwise.

In the art and antique trade, it is known as provenance – knowing the antecedents of an object greatly enhances its value, and those two musselcrackers have the most prestigious provenance going in fishing terms. They come from a place that is now strictly off-limits to fishermen. They are the last of their kind from that piece of the Bredasdorp Coast to adorn a wall. Today they would be considered Royal Game in English terms, their catching a hanging offence. So you see, their presence in the study was about much more than fishing. It is about pride, and love and loss. Those fish symbolise a life that is past and that will never return. Some, perhaps most, would applaud that. I don't, but then I wouldn't, would I? I had a son's right to fish the place. You would feel the same if once you could call Hamerkop yours.

But let's get back to the fishing. The three of us set off on our fishing expedition with all the paraphernalia that involved, drove the three hours to the barn on Johnny

A Fisherman in the Saddle

Micheler's farm, left the car and took the jeeps over the mountain to Hamerkop.

The next morning, we headed for Monument Rock, capped by a squat obelisk recalling the dead man who had washed up there. Today, there are two other spirits who watch over that coast, Ferdie and Dorothy Bergh, whose ashes are interred at *Baatjies se Bank* – the people who brought this magic spot to our attention and who joined us and others in its ownership.

It was a perfect day, a cloudless sky, the water warm and the fish biting. My father, as usual, started the day with heavy tackle, trying for something sizeable. Herman and I aimed for galjoen and proceeded to catch a few. We timed our visits to each fishing spot to coincide, as best we could, with an incoming tide that brought the bigger fish in.

As the tide pushed in, the swell rose, but this did not disturb us unduly, as Monument Rock had enough height and length to allow one to fish as if from a pier, sideways to the waves. It was just noon, I recall, as Herman called out that he was into something large. His rod certainly advertised the fact. He played the fish well. After a while we could see it in the swells before it bore down hard for the bottom again. It was a seriously big fish, square shaped and thick through the middle. Slowly but surely, he brought it closer. There would be no chance to gaff it, the swell and the waves made that impossible. So he waited for the fish to tire and then for a wave to help him lift it onto the rock.

Suddenly it was there, a mighty musselcracker, shining silver in the sun, thrashing on the rock from which the wave was withdrawing. And then the line snapped, worn thin by snagging on rock edges. The next large wave bore down on us. I was closer to the fish and did not have a rod in my hands. There was no time to think. I sprinted down, grabbed the fish by the gills and hoicked it clear of the crashing wave which drenched me and tugged with creamy tidal strength round my legs. But the fish was saved. I carried it on high to the ledge where my brother stood. We smiled. It was one of those moments in which the full meaning of brotherhood is experienced. When I see that fish hanging on the study wall, I don't think of it as his or mine – I think of that transcendent moment, a real emotional muscle-cracker.

Julian (left) with a night's catch of Kabeljou taken by him and his father Leon and brother Herman - 1967, Cape Infanta, South Africa.

Messing Around at Melkbos

Spending summer holidays at Bloubergstrand, near Cape Town, left me with a fairly jaundiced view of the neighbouring town of Melkbosstrand, five miles up the coast to the north.

I'm not setting out to make thousands of new enemies but, sadly, for me Melkbos never really cut it. Today it has a number of claims to fame: the international telephone line to Europe comes ashore here, and the town also plays host to the nuclear power industry. The first endears the place to me, for it is here that my disembodied voice reaches South Africa first when I open my mouth at home in Sussex. The benefits of the link with nuclear fission leave me cold, though I'm told that the crayfish benefit from the warming of the local water – which is icy to begin with – thanks to the amount of water needed to keep things cool when you're talking nuclear power. The fact that the crayfish probably glow gently at night is beside the point.

None of this technical stuff was an issue in my childhood in the 1950s and 60s. Melkbos was a smaller, possibly windier, flatter version of Blouberg, with fewer people and less impressive architecture generally. It also seemed to attract some strange people – *Melkbosstranders*.

But Melkbos did have one or two things going for it. The *Boeresports* on the beach just after New Year for one, when horses, mounted or riderless, would occasionally gallop into the crowd, maddened by the annual run beside the sea and, now unstoppable, or having ditched the jockey, ready, willing and able to take some more human tormentors with him or her to the land where pain is no more.

The *Boeresports* also played host to some genetic one-upmanship. Immensely strong Afrikaans boys got stuck into each other, wrestling, hurling things and in teams of tug o'war. You felt that rugby was safe in their rope-burned hands for another generation at least. Helping in the creation of the next generation were the number of attractive Afrikaans girls who attended. They were headed by the annual *Boeresports* Queen and her two princesses.

The other thing about Melkbos was the fishing to the north of the town, when we 'bundu-bashed' into the unpopulated dune country, home to the nuclear power station.

As a family, we were lucky enough to have a bright yellow beach buggy with immense tyres from a defunct Cadillac. These fat rubber giants and an 1800cc VW engine sent us along the beaches at a smart lick, whether the sand was hard and wet or deep and dry. You could go places in that beach buggy where no Land Rover could ever hope to reach.

Driving carefully off the edge of the known world onto the beach at Melkbos, you could, if you kept going north, end up in Namibia, I suppose. We were not that ambitious. We would pack a picnic lunch, strap a few fishing rods on the top, chuck in the fishing tackle box and the bait box, and be on our way.

With the southeaster behind you, adding impetus, you would career up that beach as if the hounds of hell were after you. It was great fun to show off, too.

Soon however, all signs of civilisation – even Melkbosstrand's watered-down version – would be left far below the southern horizon and you would then edge off the beach into the dunes, heading for a spot higher up the coast. In the dunes you had to start driving responsibly, as they offered a formidable challenge. Going up them was no problem, and one could always let air out of the tyres to give them an even wider 'footprint', but if you went up too fast, there was always the danger of launching into space and somersaulting down the other side if you were not careful. A very sore set of ribs, crunched on the windscreen's metal rim, where I was thrown in one such episode, had taught me my lesson once and for all.

Eventually, you would emerge from the dunes to an area of beach and rock, which offered almost virgin fishing. It was great, having less educated fish to catch. They seemed ravenous, as if they had not eaten in weeks and that redbait, white mussel, or chokka was a culinary first that merited a Michelin Star. They would hurl themselves on to your hook in great numbers, seeming to queue up for the chance to leave the sea. Those of us who today nod in the direction of environmentalism might shake our heads, but we forget what it felt like to be 18 or 19 years old. Fish were there to be caught, the bigger the better, and the more the merrier. We even fished through lunch, which with teenage appetites, is saying something. You would grab a sandwich and with fingers reeking of redbait, gulp it down as the next fish was already knocking on the line, urgently calling Valhalla.

You caught galjoen, blacktail, hottentot, steenbras, and even the odd kob. In later years, you would hear tales of the even greater catches to be made off the beaches of Namibia, 1,000 miles to the north, but I for one never made it to that happy hunting ground.

On the way home you would take it easy, exhausted by your efforts and not wanting to knock the catch around. Emerging from the dunes north of Melkbos, you'd drive demurely up the strand and carefully edge your way onto the tarmac once more. Then with hair streaming in the teeth of the Cape Doctor, you'd floor it, making the buggy fly, sometimes literally, on the last five miles home, sunburnt and happy fishermen.

After a shower and in fresh clean clothes, nails scrubbed clean of that bait smell, you would head into town for a steak. Then, sitting in some candlelit restaurant, you would fill up what felt like a hollow 44-gallon drum, wondering at the two worlds you had visited that day, and thinking how very privileged you were.

Julian fishing at Monument Rock, Hamerkop, in the 1970s

Food for Thought

'Eat it, it's good for you. Fish gives you brains!' my long-suffering mother would intone time and again as I pushed yet another piece of exquisite fish round my plate. As a child, I did not like fish.

Years later, sitting in a café beneath the fishtail crenelations of an Italian fortress on Lake Garda in Italy, I would eat crisp whitebait caught within yards of the table and its starched, butter-yellow cloth, and my thoughts were with my mother lying at peace – one hopes – in the fertile soil of Paarl which first gave her life. She had triumphed in the end and taught me to enjoy fish.

Admittedly, she had the best raw material to work with, crayfish direct from the sea in front of our house at Blouberg, haarders *trekked* from the same waters, served fried and accompanied by that strange South African invention, Mrs Ball's Chutney, or smoked and eaten warm with grape jam and fresh bread from my father's bakery. He also supplied an endless array of hand-caught fish – as chi-chi European restaurants describe it. There was kabeljou served as steaks, or cut across the bone and fried, or curried and served cold. There was *kingklip*, the favourite of many, and galjoen, fat ones, split open along the back and barbecued, their skins a delicious, crisp counter to the succulent flesh threaded with fine black veins. There were red roman and blacktail, steenbrass, and sole, all served simply and unadorned, with no fancy sauces. The freshness of the fish needed no addition but salad and rice or potato of some kind.

My favourite, yellowtail, was usually bought, for we were a family of rock-anglers and the fabled run of yellowtail inshore along these coasts from Blouberg to Hermanus was long gone. More's the pity. It was served simply with a butter sauce and its firm texture was the best thing I have eaten from the sea, though just recently at a barbecue in Cobham, Surrey, I ate a piece of swordfish that was just as good.

Looking back, it seems a fine irony that one of the greatest edible treats I've had from the sea is something we used for bait when I was a child! I have eaten calamari in Greece with my feet dangling in the Aegean or the Ionian, usually the smallest ones fried in a light batter with their tiny arms still attached, with a nutty taste that is habit-forming. This, accompanied by the traditional Greek salad with its salty slab of feta cheese and herbs, a hunk of bread and a glass of earthy red wine, and you eat like a king. And as you eat in the herb-scented dusk, at some small beachside taverna, the small fishing boats slip out of the harbour just round the headland, their lamps lit to attract the fish, shining on that wine-dark sea. Around you the ghosts of centuries and civilisations lost and gone, look on in envy.

The sea provides some strange fruit. Once, in a campsite just north of Lisbon, at a place called
Nazaré, where giant breakers curve in from the open Atlantic, and where until recently, oxen were used to haul frail fishing boats up the beach to safety, I ate something so strange that I was not sure about it at all. It was February; winter and out of season. We were one of three couples in caravans parked beneath the umbrella pines in this near-deserted campsite. The owner invited us to a barbecue where he said he would give us a special treat. He made a fire using dry pinecones, and as it burned down, he emptied the contents of a large hessian sack into the fire. Dozens of sea urchins rolled out into the flames. After a while, he hooked them out and their spines were gone. Breaking them open, he offered us their orange roe, a sweet smoky iodine taste, quite

different from anything I had ever tasted, and to be frank, not much to my liking. We ate some out of politeness and drank too much wine.

I have eaten *bacalao* – the Portuguese do it a thousand ways, they boast – dried salt cod, reconstituted in milk and then fried, stewed or crumbled like *smoorsnoek*, a kind of kedgeree, with rice and onions. I far prefer fresh snoek, a fish that is a byword in England for bad food – wartime memories of badly canned snoek haunts a generation which has overcome the nightmares of the Blitz. Yet a fresh snoek is something special and smoked it is better yet, and dried but still damp it is bliss, but I suspect it is an acquired taste if you have not grown up with it.

My father for years patronised a small Paarl fish shop 38 miles from Cape Town. As I recall, you drive to the bottom of Lady Grey Street over the bridge and left, and then it is somewhere on your right. From this unpretentious place, he got bunches of pungent *bokkoms*, wind-dried *haarders* that he ate after they have been wrapped in foil and heated on the stove. This is strong food for strong stomachs; the smell is enough to make most people gag. Yet once the taste is acquired, it is delicious. In France, this shop would be on a number of food trails and be considered something of a national treasure.

Fresh fish, even in a place as spoiled for choice as the Cape, is a very acceptable gift. Because of the amount of fish we landed as a family, there was a continual stream of gifts going out to friends and neighbours at Bloubergstrand and Cape Town. What flowed back, in return, was a cornucopia, an unstoppable horn of plenty that sometimes we simply did not have space for, and the whole redistributive process would begin again. We would give fish and bakery products from our factory, cakes and biscuits mainly. In return there would be trays of *kaalgat* peaches, the fabulous *taaipit* peaches, *mealies*, *boerewors*, legs of lamb, geese, jars of green fig preserve, watermelon preserve, grape jam, quinces and quince jam.

Once a year, we had a visit from Blouberg's two oldest residents, the Misses Kirsten, who would have been in their eighties. They dressed in clothes of times past and lived in a simple whitewashed cottage like those at Arniston, half sunk into a sand dune. Today it is long gone; where once it stood, Blouberg's only tower block monstrosity rears, an eyesore for miles. It is as if someone wished to bury their memory under a hundred tons of concrete, but instead that building serves as a gravestone to their memories.

One was stick thin, the other, fairly well upholstered. They spoke in high, cracked voices and balanced cups of tea precariously. They were probably the most impoverished Europeans we knew, but there was a pride too, a pride that required them to bring us a gift once a year. This came in the form of jars of sour-fig jam, the fruit collected by themselves, laboriously bent over the succulent plants in the dunes behind their cottage. My sister, brother and I were nervous of these two old ladies; they were seldom seen in the community and their dress and manner of speaking and their great age made them seem somehow threatening. We were convinced that they were witches.

How sad that is. Today, I would give a great deal to sit down with them and find out what took them to that desolate cottage, what caused the deep wrinkled lines in their faces, what caused their poverty in a world of white privilege? Worst of all, that gift of thanks and pride would sit virtually untouched, its taste too strange for kids and disregarded by my parents too.

But while the sour-fig jam remained uneaten, there were many things that went in seconds. There is something to be said for food eaten on a fishing trip; a fresh galjoen barbecued on the spot is hard to beat. But there is something I prefer on the coals – barbecued sardines in Portugal. I have eaten many near Faro, at a beach restaurant not far from the spot where Prince Henry had his school of navigation, and from which Bartholomew Diaz sailed for the Cape some 500 years ago, perhaps after himself enjoying a last meal of barbecued sardines. It is a nice thought.

Eating fish outdoors definitely adds something to it, I'm not sure why, but for me it enhances the taste. I recall with pleasure sitting down at a harbour-side restaurant in Cannes, beside the millionaires' yachts on the Croisette, and being served my first bowl of real Provençal fish soup, a thick, satisfying yet silky smooth substance, served with *rouille*, the garlicky, saffron-spiced mayonnaise spooned onto croutons, floated on the soup and then drizzled with grated Gruyère. Oh boy, like Oliver Twist, I held up my bowl and in my non-existent French asked for more.

Staying on that sun- and food-drenched coast, where good things to eat are probably thicker on the ground than anywhere else on earth, I also ate *bouillabaisse* for the first time and liked it, but would not call for trumpet blasts. I prefer their fish soup.

A deceptively simple dish the area is famed for is truly delicious when done well, and this is where they do it best: Salade Niçoise, that staple of a million menus the world over. Eaten here, with fresh ingredients under a Provençal sun, its freshness and delicacy makes it the perfect hot weather food.

Clam chowder, that New England staple, I can take or leave,; too much potato spoils it for me. I prefer clams the way the Italians do them with pasta, Spaghetti alle Vongole, my father-in-law's great favourite.

And there are the black mussels, which festoon the rocks at Blouberg, which I would have rather died than eat as a child, and which I even spurned as bait, the flesh too mushy to stay on a hook, and which now I pay good money for. I sat recently at a restaurant in Honfleur, just across the Channel from my home in Sussex, and ate and ate and ate. They were done in the simple Normandy style with onion, white wine and cream, mopped up with that delicious bread that is more crust than centre.

Mind you, the best mussels I ever ate were in Sète, that town famous for its water jousts, south of Montpellier. Sitting in a hotel dining room that managed to be both grand and provincial, we were served a meal with that correctness that is the hallmark of the best of France. It says first of all 'I respect myself, for I work in a *très sérieux* restaurant' and 'I respect you for having the wit to find us' and 'we respect the food enough to take it seriously, for after love what else is there but food? And when love goes, there *is* only food.'

Here, I was served a plate of black mussels topped with fresh herbs, breadcrumbs and fine grated cheese – *moules farçies*, stuffed mussels as they call them – and with it a bottle of crisp white wine. That was a meal to die for, and had the place not been so correct, I would have asked for more, but there were other good things to eat, and a diner paces himself in France.

There is a dish of prawns Jan and I ate at the foot of Montmarte, an experience that stays with me in the best way. We had looked for a place away from the tourist traps at the top of the hill and found at its foot a modern hotel, unpromising in its resemblance to a Holiday Inn. But it had a chef! He served us prawns fried in butter with thin slices of fennel, the faint liquorice taste of the vegetable marrying beautifully with the unctuous sweetness of the prawns.

But if you asked what is the best seafood meal I've ever had my answer would be instant – Lourenço Marques prawns done with butter, lemon and garlic or with peri peri. They were sublime and you could eat until you could eat no longer, they were that cheap. They came to the table in great heaps, in overflowing earthenware bowls, and you ate them like peanuts, not counting, not eking out the pleasure, just feasting. Those were the days. I've heard that the Polana Hotel is once more seriously open for business. The cost of a plane ticket from London may add to the bill, but the thought of those prawns might yet take me back to that coast. One day.

FISHING IN YOUR HEAD

The thing about fishing is that it's a drug. Bloodlust just does not come into it, or not much. There is obviously a desire to catch fish, but other things keep intruding.

The wind and sun buffet and warm you into a trance-like state, where conscious thought retreats, blessedly, and you become aware of your breathing as in meditation. The immediate objects around you take on a new significance and you enter a richer dimension. You think many things. You think of life, love and the universe, but not with the usual passion. You are content upon your rock.

As you arrive at the rock, you observe the wind, the tide, and the colour of the sea, hopefully not too clear, a sparkling sea under a bright sun seldom offers the best fishing. It's almost as if the fish reward the diligent fisherman who ventures out early or late, or at night, or in rain, wind and fog. Inclement weather seems to make the fish bold, to offer some protection, and they feed the better for it. You feel the water for its temperature, hoping for some sign of warmth for similar reasons.

You find a place that makes baiting up and working easy on your back: a ledge at chest height is ideal. You unpack the bait and place it in a crevice in the shade, so that its freshness lasts. You set out the bait board, the knives, the cotton, and the cloth for wiping your hands after baiting up. You slather suntan cream on your lips and nose.

You sit and compose yourself, clearing your mind, and offer up a prayer to the gods of fishing. You are part of a superstitious tribe and it pays to observe the rituals. There is also something in you which says, 'You've waited so long to get here, savour it, pace yourself, observe everything and store it away for the future. You may catch fish, you may not, but by watching and stealing with your eyes and ears you will not go home empty-handed. You will take back memories that will be laid down like young wine and years later you'll uncork them, and once again savour the day. Be slow, be careful of the day and the place. And above all, respect it. For the sea could have you before you have your first fish.'

You fasten your reel to your rod. It's an old friend, your Penn 49, with a three-to-one ratio, allowing you to come in fast over the kelp and the waterside rocks and snags. You thread the line through the eyes of your rod, an old brown three-quarter stiff 10-footer, feeling the line, 40-pound breaking strain, for nicks and blemishes. There are none, because the night before on the beach by the cottage you had the sense to wind on and stretch a fresh 200 yards of virgin line.

You make up a trace, a loop for the sinker and alongside it but above, a tightly knotted barbed hook – the curve almost as deep as the shank, a good galjoen hook, gun-metal blue. On it, you place a gobbet of redbait and, with elasticised cotton, fasten it on well.

Now, you watch the waves, working out where to stand for your cast. It makes no sense by the water's edge, where breaking waves will threaten your safety and distract you, nor is it any good to stand too far from the sea. You want to maximise the distance you can cast. You may well be wrong, but always you believe the best fish are furthest from where you stand. Feeling the sweet weight of the rod, beautifully balanced, the length of line and trace just two foot from the top eye, you pause and search the sea before you for the spot – the ideal spot to place your cast. There is a patch of white

A Fisherman in the Saddle

turbulent water just to the side of a dark spot in the water, denoting a sunken rock. There is depth, and movement and on the rock, there will be stuff that attracts the fish to feed; it's perfect.

Gently you swing the rod back, making sure that your line is free and not looped about the top eye. You brace yourself and then years of practice takes over and you feel the sinker flying, taking line directly to where you aimed, as you thumb the reel, avoiding overwinds. The line runs and runs. There is a splash and your line plummets to the bottom. You haul in the slack and now that you are linked to the sea, you feel the tug and release, the movement of the ocean working the line, carrying messages up the line to your arm, and two fingers, which hold the line just above the reel. You're fishing.

Thoughts turn on how to manage more of this pleasure, this space, this peace, and this freedom – this simple pleasure of being an unseen presence in a seascape. There are thoughts on self-sufficiency, of withdrawing from the world to a small farm, acres of your own, books, music, simple, white-washed walls and your own paintings upon them, jars of self-preserved jams and pickles and relishes on shelves you put up yourself.

There is a cat and a dog perhaps, and solitude, broken now and then by a woman you love and who loves you, but who gives you space. Money does not intrude on these thoughts, nor do many practical considerations. There is space for beauty and time for dreaming. And your dreams are not of great fish, but how to prolong this retreat from the world, this connectedness to nature, where the spirit unfurls, and stretches, and stirs, as if from a deep, deep sleep, and comes to life.

This is a place where speech does not have much of a role to play. Your movements are exact and graceful, for you have achieved a state of grace. The hunger for more things, for more love, for more acclaim, is quieted, and there is now space and time for happiness which, unnoticed, has crept up on you.

Why do more of us not take this road, the one less

travelled? Why are we so other-directed by the world we denigrate? Why does it have such a hold on us when it brings no lasting joy and its success is meaningless in the great scheme of things? Is it that we are such social beings that we are eternally hooked on status, seeking the respect of our peers? What a trap that is!

Yet who is the more worthwhile, the mystic withdrawn from the world, or the person fully engaged with it, who benefits others, not only themselves? It is all such a balancing act. Fishing sits at the boundaries of these two realities – a blessed space to just be.

At some point the mind returns to the present, the here and now, and the real pain in your butt where you have been perched uncomfortably long on that rock.

There are dried fish scales on your hands and blood and bait under fingernails. Your face is tight with sun and salt and your hair is flat and greasy and unkempt. These things don't mean a damn. You smell the crushed *khakibos* and peel the orange lichen off the rocks. There is a dung beetle, a bee, and a horsefly for company, and the sea, the beautiful, blessed, treacherous sea, the best company of all in solitude.

The changing light, the pristine hope of morning, the mellow satisfactions of afternoon, and the small sadness of evening. All have come and gone. There has been a deal of steady physical work, walking and climbing, casting and reeling. You realise you are tired. A mile away, the soft lights of a fishing shack blink on, promising hot water, clean clothes, food and drink, and once more you leave the outdoors and its joys for the comfort of a chair. And yes, you caught some fish too.

A Fisherman in the Saddle

DURBAN MANNERS

Each July the family would escape the Cape winter for the subtropical heat and light of Durban, putting up at The Beach, Claridges or The Edward Hotel, where the patience and impeccable manners of the waiters elicited a similar response in me. I still possess a laminated, mounted copy of Rudyard Kipling's poem 'If', given me by an elderly couple who ate at the table next to ours in the dining room of the Beach Hotel. The inscription on the back reads: 'To the little boy who attracted our attention, from Mr and Mrs H. Leeger, Houghton Johannesburg'. It is dated 13.7.1960. What attracted their attention was the sight of me, aged ten and precocious, eating a banana with a knife and fork. What can I say?

Manners, however were even more of an issue on the North Pier, where I would spend a good part of each day, fishing. Here manners were not an optional extra – you needed them to survive. Walking onto the pier you could smell the tar impregnated in the sun-warmed wood, mingling with the smell of the sea, and the bait and fish strewn along both sides at regular intervals. Standing virtually shoulder-to-shoulder were small boys with rods and handlines, teenagers and older men. But the place was dominated by the no-nonsense Indian fishermen, fiercely moustached, clutching ancient spinning reels and worn bamboo rods, sporting vicious triple-hooked silver lures and, wonder of wonders, casting backwards.

I had never seen such a thing. Instead of facing the sea as I had been taught and casting one's line straight out by lifting the rod over the top of your right shoulder, these guys did something which seemed positively mad and even madder in such crowded conditions. They stood with their backs to the patch of sea into which they wished to cast, and swung the rod and its dangerous freight in a wide sideways curve over the fast-ducked heads and dipped rods of everyone to their right, or left, depending on which side they favoured. There were brief nominal shouts of 'Coming over on the left' and then the silver projectile would whiz overhead, not taking your ear or cheek with it this time. It was barely controlled mayhem.

I soon learned that the safest position for a non-combatant in this fishing war was on your bum with legs dangling between the posts. In this way you could still fish and hopefully avoid being scalped.

If this sounds bad enough – and I thought so at the time – when the shad started biting, the tempo of shouting and casting and swearing picked up as well. It was fantastically exhilarating and exotic. I remember the wish to pee and the fear of running this gauntlet to the toilets behind the beach, holding it in being the only option. I feel that I must have done myself infinite damage, especially when these days I get up in the night for a second leak at 3am.

There were compensations – the shad themselves for starters. They must be one of the most elegant of fish. The shape would not disgrace the product of Ferrari's wind tunnel and design studio – an elongated ovoid, flat-sided, and finished in metallic silver, with a set of teeth beneath the bonnet designed to nip off a finger in a trice. Distinctly cool. And fight? Boy did those fish fight! On a light rod and tackle, they gave you the fight of your life, easily rivalling that of a galjoen.

There was, too, the great pleasure of carrying your catch back to the hotel, being stopped every ten yards by some admiring person who would congratulate you, and then the highest accolade of all, when your waiter took the fish

A Fisherman in the Saddle

from you to be prepared by the chef, bringing it back crisp and golden and telling your parents that they had an ace fisherman in the family. Holidays just don't come that good anymore.

I'm not sure quite why we moved base, but after a few years the family encamped in July, outside Durban at the Salt Rock Hotel, just north of the Umhlanga Rocks and Oysterbox hotels. The Salt Rock Hotel did not hold a candle to the sophistication of the other two, but had a laid-back style that we far preferred, and besides, strolling the gardens, snacking on whole paw-paw, were two giant Madagascar tortoises on whose backs one could occasionally ride.

The pleasures of this watering hole continued as one made one's way down through lovely sub-tropical gardens to the crystalline beach, where sand crabs made holes and ran in fear of a future as bait. Before you stretched the Indian Ocean, enclosed at one spot by a tidal pool, above which stood three fishing boxes on concrete pillars. Here, there was peace and uninterrupted pleasure, no wildly swinging Indian fishermen. It was just perfect.

I recall landing shad, and also a species called caranteen, a silver fish with lateral orange stripes, and other varieties too, whose names are long gone. This for a 10-year-old-boy was a foretaste of heaven, a private box with hungry fish queuing up to be caught. Here, too, the chef was obliging and my lunches quite often included a piece of my morning's catch.

The hotel's owners showed me another type of fishing, the like of which I have never seen since. They would thread a kite onto the end of a rod and line, with a baited trace hanging from it. With this contraption they flew the bait out over the surf into really deep water and caught shark, some of them sizeable. What the shark made of the kite as it came plummeting down on their heads I never did discover.

We used to drive up from Cape Town, until one holiday my father fell asleep at the wheel just outside Laingsburg in the Karoo and nearly rolled the car. We were saved by the quick thinking of our driver who was sitting in the front passenger seat. He grabbed the wheel as we plunged down the steep-sided culvert. After that, we took the Orange Express and I would pass the night rocking happily in my bunk, the train going shad, carenteen, shad, carenteen, through till morning.

At least once during the holiday we would visit the fabled Indian Market where your eyes, with their Cape-winter-palette of greens and greys, would explode amid turmeric yellows, purple saris and silver knives, your nose assaulted in turn by a thousand smells and fragrances, exotic fruit and beautiful women in the clothes of a 1001 nights.

All this was bliss for a 10-year-old, but it was the shad that really held my attention.

Janice, Herman and Julian at Hamerkop, 1980s

FISHING FRIENDS

Half the pleasure of fishing is the characters one meets. Fishermen are a democratic lot, giving a welcome, making space, offering bait and advice generously. If this makes them seem simply too good to be true, it's worth saying that maybe they do keep something back. There is a feeling that some things have to be earned. Information is free, but knowledge comes at a price.

Fishermen come in all shapes, sizes and styles. If supermarkets sold them, there would have to be some sort of rationalisation; a store couldn't stock them all: they are just too various. Most, however, fill a general pattern; middle-aged, mostly affable, dressed in nondescript clothes that you'd be hard-pressed to recall for a policeman. These are not the fishermen you remember.

One I do remember well was the cannabis-smoking fisherman at Kalk Bay. He was in his thirties and looked as though life had used him hard. His hands had homemade tattoos you didn't want to look at too closely; there was a scar or two on his face and a couple of earrings in one ear. He looked bad news as he sat there, a line in one hand, sucking on his broken bottle dagga pipe, red-eyed and coughing. Had he been a dog you might have thought to put him down.

He sensed my discomfort, and offered me a go at the bottleneck, laughing at my prim refusal. He said he'd lost his job on the trawlers, and that his wife had run off with another man, facts which hardly surprised me. As he said this, I mentally counted the money I had in my pocket and reckoned how much I could let him have when he asked the inevitable question. But he surprised me. Out of his back pocket he took a crumpled piece of paper and unwrapped it carefully in the lee of the pier wall, making sure the wind did not blow it away. It looked like bait.

'*Basie*, try some of this. It's magic to catch the fish.' My every instinct was to thank him and move away but, even then I was a fisherman in the making and besides, something in his gaze held me there. Whatever the paper held it smelled unspeakable, but he went to the trouble of hooking it on for me, tying it firmly with ordinary cotton he pulled from a stained reel of the stuff. 'This used to be good stuff,' he said.

I had hardly made my first cast when the mackerel began biting as if in a frenzy. After each fish was landed, I gave him a nod. He sucked on his jagged dagga pipe and held fast to his hand line. The fish kept coming and before long I must have had a dozen. Surprisingly, given their voracious appetites and their needle-sharp teeth, the bait remained firmly attached, seemingly impervious to attack. It just caught the fish.

Eventually the dagga-smoker got up and wound his line in. He asked me if he could have some fish and I said he should help himself. He took four. He wrapped them in a filthy piece of newspaper that was blowing down the quay and, stuffing them into a plastic bag, turned to go. Curiosity got the better of me. I asked him what the bait was. 'It's a piece of my heart boss. A piece of my heart.'

He said it sadly and then he was gone. I looked carefully at the bait the next time I took it from a fish's mouth. The water seemed to have refreshed it and now it was a dark red, like liver, or something similar. I did not want to touch it then but cut it off the line, along with the hook it was attached to, and threw it into the sea. I gutted my fish, packed up and went home, wiser in some ways about the ways of the world, but not really better informed.

A few years later, I did a stupid thing. I was fishing at

A Fisherman in the Saddle

Hamerkop on the Bredasdorp coast, fishing alone. It's a tricky bit of coast, deep water running into a great mass of fallen rocks, cliffs and natural piers. It is a very private place, where a twisted ankle or a broken leg would leave you in grave danger. There are baboons there and their natural enemy, the leopard. This was in the days before mobile phones put an end to the concept of wilderness. When you were alone at Hamerkop, you were pretty much alone. This was its great attraction and what made me break all the rules. I went fishing alone.

I set out in sunshine, but by the time I had made my way by jeep halfway back up the coastal range and then cut back down to a spot above The Pier, walking in the last 20 minutes, a sea fog had started to obliterate the view. At this point, my grownup self would have stopped and philosophically made my way back to the shack. But youth will have its way. I made my way onto the rocks, encouraged by the dull cover of the fog, knowing it might well improve the fishing. I was not disappointed. I caught a number of red roman, blacktail and a skaamhaai, which, despite my dislike of shark, I threw back.

I was then totally shrouded in fog and knew that I was being foolish. Of all the places on that coast, The Pier was the single most dangerous, liable on the calmest day to take any large wave over the top. You can imagine my surprise when, taking my eyes off the sea for a moment, I saw a figure scrambling down the almost sheer cliff behind me. This was private coast, and this had to be one of those people who occasionally chanced their arm, walking in from Infanta. I was really annoyed and felt intruded upon. To my amazement, he called to me. I thought, bloody cheek, and pretended I had not heard him. He called again and I thought there was something familiar about him, perhaps someone's ghillie, whom I should really recognise. I brought my line in, leant my rod against a rock wall and started climbing up towards him to ask what he wanted.

I must have climbed up the length of The Pier and started up the path behind it when I heard an enormous explosion. Looking down at the source of the noise I saw that a huge freak wave had covered the rock. Had I been sitting there I would have had no chance, I'd have been washed off and dashed to death in the turmoil at the foot of the sea cliff. I felt suddenly very cold.

'Is alright now, boss,' the ghillie said from just above me. I looked up and into the red eyes and scarred face I recalled so well from Kalk Bay. I saw in that second that he knew I had recognised him, but he was gone. The fog swallowed him up as surely as death.

That night, fairly shaken by the experience, I told Martin Tshila what had happened. He was the Xhosa employee who made these fishing trips the pleasure they were, shopping for groceries and organising bait in advance and then cooking and cleaning at the shack. The soul of politeness, he would not be drawn on this subject. All he would say was that it was a bad thing to go fishing on one's own in the fog.

After supper I stood a long time looking up at the night sky that was now clear once more, thinking that there are more things in heaven and earth than a man might imagine. Possibly there was space for a guardian angel?

Man Eater

Gordon's Bay is a pretty town situated in an elbow of False Bay near Cape Town, beneath the ramparts of the Hottentots Holland Mountains. Above the town, that marvellous feat of engineering, Sir Lowry's Pass, slashes diagonally across the mountain's face and from its vantage point provides one of the great panoramas of southern Africa – a view of two ocean bays across the neck of the Cape Peninsula and the brooding back of Table Mountain.

Gordon's Bay was an unpretentious place in my father's day, a small fishing harbour, a matter-of-fact hotel, a few businesses catering mainly to local needs and the homes of residents, with a sprinkling of holiday cottages above a beach, later known as Bikini Beach because of its popularity with the students of Stellenbosch University. But in the 1940s and 50s, it was a somnolent place, a distant outpost of Cape Town, where the real action took place. Gordon's Bay was a village where nothing much happened.

The place marked the spot where the coastal geology divided in two – starting south of the harbour a flat, featureless beach flowed 20 miles to Muizenberg, the bay's other elbow; and to the north of the town the rocky cliffs began, where the Hottentots Holland plunged its feet almost vertically into the Atlantic. This coast, all the way to Betty's Bay, had a dangerous reputation, fully deserved.

My father and Pascoe Grenfell knew this coast's reputation, but the lure of deep-water fishing overcame their caution from time to time. One Saturday in the late 1940s, they packed their fishing gear and trekked out to Gordon's Bay. They parked their car and walked down the steep mountainside to a set of rocks they had found to be a good fishing platform in the past.

They sat above the rock watching the sea with care, judging its mood, knowing it was not to be trusted. The memorial crosses erected on this coast were stark reminders of fishermen lost here. There is something on this seabed which, from time to time, helps to create a swell that reaches freak wave size. It arrives unannounced, out of nowhere, and like a somnolent cat, reaching out a lazy claw to impale a mouse, it claims lives at intervals. They knew this, yet they proceeded down the last piece of cliff to the rock, never once turning their backs to the sea, and lifting their eyes regularly while making trace or baiting up.

They tell me that they caught fish, though what kind they were is blurred in the mists of time and other things, which now take precedence. It was a sunny day, with little wind, the sea was calm, and fishing boats worked their way along the coast or in and out of the harbour. On the beach they could see people sunbathing and swimming – there was little surf. Hearing the story for the one-thousandth time, I can see it all, I know it so well, like a painting. Everything is in its place, unmoving.

At lunchtime, they packed up their gear and walked a couple of hundred feet up the mountain to have lunch in peace without the constant need to watch the sea. They unpacked and spread themselves out, enjoying the food and drink and the sunshine. After some time, they noticed two other fishermen making their way down the mountain towards them. The men stopped by to ask what luck they'd had, and they told them of their catch that morning. Dad and Pascoe pointed out where they had fished and then watched in astonishment as these two headed straight for the same place and proceeded to start fishing in the exact same spot.

Pascoe was all for going down and giving them a piece

A Fisherman in the Saddle

of his mind, but my father said it might be a simple mistake, the newcomers not realising that he and Pascoe had intended returning after lunch. It was warm and both men felt sleepy, so they nodded off for a few minutes, leaving the issue of their fishing spot for later.

After some time, they collected their gear and edged their way back down to the rocks, surprised not to see the fishermen. All the newcomers' gear was still neatly stacked on a ledge just above the spot they had been standing on, but there was no trace of them at all. It was then that my father noticed that the rock was wet. Previously it had been dry, and one or two salt-caked crevices were now full of water. Both men then realised what must have happened. Nervously they surveyed the sea; it was as calm as a millpond and the little boats continued to fish along the coast. It was a scene of utter tranquillity.

Rejecting their worst fears as simply too spooky, they looked about them to see if the men might have taken a rod each and worked their way along the coast. Everything was clearly visible; there was no easy way from this particular vantage point to other points on the coast. To move, the men would have had to walk almost to where Pascoe and my father had had their lunch and then back down to the sea. But no one had been near them.

They looked down into the water but there was no sign of the men in the sea either. Keeping their eyes on the sea, they edged their way back up the mountain to the car, packed up and drove into Gordon's Bay. At the police station they reported what had happened, the desk sergeant noted it all down but was sanguine. 'Probably in the bushes for a call of nature, or fishing behind a rock. But thanks all the same.'

The next evening's edition of *The Cape Argus* told a very different story. A trawler coming into Gordon's Bay that morning had discovered two bodies floating in the sea. The men were still dressed in their fishing clothes.

While my father and Pascoe rested after lunch on that calm and lovely day, the sea, like an impish giant, had played a bad joke on two fisherman, plucking them neatly off their rock ledge before either could even let out a shout. It was silent, deadly work. It might so easily have been my father and his pal. The fact that I am here is thanks to the sea-giant choosing two other men for its lunch.

Dad and Pascoe never did go back to Gordon's Bay after that, and they warned me away from the area as well. And if I had a penny for each time my father has said, 'Never turn your back on the sea,' I'd be a rich man.

Janice on Max, winning a showing class in the 1980s

A Fisherman in the Saddle

Subversive Activity

Have you noticed that complete idiots don't fish? This is certainly something I have observed and wondered about over the years. The flash, the big shots, the cool, don't really fish. Sure, they may now and then do a spot of fishing, some deep-sea sport fishing on an expensive charter; or holiday in Alaska to allow them to say they have caught some big salmon; or visit a Scottish trout and salmon river which costs a king's ransom before you are allowed near the water. But fishing as I know it, on your own, in unfashionable and unpretentious places, there you will not find these people. Why? I've often wondered.

My argument goes something like this: There is a kind of man who has bought into the macho trap – he's an action man and proud of it. This guy needs an audience; he needs to be part of a pack, a crew – a team. The 'boring' anti-social nature of fishing is anathema to him.

Fishing teaches philosophy, controlled inaction, environmentalism. The most superficial experience of fishing teaches one some useful things which bring you face to face with yourself and also sets you apart from the mainstream values of the world. And the more seriously you take fishing, the more different you will be from the vast majority of the human herd.

You cannot help becoming something of an environmentalist, possibly a complete nature nut, when you get into fishing. It just happens, nature impacts on you. If you're not careful, you can wind up a non-smoking vegetarian, in non-leather shoes and belt, writing to the papers about global warming and boring the pants off anyone who will stand still long enough to listen.

You may ask, quite fairly, how can a fisherman be an environmentalist when he kills fish? Fair question. But nothing important in life is simple. The better the fisherman, the more he wants to catch fish, so he soon realises that if he wants to be fishing successfully in his seventies, and have his son catch fish too, he'd better start thinking conservation of fish stocks and getting into catch and release, and looking after fishing environments. Some of the hottest environmentalists I know are fishermen.

Even more worrying for the mainstream is the fact that fishing teaches you the uselessness of all effort. It teaches you that nothing really, really, matters that much – life, death, money and ambition – it's all the same in the end; it doesn't stack up to a hill of beans. Fishing gives you this scary perspective, a distance on life that, when closely inspected, tells you that you are born, you breed and you die. If you're lucky, you get and give a little love en route, but then that's it. The memory of your achievements may last a generation or two before true oblivion. So why not grasp happiness where it can be found and go fishing!

There is a story I heard which illustrates this point well. A wealthy American tycoon spends a fortnight's holiday each year in a small Mexican resort where he hires the services of a boatman ghillie. After a few seasons, he realises the Mexican is dead smart. And he offers the Mexican a job in New York where he could make a lot of money. The Mexican says to him. 'Gracias Senor. May I ask what is your greatest ambition?' The tycoon thinks for a moment and replies that his greatest wish would be to earn enough money to be able to retire to this Mexican village to fish. The Mexican says: 'Well, senor, you and others pay me to stay here and fish all year, which I love. Why would I want to go to New York?'

See what I mean? Dangerous stuff, fishing. Imagine if

A Fisherman in the Saddle

the whole world thought like that? Fishing gives you a different take on life, an alternative reality. It's downright subversive.

Ask yourself when you last remember being truly happy. I'd venture a guess that it came to you while you were busy doing something, rather than slumped on a couch watching TV. Fishing is as much about going and doing as it is about reflection. That's a nice mix. A sure-fire recipe for happiness, I find. Horse riding is another activity that falls into this category. The trick is to be doing something – usually outside.

If fishing happens to you in your childhood, as it did for me, then you've had a kickstart down a different road, and with luck you'll always avoid being part of the mainstream, never quite one of the lads. You'll be yourself.

I've noticed that the people I like most are the ones who so arrange their lives that they get to go fishing, or riding, or skiing, when they want to. They are a pretty picaresque bunch. This life choice of course precludes having a 'career' and quite often having a 'proper relationship'. Now I am going to stick my neck out – another example of the subversive things fishing teaches. I don't want to be sexist here, but I can hear women's voices on this subject and they are speaking about a man who is 'selfish, unable to commit, a man who has never grown up'. Not a serious hombre at all.

Why be so serious? Nature has a way of defeating one's plans. My father used to say, 'Man proposes and God disposes.' Nature has a way of saying, 'No, you can't have that', which is very good for the soul. It teaches humility. Nature can't be ordered around or bullied. The economics of it, the opportunity costs, are atrocious. One has to learn to be philosophical when you fish. You simply have to, or you go mad. So fishermen learn to dance to a different tune.

Was it Jesus, possibly the best-known fisherman in the world, (okay, he wasn't a rock angler but one can't have everything) who said that unless you became as a child you would not enter the Kingdom of Heaven? Now I know you can get some pretty scary children but, even in this day and age, I have yet to meet one with a career, or one who would prefer going in to the office than go fishing.

Another visionary, Karl Marx, described the true, complete man, as one who wrote in the morning, farmed in the afternoon and fished in the evening – or words to that effect.

I love those who have kept faith with the child inside them. Some of the world's greatest artists have this quality, as do some of the world's greatest bullshitters. They are still connected to fantasy, to imagination, and the 'real world' the 'serious world', the 'grown-up-world' has never truly managed to get them hard-wired, roped in.

As I say, complete idiots don't fish.

Off Cape Point

Taking a small open boat out to sea makes me nervous at the best of times and when it's twelve to twenty miles off Cape Point, I'm decidedly anxious. Deep-sea fishing is not something I actively go looking for. But even the most dedicated rock angler has his moments of madness and, once or twice in the past, I've accepted invitations to go tunny fishing on boats out of Simon's Town.

There's an interesting phenomenon I've noticed, probably also experienced by those heading for the electric chair or a date with a hangman – the ordinary takes on the glossy sheen of the extraordinary, the ugly can look quite beautiful. I've driven through Simon's Town sufficiently often to hardly give it a thought. It's okay, I've nothing against it, but for me it always has a slightly unkempt and abandoned feel. It's like a bar the morning after, stubbed cigarettes and the stale smell of beer – probably has something to do with the Naval Dockyard there.

But in the early morning light, as you arrive at the harbour for a date with the deep, Simon's Town has a wonderful feel to it. This may have something to do with the conviction in your trembling heart that this perfect place, this jewel of the False Bay coast might be the last town on earth you see before the sea swallows you whole. I'm sure that's been true for many men. It's just that I've got round to writing about it. So, yes, Simon's Town can be ineffably lovely when one is in the right mood – a modest to full blown funk.

There is that moment when you wake up and you realise that today's the day you are going deep-sea fishing; how those words toll in your head! You get up, reluctantly, though your stomach seems not to have noticed. You drink coffee and look at the sky – a perfect day – no easy way out there. The weather forecast offers no excuse either. You drive to Simon's Town, the car behaving as though it were brand new, and you realise what a friend it's been to you and how you will miss it. With a heavy heart you park, telling yourself for the hundredth time not to be such a bloody coward, that this might be the best day's fishing of your life, that people fly in from all over the world to have a crack at this gilt-edged quarry and here you are being invited for free, as a guest, to go in search of fish history, record book material. Get a grip, man.

You realise that you are in such a state that you've left all your kit in the boot of the car; you run back and, in so doing, are made aware that you need the toilet again. Grabbing everything you see, you slam the boot down and dash for the harbour gates. At the single public toilet, you find a line of men on the same errand. They look a hard lot, tough. Your stomach wobbles and you breathe deeply and walk in tight circles.

Finally, you get down to the quay and see your friend loading up what looks like a cockleshell, the much-lauded ski-boat he assured you is the best thing based at Simon's Town. It's red inside and not more than 18 feet long with a windshield for the captain's wheel. There are two chairs bolted to the deck, bait boxes and two fairly serious looking outboard motors. A bunch of fishing rods lean over the back, two stuck in trolling rod-holders by the chairs. You grin weakly. 'Morning. Nice day for it!' you say, lying through your teeth.

'Well,' he says, 'I've just been listening on the shortwave radio. The trawlers are talking about a bit of a sea out there and they expect the wind to pick up some towards lunchtime, nothing to worry about. In fact, perfect Cape conditions. Fish should be biting. Let's go.' You cast one last

A Fisherman in the Saddle

despairing look at beautiful Simon's Town, that prince among towns, and you haul yourself down into the boat.

There is a brief moment when the engines have roared into life and the boat has climbed out of the water and is careering away from the harbour entrance, the light dancing on the sea and the small figures fishing from the quay waving to you, that you feel quite good. At least you look part of a business-like operation, even though you have the gravest reservations about your sanity. Your friend calls in to the coastguard, reporting your intentions and intended course, and then you're truly off. It's pleasant enough as you run in the lee of the land on your right, the great mass of Cape Point shielding you from the open ocean. But then that small boon is past, and you are now heading out into the real stuff and the boat begins to climb and fall, to rock and roll, to jibe and skid. And you remember in the greatest detail why you feel the way you do about deep-sea fishing.

The seagulls disappear suddenly and the colour of the sea changes from royal blue to a much more dangerous looking blue-black colour – you're in tunny water. You help to get the rods traced up and lures attached, keeping busy is good, concentrating on anything but the sea is good, anything that stops you looking wistfully back at Cape Point which is now just a small smudge on the horizon even when you are right on top of the next roller. This is not sea, these ominous blocks of flats marching down on you, relentlessly, looking for the smallest chink in your armour. You realise that if you fall overboard here, the local fish might prefer you to the lures. It comes to you that you have not got a lifejacket on. Bloody hell, what are you thinking!

'Hadn't we better put one of those life-preserver things on?' you ask hesitantly.

'Sure!' says your friend, and clumsily you wrestle yourself into one. As you do this, you think, now what happens if he's washed overboard, because he's not putting one on. You see a trawler off to your left and your mate is on the radio asking for any sign of fish. They chat for a moment and you then change direction.

Now, instead of running directly into the face of the wet black cliffs, you are half broadside on to them, climbing awkwardly, and there is an odd feeling as you crest them and descend the other side. But there is no time for that now, you must force your fears aside as you are directed into one of the fishing chairs and a rod is stuck into your sweating hands.

You trawl for hours, and, yes, the wind does pick up, and the sea with it. You manage a sandwich and a beer and instantly regret it, but keeping it all down is a small triumph. At around this point, your friend gets into a small yellowtail, or is it a tunny? You are in charge of the boat now and trying to watch the waves, and at the same time help your friend. The engines are throttled right back to make his fight easier. You look around for the gaff, but in the end, it is not needed. The fish comes aboard, thrashes some, is dispatched and put in the fish cooler. The thought strikes you that now the sea has a reason for wanting to get even. Gladly, you hand the boat back to your friend. You trawl some hours more. The fumes from the slowly working engines make you nauseous and you gag.

Finally, the blessed words come. 'Think we'd better start back.' You stop yourself from making the sign of the cross or going down on your knees, or any other form of public display. You even manage an answer. 'Fair enough. Been a lovely day.' Oh God, forgive me for lying.

Slowly, painfully, Cape Point climbs over the horizon on the back of giant waves, any one of which might crush you like an insect. Now you have a following sea, which the boat does not handle nearly as well. It slews and threatens to broach. You say to the engines, 'Good chaps, keep going please. You are doing a great job.' Your thoughts turn to Pascoe, as they do *in extremis*. 'Steady the buffs, old man,' he'd say, and you feel marginally better.

Suddenly, you are in trouble. The millionth wave of the day rises behind you and suddenly its speed and your speed coincide, or something, and the boat is careering down the face of the wave like a bloody surfboard. There is an almighty bump as you hit a wall of water with an impact like

A Fisherman in the Saddle

steel on concrete and your friend falls to the deck, his chair having ripped its bolts from the wood. You lean over and keep the boat pointing in roughly the right direction as your friend gets up with a bleeding nose. 'Sorry, double wave. Happens sometimes.'

What seems like hours pass and you finally edge into the lee of Cape Point once more. The Simon's Town harbour lights are on and you think to yourself you were right about it this morning, it is a beautiful town, the most beautiful town you've ever seen.

Julian fishing at Hamerkop in the 1970s

ON KILLING FISH

It is an inescapable fact of life that, if you fish long enough, there will come a time at which you will have to kill fish. This has never been a problem for me, though I will admit that as the years go by and thoughts of mortality increasingly intrude, I do not dispatch fish with quite the same eager relish of my youth. I do it quickly, efficiently, and with a moment of sadness.

Like the Native American, I say to the fish, 'Thank you for the fight you gave me. Forgive me for doing this. Be sure we will not waste your flesh.' Heavy stuff really. But we are talking life and death here. For all we know, fish too may have souls. It is interesting to note that trout fishermen, who generally account themselves the most superior of fishermen, kill with a small mace, which they call a 'priest'. Killing on a regular basis has that effect, makes you a mite religious.

But there is a new and worrying development, which may put an end to fishing and killing for sport. According to the latest scientific thinking, fish do feel pain. Surprise, surprise! Sometimes you have to wonder at our ability to kid ourselves. Of course they bloody feel pain, anyone who has actually killed a fish could tell you that on good authority. My fishing friends in the UK are walking softly and looking far into the distance, worrying that their beloved sport may one day go the way of foxhunting, which looks as if it's in its own death throes, after centuries.

But I suspect it will be a long time before fishing is banned. We will see anglers on South Africa's coasts for many a long year. There is, after all, a balance to be struck on the subject of killing – the more we distance or remove ourselves from the food we eat, the less we are tied to nature, reality and in a strange way, to our own humanity, our natural selves. There is a respect for food, which comes from growing or raising or hunting and killing your own.

This was a view not truly appreciated by most of those game girlfriends who accompanied me on fishing trips and expeditions. Most were quite happy to catch the odd fish between reading and looking lovely, but killing the fish was my job. Then one day I met the girl who I wished to spend the rest of my life with. She was one who did not waste time looking lovely; she just was lovely. She was a grown-up tomboy who wanted to be part of the action. She wanted to learn to fish from start to finish.

Oh! The pleasure of teaching her to cast! I had not previously realised that casting could be a contact sport. She learned fast, probably because she really did want to fish and realised early that fishing was *not* a contact sport. And with all the irritating luck of the first timer, she caught fish – serious numbers of fish. And there was the rub. She too, like her predecessors, would not kill the fish she caught.

As a fairly typical male, piqued by the numbers of fish she was catching, and irritated by the fact that I had to halt my own fishing to unhook and dispatch her fish, I got annoyed. She also got annoyed, but I noticed that the next fish she landed she unhooked herself and, crying now, she stabbed it. Then as is the way of fish, whose central nervous system lets them down in this way, it continued to flap around. With eyes shut now and crying harder, she stabbed at it some more, till it finally lay still. Brute that I was, I pretended that I had not seen a thing.

She is a tough cookie, one of the reasons I love her, and it was not long before there were no tears, just a very thorough and professional job being done on killing fish. Though I did catch the odd look that might have chilled a

A Fisherman in the Saddle

man, noting the bait knife in her hand and less sure that his love loved him.

Jan became a very competent fishing companion; I won't say 'fishwife' for obvious and diplomatic reasons. The fact is, she was damn good. There were many days that my gaze would wander from my own fishing to the petite denim-clad figure, short auburn hair scrunched under a peaked cap, fighting a fish to my right or left. The hard work doing interesting things to the view from the rear.

I recall one day in particular. There was late afternoon light accentuating her deep tan, her lips held a hook ready to be threaded on trace, there was a bloody knife in her hands, and her denim outfit was in need of a wash. She looked like a small Lascar pirate. Just the wonderful metallic lustre of her auburn hair – which owed nothing to my family's connection with Wella – glinted like new-minted copper in the setting sun, giving the lie to the male image.

She reminded me of Joan of Arc, whose tough armour hid the softness within – a bit like a crayfish I suppose. Jokes aside, where Joan finally failed to rescue the French, and paid the price, Jan did not fail and she certainly rescued me, though she was hell on the fish.

There are times now when I watch her, beautifully dressed and off to interview some City chairman, or addressing a public gathering with understated wit, that I catch myself doing something odd, I place that dirty brown lascar next to the woman in Armani and am filled with wonder. We all possess so many facets, so many masks.

There was an instance recently when the two images coalesced before me. She was hosting a writer's workshop at the Sherlock Holmes Festival in our town; something she and I helped set up, in this, the former home of Sir Arthur Conan Doyle. She was presenting one of the attending crime writers with a gift, a copy of the prestigious Silver Dagger Award. There was something distinctly fishy about him and as she lifted the dagger my heart skipped a beat.

Julian on Callum 2020

THE ROMANCE OF GOING FISHING

Fishing is a lot like romance. Now I can hear you say: 'Hell, if he thinks fishing's like romance, God help his wife!' But bear with me. When you're new to it all – fishing or romance – there's a lot of frustration involved, a lot of hanging around, and a lot of mistakes made. Later there is the full-blown passion – all-consuming, and leaving you exhilarated and exhausted. As a young man in love with fishing there is the same hammer and tongs approach.

But as you begin to appreciate the finer points of both activities, it is often those finer points that you appreciate, if you understand me. Let's say for argument's sake that a young man invites a young woman out for a meal; he is probably unduly focused on after-dinner activities and may not even taste the food or the wine. And that is a great pity. And it will be a pity for her as well, because if all he's interested in after dinner is the equivalent of the main course, he's going to miss out on all the other pleasures – and so is she – of the *apéritif*, the *hors-d'oeuvre*, the *amuse-guelles*, the joy of selecting the wine. Now, there is such a thing as having too much information, so perhaps we should draw a line here.

Let's just say that there comes a time in a fisherman's life when the mere thought of going fishing is a pleasure to be savoured. Then there is the preparation itself. How often have you fished with a reel of nylon that is over-knotted, nicked, or damaged in some way? The older fisherman cleans and oils his reels and makes sure that there is fresh line, stretched line, on his reel. He is careful about the bait he buys. He thinks about what he will eat while fishing. And he takes pleasure in getting set up to go.

Then there is the night before departure. Who said that the anticipation of pleasure was ninety per cent of the pleasure; that travelling, hopefully rather than arriving, is what everything is all about? Whoever said it was a wise man.

The next day's trip to the fishing spot is pretty good, too. If you are fishing in the Cape, and that is the patch I know best, you will drive through some of the most spectacular scenery to be found anywhere in the world. Let's say you are heading for Cape Infanta, about 180 miles from Cape Town on the Indian Ocean coast, you will head out early in the morning and maybe see sunrise from the top of Sir Lowry's Pass. Or you may leave later and stop on the way at the Firgrove Farm Stall just before the pass, to stock up on treats. Once over the mountain, and carefully avoiding the odd baboon, there will be a chance to stop too at the Orchard or Peregrine Farm Stalls for delicious homemade preserves and pies.

You are in mountain country, on a magnificent road and the car is enjoying the trip as much as you are. Just before Caledon, on your left, there is a white-walled farm, Boontjieskraal, which has a terrible story of tragedy attached to it. The farmer who owned this place many years ago was cursed by a distraught traveller who lost his wife and newborn child when crossing the raging swollen river that runs through the farm, after the farmer had refused them shelter during a particularly severe storm. The farmer and his male descendants fell to the curse, suffering tragic violent deaths, so the story goes. But you are going fishing and have no time for tragedy.

On the N2, you pass turnings for the picturesque towns of Genadendal and Greyton. Each holds memories for you. There will be the whitewashed thatched cottages, the

A Fisherman in the Saddle

romantic B&Bs, the small restaurants serving food your mother once made. There will be the tangible sense of a slower pace of life that beckons beguilingly. There will be smiles from donkey cart drivers, raised hats alongside floral headscarves, urchinss playing marbles or running hoops, there will be a yellow mongrel dog lying in the dust, too lazy to lift a head. There will be the clear rain-washed light of morning that stains the whitewashed walls soft green, or the thick, honeyed glaze of amber afternoons. In the air will be the smell of freshly made baked goods *melktert*, *vetkoek*, *koeksisters* and the tang of sweet potato caramelising. You think of pulling in, turning left towards the mountains, of leaving fishing for another day, but fishing will win out, just, and you drive on.

You drive through a country that's like an illustrated manuscript, a lot of it plain though grand, but with staggeringly beautiful capitals, and a peacock palette. And in a way it is a manuscript, for here history is written, though in a small hand. The Scottish travel writer and artist Lady Anne Barnard came this way in May 1798 on her way through the Cape, and others too. But this is a history lesson on rubber tyres at 70 miles per hour, and there is no exam at the end, just the pleasure of knowledge, of adding another layer to the many skeins of knowing that attach you ever deeper to this place, where one day you hope your dust will devil amid the new-grown corn, laying it flat like a lover's hand on a girl's hair.

All about you there is new wheat in the great prairie-like fields, or beige stubble, depending on the season. Sitting sentinel on the telephone poles will be black-shouldered kites and pied crows, while in the fields, if you are lucky, you will see South Africa's national bird, the endangered blue crane.

Eventually, you approach Riviersonderend, and brake in anticipation of the bastard traffic cops who lie in wait. This is not a place to be caught speeding; it will hold up your fishing needlessly and spoil your mood for days. You pull in for petrol and a chance to look your last on 'civilization'. You buy chocolate bars and biltong, *droëwors* and a jar of honey in the comb.

And then you go, turning off just before sleepy Swellendam, in bed below its mountain headboard, where once independence of a kind reigned for a while. Now you must keep your wits about you as you take to the corrugations of a forty-mile gravel road down to the mouth of the Breede River. Here begins a kingdom of rock and stones, in the road, waiting for a go at your windscreen if you hug another car's dust cloud ahead of you too closely, stones in piles in the fields and rocks like badly healed ribs sticking out of the cage of hills to your left and right. Suddenly there is an ostrich with illusions of grandeur, keeping pace with you at 40 miles per hour.

You keep the windows closed, avoiding grit in the car, in the eyes, in the mouth, but it comes in anyway. You concentrate on the corners, not allowing the car any leeway to slide.

You find a speed that negotiates a deal with the corrugations, but it's a bad deal and your fillings vibrate. Good German auto engineering keeps you in touch with the road surface, not something you actually wish, but which here you must live with.

You see old friends, and they come in all shapes and sizes, mute witnesses to the journeys of your life en route to fishing. There is the crooked fencepost after ten miles, the sagging barbed wire that runs alongside you, keeping you company (how can you feel what you feel for that line of wire, it is bizarre, you acknowledge that, but it is no less true for being odd), there is the first glimpse of the river between barren brown hills, and the twisted thorn tree on the last hill. And as Infanta Village hoves into view, there is something of that anxiety you feel when arriving at a party.

Fleetingly, you imagine how the sea will look, the wind taste, and the smell of the bush. A small shiver runs down your spine and you thrill a little with long-awaited pleasure. The foreplay has been wonderful, but now the main dish is about to be served. You pass Oom Piet, as you call him, who has been standing in that doorway of his two-room cottage

A Fisherman in the Saddle

for the past forty years, though common sense tells you he must have sat down once or twice in that time. You wave and he waves, as he has done for decades.

Now there is something strange yet familiar happening in your gut, a fluttering, and an excitement. The land is about to disrobe for the Indian Ocean, dropping its dust and bleak hills behind it, and striding into that deep blue sea where even now fish are swimming, fish with your name lightly tattooed on their hearts.

You roll down the window and take in a deep breath as you turn into Leon Roup Road, where your name, and your genes and your life have come together to create a little bit of heaven. You pull up in front of the cottage your father built and sit a moment looking at the sea.

You are aware that your breathing is fast and shallow, that your heart rate has gone up significantly. Controlling yourself, you unpack the car, open the cottage, rig up a rod, grab tackle and bait and stroll down to the slipway. You feel the sea caress your ankles and you know that the fishing trip, this love affair with the sea, is about to be consummated. You feel a little dizzy and you steady yourself. The balance of the rod in your hand is perfect and you cast. The sinker flies in a hard shallow curve and as it meets the sea with a wet kiss, you are at one with the ocean, and with life.

A few days later you do the trip in reverse, and there is a decidedly end of the affair feeling – a hint of sadness, tristesse, as the French name it, a regret for what has gone, for what you must leave, but also the pleasurable knowledge that, God willing, you will return.

Julian on Chancer, 2005

OBRIGADO PORTUGAL

We ran from the snow, the cold and the leaden skies. It was January 1985 and Sussex was blanketed beneath two foot of powder snow as we headed south like swallows. Indeed, it felt as though the car had wings, despite the load it was towing.

We'd been in England five years, noses hard to the grindstone, working as reporters for the *Mid-Sussex Times*, a weekly broadsheet based in Hayward's Heath, between London and Brighton. Now, finally, we had achieved Permanent Resident status and we felt we could at last go and take a look at Europe, this new continent we hoped to make our own, and which slowly, painfully, we were learning to call home.

We'd been married in the garden of a Constantia wine estate five years previously, in high summer, and we were starving for warmth, heat and southern skies. We'd bought a second-hand caravan, which towed well behind our old turbo-charged two-litre Renault 18 that we called Zorro for its dashing performance and black colour. The caravan with its many lamps – both gas and electric – we named Florence. So Jan, Florence, Zorro and I inched our way carefully over the icy roads to the ferry port at Newhaven, 45 minutes from our home, getting the feel of the car-caravan combination.

Packed somewhere in the depths of the caravan were two light flick rods and a couple of coffee grinder reels, a modest tack box with hooks and sinkers, and the hope that before long we would once more be standing by an ocean catching fish. It had been a long time since we had fished together.

The weather stayed foul as we headed down the western half of France, sleeping the first night in a rain-sodden campsite somewhere near La Rochelle. After our first coffee and croissant breakfast the next morning, we headed south once more, crossing the French/Spanish border just beyond the pretty Basque town of St Jean de Luz. We considered a slight detour to the bull-running town of Pamplona, but the call of the sun was too great, and we ventured out onto the vast Spanish plain, the Rodrigo *Concerto* providing an appropriate soundtrack to the space, so reminiscent of South Africa's Karoo.

After hours of driving, we came to Salamanca, glowing in the late afternoon light, a town that looks like its name, dramatic and romantic, its golden stone ramparts still standing after centuries, a massive brooding presence in all that flatness. The road was arrow straight and there was no traffic as we approached it, as so many before us would have done on their pilgrimage to Santiago de Compostella.

Too tired to go exploring, we headed for a shaley campsite open to the four winds, a few miles from the city, made supper and discovered a gypsy truth. If nowhere is home, then everywhere is your home. We had our home with us, like a snail. We travelled complete, transport and home in one. It is a very good feeling. As a species, we are not naturally residents of just one place; three thousand years have not wiped out the hunter-gatherer in us. It was good to be abroad, going somewhere. We drew the curtains on the world and slept.

The next day, we continued south-by-south-west on into the mountainous border with Portugal. The car behaved well, tackling the mountain pass like a good 'un. The pass once crested, we headed down through blue gum forests to Coimbra, the old medieval university town. The friendliness of the people struck us immediately. Though Portugal is Britain's oldest ally, we had no common language, but we with

A Fisherman in the Saddle

our British plates got a warm reception everywhere. We set up camp next to a sports stadium and went into town to find supper. We ate in a cool, whitewashed restaurant with the vivid white and blue tiles of Portugal, hard by the river bridge. At the end of our meal, huge goblets of port were pressed on us, compliments of the house. This, one felt, was a country worth getting to know.

We walked round Coimbra the next day, its vivid market and its magnificent university, struck by the good looks of the people and the familiarity of the shop names, our contact with the Portuguese community in South Africa creating a sense of comfort. We felt at home, in a strange way.

Our plan was to head as far south as we could, with Faro on the Algarve our ultimate destination, but we stopped a day or two in Lisbon. We visited the Gulbenkian Museum, where we saw more beautiful things than most people might see in a lifetime. We listened to fado, the sound of heartbreak made into a music of love and loss and longing, so close to my own feelings, and rubbed it in some more with a Leonard Cohen concert. Later, watching fisherman busy at the harbour, right at the foot of the main street, I felt happy.

We explored the nearby coast once the caravan was safely ensconced in a pretty tree-lined site, more like a garden than a campground. We found Cascais and Estoril and the palace of the Portuguese kings, and just a few miles further round the coast at Praia das Macas we found royalty itself. We drove into a small seaside village and down to the harbour wall. Walking along it, we passed a single fisherman whose car had British plates, though his dark aristocratic features were unmistakably Portuguese.

As is the way with fishermen the world over, I asked if he had caught anything. He was charming, spoke perfect English and we chatted for a while. He had worked for many years in England and Scotland, he said, but had now retired to his roots in Portugal. We introduced ourselves and told him about our journey. To our astonishment and delight, he then invited us to go home with him to meet his Scottish wife and their family. His name, he said, was Fernando. His wife,

Margaret, gave the lie to the myth of the dour Scots; she was hugely welcoming, warm, kind, and full of life, and she seemed not at all surprised by such unexpected and unlikely guests; we might just have been another part of Fernando's catch. And I suppose, in a way, we were.

These lovely people made us feel so at home in their beautiful house that they stole our hearts. They insisted that we phone our parents in South Africa and would not hear of payment. They fed us magnificently and took us to a local restaurant whose speciality, barbecued *cabrito*, young goat, brought the great and the good to its doors. Uncertain at first, we tasted and found it delicious, and ate like kings.

Then we were told to go and pack up the caravan and move into their guest suite, which we did, luxuriating in the space, the hot baths, proper beds, the company and the kindness. It was magical and a little like falling in love. When you find friends like this, it is like stumbling on a gold bar in the dust, as astonishing as it is unexpected. We were overwhelmed, bemused, and very grateful. These people knew us not at all, for all they knew we might have been murderers, drug runners, God knows what. Yet they invited two total strangers into their family as if this was an everyday occurrence. We spoke late into the night and a great friendship was sealed.

As a couple, they were like the moon and the sun. He was first and last a gentleman, a very private man, and there was at his core a reserve and a hint of steel. He had managed large casino operations with big staffs in the UK and one could tell that he had lived hard and was not unscarred. But though he was worldly wise, he was still open to life. He took a delight in people and had an immense gift for friendship. We felt flattered that such a man wished to be our friend.

Margaret was like the sun, with a laugh and a warmth and kindness that just took your breath away. There was something capable and strong about her. She had a personality that reached out to you, that came more than halfway to meet you, as the decision to leave her home and country to follow the man she loved, proved conclusively. She was gra-

A Fisherman in the Saddle

cious and her home reflected this – her love of beauty and beautiful things was all around us.

They both had a wonderful tact that did not presume on friendship. They were well-matched, and we felt warmed through by them. We bought their children a few simple gifts and reluctantly went on our way after a day or two. As we drove away, we passed the village beach. Across it, a fisherman was carrying a fish of some twenty pounds he'd obviously just landed. I looked at him enviously and then brought myself up sharp; this coast had offered us a gift so much greater than any fish, that it would take us a lifetime to truly appreciate it.

We would not meet again for fifteen years but that bond of friendship was never broken. Many miles and many changes would occur in our lives before we spoke again, but we talked of them as they did of us, recalling that magical weekend, when people of like mind found each other.

Meanwhile, we headed down to the Algarve and stood in amazement on the site at Sagres where Portugal's coast turns north, and where Prince Henry the Navigator founded his school of navigation. It was from this point that our South African home, history, and culture had all begun, thanks to Portuguese sailors with lion-like courage. We saw that this quality was still alive in the Portuguese, as we watched the crazy antics of men tied to ropes leaning out from cliffs hundreds of feet high, fishing above the hungry waves of the Atlantic, which clawed and roared at the cliff face. Even more remarkably, they were catching fish, dropping rope gaffs down to haul the catch in.

We too finally fished, but on a placid beach at the mouth of a river, not unlike Infanta, called Vila Nova de Milfontes, where we stood fishing in the lee of a fabulous Moorish Castle on the River Mira, an estuary reputed to have harboured Hannibal and his Carthaginian hordes during a storm. And we caught fish too. In some indefinable way, we felt just that little bit more at home in Europe as a result.

Years later, we had a telephone call out of the blue. Fernando and Margaret had kept my father's number and phoned him to ask if we still lived in England. He gave them our number, they called, and we talked and talked. They had moved to the Algarve for better weather, they said.

We thought about this call for a week and then booked a holiday on the Algarve. We decided to say nothing, just to call them from our hotel. Once we'd unpacked and had a swim, I made the call. They could not believe that we were just up the road. There was a strange sad, bittersweet moment when they walked onto the hotel terrace where we waited for them with our children. The years rolled back as we hugged and looked at each other, unable to say all we wished to. But we ate and drank and talked, trying to fit the news of fifteen years into an afternoon.

This was a friendship that had lasted the test of time, though there had been no contact. Fishing has brought many gifts, many joys, but Fernando and Margaret are among the best. We had gone in search of sun, of warmth and light, all those years ago, and indeed we had found it. But we also found warmth and light that had nothing to do with the sun, but which shone day and night though unvisited for all those years and was still there when found once more.

Some friendships are like that. They are like a precious gift, seldom removed from its box, the lustre and beauty remaining untarnished by time and familiarity – the wonder of the possession never palls. Truly, sometimes, less is indeed more.

The next evening, we joined them in their new home and found that Fernando had driven over the border into Spain to buy special prawns. When we sat down to eat, I was overcome. It was too much. Before us on the table were six ornate ceramic crab plates, complete with huge legs and knobbly carapaces. I looked in wonder, they were an exact match of six such crockery crabs I had seen in just one other place on earth – on my beloved mother's dining table, thousands of miles away in Cape Town. She had died three years previously, and seeing those rare, unlikely things on the table of our special friends in Portugal, it was as if my mother spoke to me across time and life and death, and her words were

'Yes, these are special people. Treasure them.' Good as those prawns surely were, I did not taste them, for all I tasted was the saltiness of tears, happy ones.

Julian on Chancer, 2005. Ashdown Forest, East Sussex

A Fisherman in the Saddle

THE ONE THAT GOT AWAY

Max Kansky was a bear of a man. He had walked out of the Ukraine to avoid conscription into the Red Army, found his way to Holland and there boarded a ship for Australia, signing on to work his passage. But Max was so seasick that when the ship docked in Cape Town, in February 1927, he decided enough was enough and jumped ship.

The world economic slump was not making things easy at the Cape and Max had few skills, but he was hugely strong and hard-working and found work carting goods around the Boland, Cape Town's back country. Years passed and he made a life for himself. In the late 1930s, he was driving wagons between Paarl and Cape Town, hauling stone from the quarries in Paarl to the stonemasons yards in the city. One day, returning to Paarl with an empty wagon, he came across a young tea salesman with an Austin Seven that had a puncture. Max hauled his team of mules to a halt, jumped from the wagon and with one hand simply picked the side of the car up while the bemused salesman changed the wheel. That is how Max met my father.

salt, which he crushed with a stone. When he had finished the bread and the chops, he drank half a pail Max became a welcome and regular guest at my father's parents' home in Paarl where he became part of the family, like some long-lost cousin. He had an enormous appetite and would eat astonishing amounts of food. One day, sitting under his wagon out of the rain at the Maitland stonemason's yard, he got stuck into a chicken and a bottle of brandy. When he had finished both, he gave his African assistants some money and asked them to get him something else to eat. They returned with three pounds of lamb chops and two loaves of bread. He made a barbecue under the wagon, salting the chops with the mule's rock of water, got up and said in his thick Russian accent, 'That was a good appetiser!'

He was not tall, I suppose about 5ft 6in, but with an enormous chest and awesome shoulders, and he walked with a bandy sway like a seaman. The only things he missed about his homeland, he said, were the vast spaces and the river fishing he'd done as a boy. My father promised to take him fishing one day, a promise he came to regret.

My father made a financial success of his life in the flour-milling and baking industries, and with his first real money bought a 70-foot yacht, in the years before prudence set in, and extra cash went into property. Knowing nothing of yachting, he took on an Englishman, Jimmy Thomas, to captain the boat, and they and their friends and girlfriends would cruise the waters off the Cape, sometimes as far north as Saldanha Bay.

On these trips, they would come across the endless sea life that teemed in this ocean, sea birds, seals, dolphins, whales and now and then one of the massive basking shark, gentle giants that fed on plankton with mouths that would accommodate a truck. These would often be found, as their name implied, basking on the surface, and it was a favourite trick of Jimmy Thomas's to bring the yacht right alongside, a tricky manoeuvre when the animal was almost as long as the yacht. According to my father, Jimmy was 'mad', which made one wonder about his own sanity, employing him to captain his yacht. In fact, Jimmy distinguished himself during the Second World War as the captain of the first minesweeper to make it to Tobruk.

A Fisherman in the Saddle

Sometimes things happen when a group of high-spirited young men gather together, young women and some alcohol is factored in, and the sea is involved – the mix has been known to have fatal results, and one such incident stands out from this time when my father and his friends cruised the Cape aboard the happy yacht *Senta*. If I have said this was a big yacht at 70 feet, it does not really do it justice. There were staterooms and cabins, which had an Edwardian level of comfort and spaciousness. Where the mast entered the main saloon, it was so large that a grown man could not get his arms round it. The wooden-hulled yacht weighed well over 100 tons. This was no light-weight racing skiff.

I'm not sure how my father persuaded Max Kansky to join him on *Senta*, but despite his well-known problems with seasickness, Max accepted the offer and was bewitched by the experience. More than anything else, he said he wanted to catch one of those basking sharks. The impossibility of this was explained to him, which only made him that much more determined. It became something of a joke. If you catch it, you'll have to eat it yourself, they said, and Max was teased mercilessly. So often that is the very breeze which fans the spark of an idea into flames. And that is just what happened.

On his next outing aboard *Senta*, Max came prepared. He brought with him a whaling harpoon and 200 yards of brand new two-inch manila rope, spliced to it. He was not messing about; everyone else thought it the funniest thing they had seen, this Russian bear getting ready to claw a giant fish out of the sea. And, of course, they played along. They went in search of a basking shark and it was not long before they found one.

Jimmy ghosted the yacht alongside the shark and Max readied himself in the bow. In the excitement, no one took much notice of the fact that Max had knotted the end of the rope to the forward bollard used to fasten the yacht to the quay when in harbour. Max with his harpoon at the rail had everyone else on board in fits, but the laughing stopped when with all his great strength he plunged the harpoon into the back of the shark. The remarkable thing was that nothing happened for at least half a minute, said my father. It took that long for the shark to realise all was not well.

Then, slowly, it began to swim off, taking rope with it as it went. Soon the end of the 200 yards was gone and the shark began to tow the yacht and the boom swung round. Suddenly the joke was over, Jimmy Thomas and my father yelled at Max to cut the rope, but Max stood by the bollard, grinning madly. He had no intention of letting his catch go – that much was evident. Gradually the shark picked up speed and the yacht with it. It was bedlam aboard with shouts and yells, the sails flapping, but Max would not hear of releasing the shark.

By now, the shark must have begun to be seriously irritated by the load it was towing and sensing sufficient sea-depth beneath it, dived. The yacht spurted forward at the pace of a speedboat and then the bowsprit dipped into the sea. For one terrifying moment it seemed as if the yacht must be dragged under. The whole length of the boat lifted before Max took an axe to the rope. The yacht came back to an even keel with small lateral waves washing away from her sides.

Smiling sheepishly, Max said, 'He got away.' The story went the rounds of the Royal Cape Yacht Club and entered the annals of myth. It was the end of Max's fishing.

Many years later, when my brother and I were both over six foot tall and having the odd argument, Max, now in his seventies, would grab each of us round the waist and lift us both off the floor, ordering us to stop arguing. It felt as though a steel hawser had encircled your waist and clasped it to a steel drum. He was a hard old man and I felt that the basking shark had got off lightly.

A Fisherman in the Saddle

LUANDA 1967

I was 17 years old and away from home for the first time with an American classmate of mine. I had been invited to spend three weeks with him and his family in Angola, where his father ran the Kabinda oil fields for Texaco. I was not that sure about it, but I had been promised some great fishing and that clinched it for me.

The heat struck you like a wall as you stepped from the air-conditioned Fokker Friendship out into the West African sunshine. It was seriously hot. A thick, wet, cloying heat that made the air seem tangible. You felt as though you were pushing through some foreign substance that yielded, just, to force. On the airport concourse there was evidence of another force; troops in olive green fatigues were everywhere, carrying Uzi submachine guns. On the way through the city approaches, we saw bullet-riddled traffic signs, where these young Portuguese conscripts had been doing a bit of target practice.

I was still trying to regain my equilibrium, lost as the aircraft dived over the statue of Christ on the hills above Suda Madeira, a few hours before and a couple of hundred miles to the south, re-fuelling and picking up more passengers for Luanda. We had also stopped briefly at Windhoek in South West Africa. I felt far from the Cape and into Africa proper.

The drive from the airport down the escarpment to the sea was pleasant. The city glittered in the heat, a hard white against rampant vegetation with a deep blue bay beyond, graced by a palm-fringed barrier reef island. It seemed as if most human life here came on two wheels; there were motor-bikes everywhere, like schools of fish round pavement café peninsulas. Parked in their thousands, they formed effective crash barriers between strolling pedestrians, motorists and more motorcyclists.

The pace was slow, pedestrians did indeed stroll, it was a languid pace. The place had something of Lisbon and Nice about it, a shared cosmopolitanism, though it would be many years before I could make that judgement myself. The shops were chic, and the pedestrians predominantly short, dark Portuguese men in cream tropical weight suits. Their hair, moustaches and shoes all shone immaculately. There were few white women about. The black residents of Luanda looked decidedly less cowed than those in my country, though soldiers lounged on street corners, guns slung casually from shoulders, looking bored. The boredom would not last; 500 years of simmering colonialism was on a rolling boil. The masters were about to be mastered, looking back briefly at paradise lost, and then going.

But for now, the war was 300 miles inland, and Luanda was at peace, or seemingly so. Carlo Ponti and Sofia Loren had just built a house next door to the Club Nuval on the waterfront. The place was exotic yet off the map, a great hideaway for those in the know.

The car pulled up at a white house almost overtaken by its garden, lush rubber plants, tall palms and bougainvillea. We unpacked, showered and then headed down to the harbour to inspect the family's speedboat at the club. It was an unostentatious but perfectly serviceable speedboat which in the days to come would carry us backwards and forwards to Mussulu, the 25-mile long reef islad which followed the coastline about three miles offshore. This reef was a pristine, white sandy paradise covered in palms, some of which leaned almost horizontally out over the inner lagoon side beaches. The place was not more than 10 feet above the lagoon it had created on its landward side and the Atlantic, 100 yards beyond. It was home to a fishing tribe that scratched a living here, with a few chickens adding some difference to their diet. There was the odd mongrel and many small children.

We would start each day by taking the boat over to one or other of the villages on Mussulu to arrange lunch, barbecued chicken or fish or squid. Then we'd spend the morning fishing, swimming and water-skiing. It made for an idyllic holiday. If you had had enough of the boat, you could be dropped at one of a hundred beaches with a book, a cooler bag of Cokes and beer, and in places, blue mangrove crabs for company.

It was all low key and very relaxed. In town, we were shown around the astonishing botanical garden where thirteen shades of bougainvillaea, from purest white through cream, to salmon, to peach, apricot, and pink finally reached a deep burgundy. We walked round the fifteenth century fort built by the Portuguese to command the harbour and roadstead and visited the astonishing Catholic cemetery where many of the dead had better above-ground accommodation than the city's slum dwellers. The cinemas came as a revelation, marble, mahogany and ivory, with deep, velvet, plush seats, but without a roof, just the magnificence of the southern night sky. The short rainy season made this possible, a simple temporary roof needed to last no more than a couple of weeks.

But as usual, it was the action in the water that really gripped my attention. The sea world below that blue mirror of the bay hid myriad treasures, two of which would remain with me for life.

One morning, as usual, we took the boat over to Mussulu and at our favourite village asked if they could arrange lunch for us that day – squid for a change. A few hours later we tied up again beneath the overhanging palm tree and saw a line of men each with a ten-foot pole, marching one behind the other into the water. They walked out until they had created a wall of men in the shape of a 'u', starting with one man just ankle deep off the beach at each end of the curve, the rest progressively deeper with the deepest showing just their heads above water.

This human 'u' then began drumming the poles on the seafloor and walking slowly in towards the beach. As those who had been furthest out reached waist height, the colour of the sea within the 'u' began to darken. I wondered what this could possibly be. I did not have long to wait. As the back wall of the 'u' reached the beach, a few dozen squid shot out of the water and up the beach, still pumping their black ink behind them. They were dispatched, cleaned and grilled on the spot over charcoal. It remains the freshest calamari I have ever eaten.

That afternoon, I hooked and landed a bonito, a fish I'd not heard of before, a tuna-like fish that we ate that night with fresh limes from the family's garden.

On our last day in Luanda, we experienced something of an epiphany provided by the natural world. Once more we were out on the boat, this time past Mussulu, in the ocean proper. It was evening and a low sun shone a gentle light into the sea. Someone shouted, 'Look!' and as we looked down into the water, we saw massive black shapes gliding beneath us They were Manta rays, black on top and white underneath, swimming in a vast school of hundreds. They were so close to the surface that the water seemed to form a fine skin over their bodies, and as their wings lifted on the upward beat, all around us were hundreds of white 'hands' raised as though in farewell. After that initial shout there was total and complete silence on the boat, despite its load of teenagers. We stared in awe. When the last of the rays had gone, still quiet, we turned and headed back for the harbour, home and school in South Africa.

A Fisherman in the Saddle

TRAWLING FOR CHEESECAKE

I have fished for some strange things in my time and have caught some odd fish, but the summer I trawled Clifton Fourth beach for cheesecake must be the weirdest of all.

I was working on the *Cape Times* as a trainee reporter in my university holidays, having a break from my Bachelor of Journalism Degree at Rhodes University. I was still recovering from the brouhaha that had followed my opening shot in the *Oppidan*, the University's magazine for students who lived off-campus. The article appeared just before a big debate on censorship between the Vice Chancellor and the student body. In the article, I had explained how I had arrived, at the grand old age of 27, to do this degree after taking advice from Professor Piet Cilliers, the editor at that time of *Die Burger*, and a near neighbour of ours at Bloubergstrand.

I had gone to see the great man in his office in Cape Town. Outside the office on a marble plinth stood a bust of Dr Verwoerd, one of the main architects of Apartheid, perfect in every way, right down to the large porcine nostrils. Nervously I entered and explained that I was thinking of studying journalism and asked what would his advice be in the circumstances – there were options at UCT (University of Cape Town), Stellenbosch and Rhodes.

He asked me how many *cum laudes* I had achieved in

my matric at SACS. I explained that I had left SACS in Standard Eight (at 16 years old) and had matriculated, sort of, at Progress College in Claremont, home of scholastic oddballs and those of us too creative for our own good. And what exactly was a *cum laude?* I asked Looking at me benignly he smiled, waved his pipe in a dismissive manner and said: 'Ag, ou kêrel, jy moet maar Rhodes toe gaan!' ('You'd better go to Rhodes then, old chap!')

I took his advice and went to Rhodes. And felt that I had been reborn, from the biscuit salesman I had previously been masquerading as; I felt that I had found my calling. Writing feverishly, I outlined the above story for the University student magazine, *Oppidan*. The day of publication coincided with the big censorship debate at Rhodes, which took place in the Great Hall before a packed audience of students and academics. I sat near the front.

The Vice Chancellor rose and spoke. Halfway through his speech explaining why he felt the need for censorship, he explained that, in certain quarters, Rhodes 'enjoyed' something of a strange reputation. This was, he said, well captured by an article that had just appeared in *Oppidan* that very day. I sank low into my seat, knowing what was coming, my life flashing before my eyes. He read a few paragraphs of my article, ending with *'Jy moet maar Rhodes toe gaan.'*

I fully expected to be called on and asked for an explanation in front of that heaving mass of people. As luck would have it, I was not, but as I slunk out at the end, I was aware that I was considerably lighter than when I had gone in.

My Professor of Journalism, Tony Giffard, caught my eye, smiled, and commented, 'That, Julian,' he said, 'was a perfect case of the first rule of writing: publish and be damned!' I never looked back. But it must be said that when I arrived at *The Cape Times* in the summer of '77, and was ushered into the open-plan newsroom, chock full of busy journalists, after a brief chat with Tony Heard, the Editor, I was not brimming with confidence. My first assignment did not help either. In my dark suit, white shirt and tie and gleaming black lace-ups, I was sent in search of 'cheesecake', as the news editor put it, – the term then used to describe beautiful young women in bikinis on the beaches of the Cape, whose photographs ran on the front page of every edition. My companion was a one-eyed photographer, a former circus trapeze artist, who had perfected the necessary and life-saving technique of never blinking.

Imagine the scene. It is 90 degrees Fahrenheit (32 degrees Celsius) in the shade and the sweat is trickling down your back as you trudge through the super-heated sand of Clifton's Fourth Beach. Your task is to ask the prettiest bikini-clad young women you can find if they will mind you asking them for a few personal and intimate details and getting their photographs. It would have been a dream assignment for someone with more *savoir-faire* than I was able to muster. I simply felt an idiot.

It must be said that the young women did all they could to help. For the first and only time in my life I knew what it must feel like to be Paul Newman – a babe magnet. Beautiful young women wearing little or virtually nothing and who well understood our brief, angled their way towards us, coyly or boldly. It was a cinch. By day three, I was blasé and the photographer was so cheesed off with the cheesecake job that he had phoned half a dozen girlfriends of his, all professional models, and was shooting them at appointed times, toe deep in the sea or with one of the massive granite rocks for backdrop at Llandudno beach, well out of the Clifton scrum. Nobody ever rumbled us. I would get the girl's name, age, vital statistics, address, job description and interests, and then the former trapeze artist would swing into action. And so I learnt my first lesson of journalism. You cannot believe everything you read in the papers.

Having been 'blooded' and having produced the goods, I was ripe for a new assignment. The news editor called me over one morning and threw a file at me. I wondered why there were sniggers all round as I caught it, fair and square. When I got to my desk I understood. I was to interview Fiona Richmond, who was in Cape Town for the British porn mag, *Penthouse*, doing the latest in her series

'Road-testing men like they road-test cars!'

I paled beneath my Clifton tan. This surely was stretching journalistic dedication too far. I had experienced an instance of publish and be damned, but this was a case of 'damned if I'll do it'. I marched up to the news editor and with my voice rising an octave, asked if I was merely to interview her or if a 'road test' was part of the deal? The newsroom had been waiting with bated breath to see just how long it would take me to ask this question and fell about laughing fit to burst. The news editor played along: 'I leave it to you. But think of the story you'll have!' I left the *Cape Times* feeling pretty much like a lamb headed for the abattoir.

When I got home that night I was in hot water, but not for obvious reasons. Everything had gone swimmingly. My trapeze artist had been so enamoured he'd blinked for the first time in years, he said, as he photographed Fiona in a diaphanous, virtually see-through shift, against the glare of the sun. The interview was also a pleasure; Fiona was beautiful, articulate, witty and amusing. Making a joke about South Africa's fear of Reds-under-the-bed, she said she was having problems getting red-blooded South African males out from under the bed and into hers for a road test! I did not volunteer, for travelling with her was her fiancé. Truth is truly stranger than fiction at times.

When I got home, I got a rocket from my girlfriend, another would-be journalist and a founder member of the Cape Town chapter of the Women's Liberation Movement. I explained that, despite her reputation, Fiona Richmond was a lady and a delight. This elicited a tirade about double standards and men having reputations enhanced by each conquest, whereas women on the other hand ... I crept away as meekly as I could. Trawling for cheesecake could be a bloody dangerous business.

A Fisherman in the Saddle

THE DOLPHIN'S DAUGHTER

I'm not sure what comes first, fishing or philosophy, but it is an incontrovertible fact that the two go together. Whether people of a philosophical nature are attracted to fishing, or fishing itself brings out the philosopher in one, there is a strange symbiotic relationship between the two. I am no philosopher but am definitely subject to philosophising. So if that is not your thing take the next exit and head for a story that is actually about fishing. But if a spot of philosophy does not horrify you, grab a drink and let's talk about the strange business of the dolphin's daughter, fatherhood and life.

As you can see by the above, I am not averse to putting my fishing rod down; some would say I hardly ever pick it up. This was the case one day as I turned my back on fishing for a few hours to enjoy a simple early morning walk up the beach at Hamerkop, kicking sand, collecting shells, bits of driftwood, the odd glass float from some massive net, and cuttlefish spines for our canaries.

The beach was long and isolated, visited only by the few fishing types who had access to it. On this particular day, I was alone. About halfway along the beach I looked ahead and saw a dark object lying just above the waterline. I presumed that it must be a piece of driftwood, but as I approached it, I saw that it was a large fish of some kind. In fact, it was a young dolphin, still alive but only just. There were no visible markings on it that might have indicated an attack by something else, but it did not seem to be in a good way. As I leaned over it, I thought I heard a strange noise and got a shock. Just feet away from me was an adult dolphin that I can only assume was its mother. She had her head out of the water and was making the clicking noise that they do and also something higher pitched. It seemed to me as if she was asking for my help.

I was a city boy, born and bred, brought up in Cape Town. My contact with nature was limited. Standing on that beach holding a young dolphin, which for some odd masculine reason I thought of as female, and the adult dolphin, as its mother, I felt rather like Alice, when she fell down the rabbit hole. Everything seemed a mite topsy-turvy and I wondered if all this were truly happening or if last night's wine was having a delayed reaction.

I lifted the young dolphin gently and keeping a close watch on the adult walked it into the water. The adult came immediately to its side, motherhood overcoming any instinctive fear it might have had of me. Conversely, any fear that I might have had that I would be attacked if I went into the sea with the youngster disappeared. The mother dolphin and I worked side by side alongside the baby trying to keep it afloat. Sadly, we failed.

Whatever had caused its injuries if that was what it was, for it might simply have been sick, we did not succeed in saving it. After trying to swim/walk the youngster in the shallows for half an hour or thereabouts, it became obvious that it was dead. I carried it out and laid it down on the beach. As I sat there beside it, I felt a flood of mixed emotions, sadness, anger, bewilderment and wonder.

The mother dolphin continued to patrol up and down before me, quieter now, as though she realised all was lost. I felt an intruder then and got up and walked away. I wondered how it must feel to be a creature of the sea and to have to leave your child in another element, on land. I did not fish

A Fisherman in the Saddle

that day and at dusk I returned to the small dark shape on the beach. The adult had gone and it was evident that seabirds and other creatures had begun their recycling work; the great wheel of nature, which grinds us all down and reshapes us, was turning slowly.

Many years have passed since that day and I am a father now. I have a son and a daughter. My love for them is such that I am more vulnerable than ever to, as Shakespeare put it, 'the slings and arrows of outrageous fortune'. The worst thing that can befall a parent is the sickness, suffering or loss of a child, and I, like every other parent, worry constantly. I remember my mother's oft-repeated words: *'My kind, as jy kinders het, is die koring op jou land altyd groen.'* My child, if you have children the corn on your land is always green, never ripe and safely harvested, always subject to rain or hail damage. The farming wisdom of those words have taken years and fatherhood to be understood. But now I do. To have children is to be like a farmer whose corn is always green, subject to damage by rain or hail, insects or disease, never harvested and safely in the barn. It is a fearful thought.

I live in England now, so very far from Hamerkop, which is triply removed, by time, space and law. Yet I still think of that mother dolphin, clicking her fear and concern on that beach, prepared to accept help from anyone and anything, which might return her child to her. And I pray that I will never know what she knew; that one day my corn will be safely harvested and in the barn, but I know that is a vain hope.

Now and then I take my children fishing. We drive the 45 minutes to Newhaven where the big red and white ferries slip out of the river harbour for France, crossing the busiest waterway in the world, playing 'dodgem-ships' with tankers, ore freighters, container ships, passenger liners, other ferries, trawlers and pleasure craft, before they dock at Dieppe. We do not catch much, now and then a mackerel in the spring. But I feel the pull of the sea through my fishing rod, and smell the sea, and I watch the sea. And I try to fish instead of philosophising. But I don't always succeed.

Chancer and Dexter, Irish Draughts, being shod in the 1990s

IDAHO ICE FISHING

The Rocky Mountain lakes in Idaho are not the sea, by any stretch of the imagination, but some of them are vast. Lake Pend Oreille, north of Lake Cœur d'Alène is so big that the whisper on the wind is that the US Navy tests its latest generation of subs here. Who knows? It may be true. There are some big fish in these lakes.

There are huge cutthroat trout (the Idaho record is 19 pounds), giant lake trout, known as Mackinaw, which grow to 30 pounds, also rainbows and brookies, there are bass, smallmouth and large-mouth, there are perch, and there are double digit pike here too. But the most astonishing thing in these lakes and the rivers that feed them are the land-locked sockeye salmon, called *Kokanee*, who change colour from their normal silver when they spawn, making the rivers run red. It is an amazing thing, watching these large red fish and the bald eagles and bears that feed on them in this annual autumn bonanza.

Summer fishing with a near-silent electric motorboat, trailing a lure while you sit, a rod in one hand and a beer in the other, is a popular pastime. But it is when the great winter storms sweep in and ice up these lakes that a really rather strange form of fishing takes place. With ice-blue skies overhead and the country clothed in bone-dry powder snow, Idaho is a winter wonderland, a holiday paradise, and fishermen struggling with the onset of cabin fever grab a rod and head for the lakes.

The experts will tell you that you need a minimum of four inches of ice to be safe walking and fishing on the lakes. The equipment needed is relatively simple. You need a drill to get through the ice to the water (some use a powered ice drill), a sieve for keeping the hole open, scooping up ice bits, lots of warm clothes, rods, reels and lures for 'jigging' with. This is a part of the world where twelve to twenty feet of snow in a winter is no big deal. People hereabouts live for the winters. There is hunting – $40 buys you a licence to shoot a bear if you are so minded – fishing, skiing in some great resorts, or simply whizzing round the place on snowmobiles. With over 7,000 miles of snowmobile trail in Idaho alone, there is space aplenty.

Others prefer to get around on skis and the sight of cross-country skiers on the lakes is a lovely sight, as they glide silently past your lakefront deck or veranda. The air is champagne-like and your pent-up energy is just raring to get going. Many take to the lakes for ice fishing.

Now this can be done simply with a fishing rod, a box to sit on and a thermos of hot coffee, possibly spiked with something to hold the cold at bay. But temperatures of minus 20 degrees are common, even before the wind chill factor kicks in. So there are those who want the comforts of home on the ice and this is a story about them.

The purist fly fisherman who told me this story is a largely truthful source, but he holds ice fishermen in low esteem. He says ice fishing is as boring as hell, so he is not an altogether unbiased observer. However, his tale was backed up by a news story in the local paper, the *Spokesman Review* out of Spokane, so I think it can be trusted.

A couple of good ol' boys decided to go ice fishing out on Lake Cœur d'Alène, aiming for big pike, so they loaded a wooden garden shed onto a pair of sleds and towed it out onto the ice with a pick-up truck. They put in a couple of easy chairs, a gas brazier, and even a carpet to keep their feet off the ice. They brought a case of beer, plenty of food, a portable TV and their fishing gear. They fished all day and did

A Fisherman in the Saddle

okay, with a few small fish. That afternoon they made themselves lunch and settling back in the easy chairs with a beer or two, began to tell ghost stories. The fishing had gotten real slow.

It was quiet out there, with no sound but the hiss of the gas heater and they dozed off from time to time, dreaming of goblins and giant pike. What they did not realise was that just round the headland, another couple of ice fishermen had made a similar camp with one single addition. They had a black Labrador dog with them. This was a keen fishing animal, an alert dog that took an active interest in fishing and would keep a close eye on proceedings.

At around 4pm, as dusk was coming, his master got into a decent pike and the dog stood trembling and eager by the hole, giving the odd woof to encourage things along. After a stiff fight the pike was brought to the hole and as its huge head emerged it gave one last struggle and gnashing its razor-sharp teeth, severed the line. It dropped back down the hole and out of sight. This was too much for the Labrador who, brave dog that he was, dived straight down the hole after the pike. His master, drained by the fight, was collapsed into his easy chair, and in no position to stop him. That dog went fishing.

Now remember the water in those lakes is around 32 degrees F (zero in Celsius), and even a well-padded dog will not want to stay in long, but he was a dead keen fishing dog and he sped after the pike. Within seconds the pike was gone, and the dog disorientated. He swam round in circles under the ice, in imminent danger of drowning, when at last he spotted the dim light of an ice hole and swam strongly for it.

As he swam for his life, the two fishing partners above this hole were watching the evening news on the portable TV. Both smiled when the newsreader touched on a subject dear to the heart of all hunters in these parts. He said that reports were coming in of a sighting that day, near Cœur d'Alène, of Big Foot, the mythical man/ape monster some believe really do haunt these parts.

And it was at this point that the dog erupted from the

hole, the wrong hole as it turned out, gasping for breath, and shaking water off his coat. The two dozy fishermen lurched backwards upsetting their chairs in a desperate attempt to exit the garden shed/fishing-shack before this monstrous thing from the deep could get at them. Despite the weight of their clothes, and the amount of beer they had drunk and the fact that they dead heated for the door, the fishermen managed to exit in double quick time, crawling and running on the slippery ice for all they were worth, pursued by the terrible noises of this hellish thing still inside the hut. Round the corner of the headland they spotted salvation: another fishing cabin, with two men at the door.

As they ran, they were overtaken by the Labrador delighted to see his master waiting for him. What the first two fishermen told the others remains shrouded in mystery. The reporter from the *Spokesman Review* said the Labrador owner gave one version, and the other two fishermen something rather different. The newspaper quotes were dotted with expletives deleted, which made it difficult to understand just what had been said. But one thing is clear; Idaho ice fishing does, after all, have its excitements.

A Fisherman in the Saddle

THE SPIRITUAL FISH

Fish, when you come to know them intimately, have, I am sure, many fine qualities, but it would be a brave man who would venture the view that they are particularly spiritual animals – though you can never be sure. It must be said in their favour that they have a 'spiritual' effect on others. I for one have neared spiritual bliss on tasting my first bloater, and I'm very fond of kippers too. Yellowtail also does it for me, and smoked wild salmon is a foretaste of Heaven. So, yes, I suppose fish and spirituality do have links in a way.

There is a serious subtext here. I have knocked around the world a bit and have spotted fish in places significantly linked to spirituality. Come with me for a trip that will take us to the Greek Islands, and you will see that fish and the spirit do have links. In any case, it's not a bad itinerary for anyone who loves beautiful places and who might be planning a trip. You could even take a fishing rod along, but don't expect to catch many fish. For me, this journey represents an end to fishing, or at least the kind of fishing which actually sets out to catch fish.

The fish carries a heavy burden on its slim back, being associated with the early Christians. The Disciples as we know included fishermen, and Christ entreated them to be fishers of men. The sign of the fish in the sand was an emblem and signal of a Christianity that had to remain secret, that sign of the fish we see to this day on the back of cars advertising the driver's link to that religion. And one can trace the spread of Christianity westwards from Israel with stops for fish.

St Paul took the religion to Greece where, today, it is omnipresent. On any Greek island, no matter how remote, there will be a handful of small churches, some no larger than a stable. My family and I have a particularly good relationship with an Island called Skopelos in the Sporades. It is a heavily wooded island with two white towns. An English writer, Michael Carroll, sailed in there many years ago and wrote a book, *The Gates of The Wind*, and his house remains there alongside one of the most picturesque moorings in the Sporades, next to Panormos Beach.

Skopelos is mountainous and as you feel your way cautiously round its length and breadth, there are views from the heights of jewel-like, azure bays cradled in dark green pines. To reach this island, which has wisely refused its own airport, saving it from the tourist hordes, one must fly into its neighbour, busy, cheerful Skiathos, and then take a ferry or the Blue Dolphin hydrofoil, which does the trip in half an hour.

Skopelos is no Mount Athos where monks have been in residence for 1,000 years and where women are forbidden to set foot, but it too has its monastery. Entering a monastery to participate in the contemplative life might be going a bit far for most people and there are other secular options. There is a beach on Skopelos where you can get away from most people, where the water is gin-clear and in July around 80 degrees F (26 degrees Celsius), bliss, for anyone who, like me, found the Atlantic on South Africa's Cape coast much too cold.

You can reach this beach – which shall here remain nameless – by bus from Skopelos Town or you can hire a scooter or a small jeep. Then it is half an hour's drive, first through vineyards and olive groves, then up twisting mountain roads into the pines and plane trees, and then down to the beach on a gravel road. Walk to the far end of this lovely beach and set up camp by the cliff, which provides some shade. Now, if you take a piece of stale bread and walk into the water, throwing bits about, you will soon be at the centre of a milling school of mullet. After they have finished the bread, the braver ones among them will investigate your legs, giving gentle nips. It's an odd feeling; and for a fisherman to be his own bait is an even odder feeling. I'm unbarbed bait though, as I have no intention of catching these friendly fish.

You cannot sit long in this place before its history comes pouring down the mountains and racing over the sea. It must have been a bloody, hard and merciless place to have lived in the past. The view, though lovely, would have been little protection from seaborne dangers. And, of course, the Greek Gods disporting themselves here were not much help. Today, however, it is an island known to the more discerning Greek traveller and some families spend part of the summer here. At dusk, sitting under the mulberry trees of the town's open air jazz café on the waterfront, listening to cool piano music, drinking a beer before supper or a glass of Metaxa Three Star brandy, afterwards (I like the semi-rough quality of three, Five Star is too refined), there is a satisfaction to be had, knowing that you have arrived. You are no longer travelling towards a wish, a hope, a desired destination. You are there. And you can relax.

You might well eat fish for supper, one of the silver or red ones lined up on ice before every taverna, and as you eat, a priest with a long black beard and a long black *soutane* and a strange boxy hat will walk past you, and for a moment, Christ, Christianity, St Paul and fish will come together in this place and you will have a feeling, that might not last, that for a minute you understand more, though what and how will remain elusive. It's partly what takes us back again and again to the Greek Islands. It is a place where you are doubly refreshed, once in the sea and once in the spirit that inhabits this place. It is a baptism of grace. And for me, the presence of fish is a happy bonus.

Julian on Max, in the 1980s

East Pier Newhaven

This can be a tricky place to fish if the incoming ferry from France misjudges things and ploughs into the pier, as it has done on occasion. This puts a bit of a downer on a day's fishing, but certainly perks up a slow day on the pier when the fish just won't bite.

It's a slightly tricky place to get to, is the East Pier at Newhaven. You can park at Seaford beachfront and walk west the mile along the beach to the pier but that is hard going on the pebbles. The easier way is to park in the Newhaven industrial estate near the railway station and walk in from there, putting your concern about the safety of your car to the back of your mind. You cross the bridge over the railway line and then walk through a landscape of semi-rural semi-urban decay which at dusk or dawn can feel a little threatening.

The outskirts of this small run-down coastal town, huddled round its harbour and river ferry port, speaks of hard times and its margins to the east are not salubrious. Back of the river's eastern wall, fenced off with a single strand of sagging rusted barbed wire, bearing bits of string and an unintelligible tin sign, the place runs into a flat, scuffed, grassy scrub, burnt by the salt winds that scour this bay and its hinterland. You are as likely to see plastic bags and rubbish blown around here as the hardy blooms of plants just able to survive the salt laden air and soil. You walk through it as quickly as possible, keeping a wary eye out for lounging youths and tough-looking dog walkers sporting tattoos.

The first sight of the pier piercing the bay is a welcome one and you feel a certain sense of sanctuary attained. The company of fishermen is one I grew up with and my experience of it and them is always one of welcome to a fellow addict. And there is a thin sprinkling of the tribe evident on the pier, well-spaced as ever, the fisherman's unspoken code of peace, space and privacy honoured until the fish start biting in one area and then the tribe is drawn in by the hunting instinct as if by a magnet. But this morning it is too early for most and those on the pier are either overnighters or up-with-the-lark types like me this dull overcast morning.

In my rucksack, I feel the weight of water and coffee, bait bought at the local fishing tackle shop a few days before, my reels and lures, knives and bait-board, the small paraphernalia kept as light as possible because of the walk in and out at the start and end of the day's fishing.

You nod a greeting as you pass the silent backs on the pier. They are a motley crew as ever, but fisherman every one. They spent the night here, not in a pub, or they got up even earlier than me. A hardy bunch. Committed. Youngsters in their late teens and twenties, some fathers and sons, a few fishing friends and as ever the loners like me, older men, grizzled, with an air of failure about them and a certain toughness too. But everyone returns your nod or greeting. You are welcome here, just as long as you give each other space. For this pier is not just for fishing, it is a dreamscape too, fathoms deep at the far end, a place of escape from reality, wherever you place yourself on its length.

To the west are the cliffs that block out the view of Brighton, further up the coast. To the east, the long open beach reaching to Seaford and its chalk cliffs beyond. You are part of a port, modest in every way, as are its seaborne visitors, modest trawlers and day fishing charter boats, small rusty freighters and one single yellow and white ferry for those who choose to access France from this humble place, like a fly taking off from a shabby bouquet for a banquet

A Fisherman in the Saddle

across the room.

The place's saving grace is the sea. It lies all about you, encircles you, in a soft pearl grey oily calm with a gleam here and there off the rising sun behind the cloud cover. It heaves and sucks gently at the pier and the few small waves on the shore are quiet and self-effacing. The calmness of the sea soothes you as ever and you look at it, bewitched once more. Your walk to get here through the shingle shore and its flowering sea kale, yellow horned poppy, sea-beet, viper's bugloss and woody nightshade at Tide Mills is now behind you, and the sea offers its open-handed promise of a day's pleasure, just enough removed from the everyday world to allow you easier breaths and a less turbulent mind.

The 40-minute drive down from the inland heights of Crowborough in the Weald already seems a dim memory. Mist-wreathed cows and horses in fields. The passage through the Cuilfail tunnel at Lewes and along the humpbacked Downs, and then into the open grassed landscapes, no longer wooded.

You drop your pack and lean your ten-foot fishing rod against the railings close to the far end of the pier, at a spot enough removed from other anglers that their conversations, such as they are, dim to sibilance. As you tackle up, the fisherman's telegraph briefs you on the night's doings as fishermen move up and down the pier in search of a leg stretch or a need to pee at the beach end of the pier, or those calling it a night. 'Decent fish for a bass, three pounds.' 'Best he says he's ever taken here.' 'Waste of time, tiddlers and bloody crabs.' 'Not bad for a codling at this time of the year.' 'Well, if you can be bothered to eat the damn things.' 'Mixed bag last night, but not bad, pouting, gurnard, couple of silver eels and Jonny's sea bass. Best catch of the night. Reckons it's over three pounds.' Jonny, it seems, is the night's hero.

This overheard litany reminds me always of the UK shipping forecast, but this time, fish not weather: 'Viking, North Utsire, South Utsire, Forties, Cromarty, Forth, Tyne, Dogger, Fisher, German Bight, Humber, Thames, Dover, Wight, Portland, Plymouth, Biscay, Trafalgar, FitzRoy, Sole,

Lundy, Fastnet, Irish Sea, Shannon, Rockall, Malin, Hebrides, Bailey, Fair Isle, Faeroes and Southeast Iceland.'

If I stopped the fishing telegraph long enough to say 'it's poetry' they would understand, nod and smile and walk on muttering, 'Silly sod. Daft bugger.' There are rules, unwritten but no less real for that.

I bait up with fast defrosting worm and tie it on tight with cotton thread and hurl it out east towards Seaford. The pebbled beach now has two lone fishermen at a quarter mile from each other, more in need of space than those of us here on the pier.

The day opens up now that I have a line in the water finally. I am little troubled by my old hunting instinct. I am more focussed on the light on the water, the mood of the great sky dome and a certain Turneresque cast to the clouds. The spring day is a gift I have given myself and I intend to savour it.

In my food bag there is cider, cheese, apples and tuna salad on sourdough sandwiches. And two KitKats with a flask of coffee. It does not get much better than this, and there is not a drop of wind.

I catch fish almost as an afterthought, too small to keep, dogfish and dab, but it keeps me occupied. Cast, wait, reel in, rebait, cast. And then the highlight of my day – I land a huge orange spider crab, early in the year this May Day. A few of my neighbours move it to look at its vast size. 'Bloody hell, he's a big bugger!' 'You gonna keep him?' I say no and ask them if they want it. They are two brothers, and they laugh: 'Our ma would kill us if we took that thing home!' and I return the crab to the sea, into which it sinks slowly to the bottom.

People pass by at intervals, some ask: 'Catch anything?' and I shake my head: 'Tiddlers is all.' And they walk on. The day passes slowly, the hours like the turning of a page in a much-loved book that you return to from time to time. You know the ending but that does not make it any the less enjoyable. The sea has risen with the incoming tide and the breeze that lifts and ruffles my hair. The water is now a danc-

A Fisherman in the Saddle

ing blue as the cloud cover has lifted and the water looks altogether more inviting.

I take a chance, leaving my line out as I knock off for lunch. I put the reel's ratchet on and brace the rod in a hole in the concrete floor of the pier. I tell two lads who are precariously perched opposite me on the concrete trellis work that runs up the eastern side of the pier, that I'm going to have my lunch on the beach and that they should wave if my ratchet goes off, I will keep an eye out. They wave and nod agreement and I heft my lunchbox and walk the hundred yards to the pebbly beach. I know my kit will be safe.

As I eat, I notice some swirls under the pier, just ten foot from the beach. Looking closer it looks like a few decent bass are feeding there. No need at all to walk halfway out to sea, one could sit right here and fish. I let the fish be and eat my lunch, enjoying the tuna salad.

The image of tuna takes my mind hurtling south, six thousand miles, to my first thirty years in South Africa's Cape and my fishing days there, where I cut my teeth in this ancient practice. It is now forty years since I have fished the beaches and rocky ledges of that faraway place, but they are inscribed in my heart and mind as if in detailed blueprints. If for some reason they were obliterated, I would quite certainly and deftly be able to rebuild them from memory, given the time and the right materials. They are as much a part of me as my own body. So much of what is past I took for granted, not appreciating it at the time. I cannot say this about my fishing days in Cape Town and up the east and west coasts north of the city.

But with time, a new and deeper appreciation comes to you for something you loved, which at the time, you didn't see for quite the gift it was. I am thinking of how Strandfontein, Swartklip, Betty's Bay, Hermanus, Hamerkop, Cape Infanta and Blouberg gave me the most solid foundation through its people and landscape that anyone could wish for. It was a treasured time, but now it has become a fabled time, glossed and polished with memory so that it fairly glows in my mind.

And how strange the connections one makes across time. Sitting here a mile from Seaford,
I remember now the name of a tunny boat we went out on that was called the *Seaforth*.

My eyes stare out at this cool English sea, but it is Simonstown in the 1960s that I see and the gracious lines of the *Seaforth*, hugging the quay close to the naval dockyard. On board getting the stern deck ready for the day's outing twenty miles offshore in the deep blue water the tunny prefer is that Cape Town fishing legend Jackie Wheeler. A slight, wiry figure, good looking in a boyish way, blonde and tanned with sky-blue eyes. Delightful company, fun, enthusiastic, I don't think he had an ounce of ambition, other than a fever for fishing. A kind of boy-man. Jackie was a legend in his own lifetime. His exploits would fill a book. He landed big tunny off the ledges of Rooikrans and out at sea as well.

The Cape fishing families still speak of him. Jackie Wheeler sold office stationery when he didn't actually have a rod in his hand. He held the Marlin Trophy for ten years. The fish that secured this title for him he played for sixteen hours before bringing it alongside the boat. When they at last gaffed it, they half lifted the great creature out of the water to make sure that no shark would be able to get at it, then they set off back to the harbour at Hermanus.

The captain had radioed the news of the catch ahead and the place was in a fever of excitement with everyone taking photos as the giant marlin was brought onto the quay, and then with a special crane hoisted for weighing. The great marlin weighed in at just over 1,000 pounds – a record at the time. Newspaper reporters had been despatched to the scene and they were frantically scribbling notes or recording the event on camera and film. Everyone was utterly amazed at the size, and the fish's giant sword.

Then, someone asked: 'Where's Jackie?'

Jackie was nowhere to be found. He was not on the boat, nor chatting to reporters in the big crowd that thronged the scene. But he had not left as his car was still in the parking lot. A search party was despatched and, finally, Jackie was

A Fisherman in the Saddle

found, fast asleep, curled around a bollard, just a short way down the quay, utterly exhausted by his fight with the giant marlin. A boy-man of just 150lb had landed this monster, having given it his all. And now he slept on concrete. Dead to the world.

A seagull screams overhead and suddenly I am back in England, an old man now sitting on a pebbly beach a lifetime away from where I had just been. The sky is grey once more and the words of a song come to me, *California Dreaming* by the Mamas and Papas:

> *'All the leaves are brown*
> *And the sky is gray*
> *I've been for a walk*
> *On a winter's day*
> *I'd be safe and warm*
> *If I was in L.A.*
> *California dreaming*
> *On such a winter's day.'*

I pack up the remains of my lunch and toss some crusts to the sea bass under the pier. My rod and line is just as I left it but there is no sign of the lads opposite. It is three o'clock and I decide to call it a day. The fishing has been slow in one way and record breaking in another. It's enough for anyone. And then a small consolation prize as I reel in my line. I find a one-pound bream on the end and I decide to keep it for my supper.

As I walk slowly back to my car through the yellow blooms of the seakale I stop and pick a blossom for my hat and walk on, lightly, despite the weight of memories I carry.

At home, Jan congratulates me on my day's catch which I fry in butter. It is fresh and delicious, and I don't mind the many small bones too much. After all, this is bounty from Newhaven East Pier not Cape Infanta or Simonstown.

Julian on Obi Wan Kenobi, 1990s

THE SEA, THE SEA

When talking fishing, the focus is understandably on the fish, not so much the water in which the fish swims, but it is the water that a fisherman first falls in love with.

The sea has a hypnotic effect on us all that even the most landlocked man, woman and child will acknowledge. For those like me, lucky enough to be raised by the sea in South Africa, it took hold of my heart early on, even before I realized what was happening at around the age of six.

Each year, as the school summer term ended before Christmas, we would decamp from our home in Newlands and later Bishopscourt, two of the green suburbs tucked into the rear slope of Table Mountain, and drive the seventeen miles to another world, our summer home 'Just Ashore' at Bloubergstrand, across Table Bay from the mountain colossus that brooded over this southland of the African continent.

As we turned left in Milnerton to the lagoon and its lighthouse, we would get our first glimpse of the sea. It would then disappear behind the line of coastal dunes until about a mile from the small isolated coastal village that Blouberg was then. And suddenly, to our left, the sea would re-emerge, a plain of blue all the way to the horizon, holding Robben Island in its clasp. No two days are alike by the sea and our first glimpse would tell us exactly what mood the sea was in as quickly as one look at a parent's face.

A combination of wind, tide, cloud, current and time of day were all factors which etched in the sea's mood. Usually its colour was two-toned, a lighter blue inshore and a deep navy out to sea, and as this is a notoriously windy coast there were more often than not whitecaps and surf running hard to the beach. But now and then the sea would be in a breathless calm with not a puff of wind ruffling its surface, then it was like a restless animal that was suddenly at peace and which welcomed your stroking hand.

But mostly, as we opened the car doors after pulling up at the cottage the whitecap warning would ready us, for the grasp of the wind taking ownership of the door and childish fingers had better beware. We would run into the cottage, smelling its welcoming aroma of damp wood and carpets and pass through the place quickly to the front deck, which offered an overview of two large tidal pools that would tell us by their fullness or emptiness the point of the tide we were at. At their lowest, they would hold no more than a ten-foot stretch of water; when full, the two pools would become one, nearly 100 foot long and 30 foot wide. And it could be a wild maelstrom in there, with two exits to the sea pushing and pulling at the water, in and out, and slapping the front retaining wall of the house, sending a fine sea-mist as high as the A-framed roof.

That night, the sound of the waves would keep me awake, excited to be by the sea once more for a few months. The sea and the sea winds dominated everything there from the moment you woke till the last thing at night.

My siblings, a younger sister, Janine, and a brother, Herman, five years younger than me, still talk about the freedom we enjoyed there, free to run on the hot melting tar roads and on the mile-long rock topography that made up the shoreline, with its mix of rock pools and tidal pools small bays and rocky peninsulas and two flat fifty-yard-long aircraft-carrier-rocks to the left and right of the cottage. We knew every single inch of this place and our scarred, leather-soled feet bore witness to that. Some of the small beaches were sandy, some pebbly, some a mix of crushed seashell and sand,

A Fisherman in the Saddle

and here and there were places where the tide deposited the best shell middens, areas which offered treasures.

This place was our playground, but it was also a larder, a sea cupboard of edible delights, black mussels, crayfish, octopus, limpets, periwinkles, rockfish, sea anemones, spiky green or purple sea urchins. Further out in the sea-kelp forests there were blacktail and bream, galjoen and red roman, wildeperd, Hottentot, and small shark, skaamhaai (shy shark, so known because they would curl up into a circle as if to hide their head in their tails when caught). And there were silvery, skittering schools of mullet, haarders as they were known hereabout, and now and then the scary blue electric eels which we feared most when putting a hand deep into rock crevices and crannies to feel for crayfish. Herman was braver than me and he became the family's crayfish catcher.

And all the while, as we played in this magic realm, our knowledge of the sea increased with each season we spent there. Barefoot, and wearing nothing more than shorts and a T-shirt or simply a bathing costume, we would roam freely, away from commanding adult eyes. And all the while the thump of the sea and the wind's threnody would fill our ears.

I am still not sure what possessed our parents to release us in this way – exhaustion maybe – but we had servants and nannies. Incomprehension of what dangers lurked here on the shore? Not really: our father was a keen fisherman and knew the risks intimately. But whatever their motivation, we ran free, admittedly with admonishments to keep an eye on the sea, but free in ways we would never entirely allow our own children. We were more fearful or more careful parents when our time came.

And so each day unfurled with swimming, canoeing, fishing, netting haarders, making dried sea kelp trumpets which gave forth, once mastered, a long melancholy sound not unlike that of the Milnerton lighthouse foghorn. We played with friends, tasting sour figs, building sandcastles with the small incoming waves filling the moats and wetting feet and thighs and buttocks. We lived wet and salty lives and when guests came visiting, our mother would pull down our costumes to expose our white bottoms in stark contrast to our deep chocolate tans.

I wonder now if we knew enough to be aware of being happy and to register the fact, but I fear not; we were as unthinking as the rocks we played on. The only interruptions were the calls to lunch and supper, and such was the appetite built up, we did not have to be called twice.

And so we lived at the edge of the tide; as the blood tide rose and fell within us, so did the sea tides without. We were creatures of the tides.

And, by and by, the years crept past and fishing rods stood by our beds on Christmas mornings, and fishing reels and bait-boxes with knives and hooks and lead sinkers and cotton thread. And so we began to know our fishy neighbours more intimately, what they ate, where they hid, how they fought and how they tasted when they made it to our plates. The crayfish fought a losing rear-guard action to my brother's clever, knowing hands and even now, a man in his sixties, he can stand on those hallowed rocks at Blouberg when he returns from his shoreline home in Santa Barbara, California and the great-great-great-grandsons and daughters of their crayfish forebears he caught, go deep inside their dens and tremble and their feelers twitch as the word gets out. 'Its *him*, he's back!' And terror stalks the rock pools once more.

There are places on these rocks where the waves came at you directly, as you sat holding your fishing rod and crashed in shuddering impacts below you, drenching you if you misjudged the distance the seventh wave in a set could reach. And then there were places, like the one that overlooked the tidal island and Big Bay where you sat sideways on to the incoming waves and they could hypnotise you with their rounded, muscling backs sweeping into the bay, line after line after line. Now and then, a school of porpoises would surf in on a big one, turning away as they reached the brown, bobbing lines of the kelp beds. Sitting here, you faced north, Robben Island to your left, in the west where the sun went down. As I sit now in England in our south-facing cottage in Sussex I imagine that with a super-vision that could

A Fisherman in the Saddle

penetrate time, I would be able to see my ten-year-old face staring north back at the man I would become, looking north up the length of Africa's Atlantic coast, as the waves of the past and the present continue to bore into Big Bay.

The quality of those waves was known to me. In time, I could read them in a way a jeweller can read a gem through his eyeglass loupe. I knew their heft, their weight and the depths they covered. I knew the currents they crossed by the lines of foam that marked them out like sinews in meat. I became a connoisseur of seawater, as did my brother. I learned to respect them and to fear them more than a little. Each year there, would be another drowned body on the beach, of a child usually, who had ventured in too deep. These blue rounded hills of water were not benign, but they hid our quarry, the fish, so had to be dealt with and understood and respected.

And, strangely, sitting by them as they passed by in their never-ending serried ranks, I was more and more at peace. The danger they represented was just one part of what they were, much like the horses I would next fall in love with and spend a lifetime riding, the danger was part of the deal.

By our early twenties, Herman and I had fished the many beaches and coasts that the Cape offers a fisherman, a never-ending bounty of blue and white. And the rocky promontories too, where we'd caught a great many fish. We could look at water and know its viscosity, its temperature, its treasures, and make an educated guess as where best to plummet its depth to find those.

We carried this knowledge lightly. We had not worked or studied to have ownership of it. But it had come to us anyway, a gift out of our pleasure in the sea, by its side these many years. It was part of the load of fishing tackle we carried each time we went fishing alongside the rucksacks and the rods and the gaff, the knives, the bait and bait-board. It was the lightest part, but this knowledge was the most profound, the most important part of the load.

On one particular day that lives on in my memory, we walked along the rocky shore at Cape Infanta, 180 miles north east of Cape Town, where our father had built a fishing cottage just beyond the deadly bar at the entrance to the Breede River. On this day, we put the river behind us and walked as though going out to sea. On our left as we walked, we passed the boat launch ramp, a concrete slipway where fishermen launched their ski-boats for a day of fishing out at sea. I for one did not envy them. Their experience required too much of everything, including the managing of a boat in a treacherous sea. I walked content behind my brother. Slowly, carefully, but with the fluid agility of youth and two decades of knowing just where to place your feet on seashore rocks, we too headed out to sea but with feet on dry land. After a good hour's hike, we reached the point where the coast veered right, to the south.

Now we stood at a point high above water, whose movement told of great depth. It was as if ten thousand men held a flag of blue, ten miles square, and gently lifted it and lowered it, the sultry waves of blue silk just twenty feet below us, pulsing, rising and falling, hiding great fathoms. Carefully we debouched before this ocean plain with military precision, knowing our lives depended on it. In situations like this, you move with the educated care that a mountaineer three-quarters of the way up the Himalayas would use, with care, great care. We watched and counted the waves rolling in, not breaking, just curving past, and when striking the rock wall on which we perched, suddenly rising, reaching high, ready to pluck the unwary off their ledge.

We looked for those places where we could best cast from, seeking those points at which we would be at the least danger from a slip, a precipitous fall, which inevitably would mean a drowning. And excitement flowed within us, because we knew we were in the realm of the truly great fish, the giants that patrolled this coast, particularly at the mouth of this giant estuary. We were in deep, in more ways than one.

With shaky fingers we traced up, fifty-pound breaking strain line, wire trace for the hook, a middleweight flat sinker, a whole bait fish threaded onto a hook half the length of our hands. Then some minutes more observing the sea and finally a first cast, often misjudged because of tension, then a rewind, the bait rechecked and a better-placed cast, taking the bait eighty yards out into the blue, blue sea.

When both of us were finally well placed, our lines out and taut, we found fighting positions close to each other, where we could brace our legs and play a fish to the end. And now we waited, relaxed yet alert, and read the signals telegraphed up the line. Finesse would not be needed. What we were fishing for would not come on tiptoe but with a slamming attack like a mugger. You would be hit before you even knew what hit you. And so we waited, happy to be there and grateful for the day and each other's company. Drinking in that sea like an alcoholic on the ultimate bender, just taking it in, taking it in.

Not much happened that day. Herman got hit and played the giant fish, most probably a shark, a bronze whaler, a bull shark maybe, for half an hour and almost all his line slowly and steadily heading out to sea for all that he did to try to slow his drag, the rod bent into the shape of a C, the fish just swept on till finally the line pulled to breaking strain touched a bottom rock or reef and sighed apart, ricocheting back a few hundred yards, and it was over. We fished on into the afternoon, eating our sandwiches and drinking our beer, comfortable and almost at home in our eyrie above the sea.

As evening came, we called it a day, packed up and went back the same way we had walked in, with homegoing ski-boats passing us to our right. At the shack, we washed up, scrubbing our hands hard with soap and water. And finally, tired legs stretched out as far as they would go, sipping a beer in the sunset.

Silence between us and a great content. We'd caught no fish, but we were filled with ocean, the sea was in our eyes, our hearts, our veins.

Julian on Obi Wan Kenobi, in the 1990s

A Fisherman in the Saddle

Swinging the Lead

My fishing days are now past, but the memory of them lives on in my mind, like an aquarium of fish in bright, pulsing colours.

Each fish has a haiku attached to its tail, sown on with gossamer line and a label in waterproof ink. Starting with the first and the smallest it says, 'Klipvis. Bloubergstrand, small pool in front of the house. December 1956'. Or 'Kabeljou, 16lbs, Swartklip, 1962'.

Alongside these fishy memories I also carry a freight of guilt and sadness for the many fish I caught and killed in the days when catch and release had not yet been thought of. A time when our seas teemed with fish of every kind and helping yourself was both a pleasure and a good way to feed your family.

I still eat fish and meat and feel some disquiet about it, but, like St Augustine, I say, 'Make me pure Lord, but not yet.'

It seems that the Bible is right in its summing up of man's time here when it says in Ecclesiastes:

'For everything there is a season,
A time for every activity under heaven.
A time to be born and a time to die.
A time to plant and a time to harvest.
A time to kill and a time to heal.

A time to tear down and a time to build up.
A time to cry and a time to laugh.
A time to grieve and a time to dance.
A time to scatter stones and a time to gather stones.
A time to embrace and a time to turn away.
A time to search and a time to quit searching.
A time to keep and a time to throw away.
A time to tear and a time to mend.
A time to be quiet and a time to speak.
A time to love and a time to hate.
A time for war and a time for peace.'

My days of killing fish are over and now I feel it is a time to look back at the primal hunting instinct that gave such joy to my fishing, to casting a line in the sea, such pleasure in swinging the lead and my bait far out beyond the breakers in search of fish. It is a time to keep, in mind at least.

These days, I view YouTube videos of fishing charters in South Africa, the US, in Mexico and the Caribbean with some misgivings and am not a little repelled by the tribe of skin divers who give the fish very little chance of escape, taking the life and death struggle under the water in search of prey. I listen to the crowing voices of boat-borne anglers as the shining harvest is heaved aboard. I can still recall the feeling of dread that the fish would escape and the primal joy when it lay safe at my feet gulping for air. I've done my share of killing, so my distaste bears a freight of hypocrisy.

Fishing for me was always about more than catching fish. There was so much more about it that I loved.

The equipment is the start of the magic. The understanding of what will bring a fish to strike is a kind of crash course in Marine Biology and Oceanography. The beautifully made fishing rods with their colour-whipped cord, cork handles and ceramic-lined iron eyes, the technological marvel of the fishing reels, the varieties of hooks and lures and the breaking strain of fishing line and wire leaders for those fish that would shred anything less.

In my father's comprehensive tackle box there were compartments filled with small plastic bottles that had previ-

A Fisherman in the Saddle

ously held tablets, now filled with a range of hooks, each in its own bottle, from tiny hooks for rockfish to the bent-over hooks he favoured for galjoen, that tough-jawed street fighter of a fish that looks like a bigger version of the meat-tearing piranha of South America. There were silver hooks and brown hooks and blue-black hooks, and those with differing shank lengths, long for impaling and wrapping bloodworm and coral worm and the huge hooks for catching the supreme, longed-for targets of every fisherman on the Cape coast in South Africa: kabeljou, yellowtail, mussel-cracker and steenbras.

Alongside the hooks there were reels of cotton for tying on bait: plain cotton thread in white and in black and elasticised cotton thread for securing the squishy redbait, which would fall off after one bite if not properly secured with this stretchy thread.

There were some tools, sharp bait knives, regularly honed, and smaller knives for trimming nylon trace close to the knot used for securing it to your line. There was an array of bottled oils for lubricating the fishing reels and a separate, backbreaking leather bag filled to bursting with six different kinds of lead sinkers. The traditional flat spoon-shaped ones, small round balls of lead with a hole through the middle for rocky places, sinkers with wire 'legs' for gripping a sandy bottom and diamond shaped and lozenge shaped sinkers for every strength of wind and for every kind of sea bottom.

And then, most crucial of all the cargo hauled to the beach, were the coolboxes of bait with their selection of frozen sardines, redbait, white mussels, *chokka (squid)* and usually some small fish for putting on whole, and haarders for a 'mixed grill', when partnered with *chokka*. There was something for each fish variety being targeted. And as a failsafe, there were a range of silver, copper and coloured lures. And tucked into the side, a sand-scoured board for cutting baits. It made up quite a load to lug from the Land Rover down to the beach or along the rocky shoreline to our favourite spots.

It takes years to understand all of this, and the arcane knowledge is something that comes out of a love of the subject. It is not so much about studying, but instead it is absorbed through your skin, eyes, ears and hands. The colour and temperature of water, the right place to choose to fish on a mile-long sandy beach, which looks to the untrained eye much of a muchness, but is not. One has to watch the movement of the sea for some time to understand that there are eddies and riffs and steeper drop-offs, where fish like to congregate in the current, waiting for the passing prey. There are both crowds and deserts just offshore. The trick is knowing what to look for. The same applies to rock ledge fishing. You need to keep an eye on the sea to avoid becoming fish bait yourself, to find a place where landing a fish is feasible, and to look out for reefs and sea kelp, which will either carve up or tangle your line or provide the hooked fish with a quick means of escape, rubbing the line against sharp rocks to snap it.

So when you see a tramp-like figure carrying his fishing rod and a pack on his back, don't be confused, understand this; you may be looking at someone who owns as much information about his subject as any professor.

There is a strange phenomenon that goes with fishing, an elasticity of time. When your fishing day starts, you feel a pressure to get to the sea that is utterly compelling. It is a demand that *must* be met and immediately. When you arrive at the beach, a kind of fishing fever then seizes you and there is a slight tremor to your hands as you fit reel to fishing rod and thread the line through the eyes of the rod and make up your trace with sinker and hook, on separate pieces of heavier breaking strain line. Baiting up seems one final challenge, but then you are ready. You scan the sea, watching it closely, reading it for the best place to send your bait. Then, in synch with the rhythm of the incoming waves, you wait for a lull in the sea's pulse and as a wave pulls back hissing, you run down the last incline into the water up to your thighs and with a practiced swing much like a golfer but going the other way round, from behind your back up over your head and away in a long, slightly arched trajectory, with a velocity like something shot from a cannon, you watch as the sinker leads the

A Fisherman in the Saddle

bait out, out, out, to sea, beyond the line of breaking surf. You gently thumb the spinning reel and feed line out till the sea bottom has been touched and then you click the gear to lock for reeling. Now you are set to reel in, and you do, just enough to lift the slack out of the line so that any fish touching your bait will send an electric current up the line to your hands instantly. You release the line once more and run up the beach, just beating the incoming wave, and now you wait. Time slows now, but it's a pleasure. You are relaxed but alert, you now inhabit the hunter's mind, an active, tensed, focused waiting. Your mind is in the water with your bait. And so the day goes: run into the sea, cast, wait.

The sun moves across the sky and you have time to watch the gulls riding the updrafts off the waves and the little flocks of sandpipers doing their run stop, run stop dance at the edge of the hissing, beach-climbing waves, finding that place just where the water's energy expires.

Time now is limpid; you are utterly in the present in a kind of wakeful meditation, only interrupted if there is a telltale knocking on your line. You rebait and rebait and send your casts out in a fan that covers your whole position. And then at last you are into a fish that has taken the bait and after a heart stopping fight, it slides up the beach like a talent of silver, a gleaming bar of pure energy, flapping and fighting till the end.

Lunchtime comes and you eat with peculiar appetite, a faint reek of fish still on your hands despite the sand and water scouring you gave them. Coffee and back to fishing. Now the morning's clarity is gone and there is a slight haze over the sea and the sunpath dazzle is subdued. You fish on and on and you feel this day will last forever. Nor would you have it any other way.

The late afternoon brings a moment when you have a run of rubbish fish, blaasoppies and small reef shark. You throw them back into the sea and take the time to have a cup of tea. Maybe now you change tactics and put a whole fish bait out there on a much bigger hook, seeking some wild action which may or may not come. And then, suddenly surprising you, it is dusk and you have a moment of intense sadness that the endless day has passed. You cast once or twice more with less energy than before, but with just as much hope as ever.

And, finally, you call it a day and leave the beach with the same sadness you will know later in life at leaving a lover on a railway station or airport. You long for her return even before she is out of sight and the beach seems suddenly empty and cold. You shiver and pack up your tackle, load up the rucksacks and head slowly up the beach, weighed down with fish if you've been lucky, with regrets if not.

There are places where I have left my heart as well as my blood on the beach or the rocks, pricked by hooks, cut with bait knives or scraped a knee in a fight to land a fish. These heal soon enough. But if you really have fallen prey to the passion that is fishing, then your heart may well stay behind on those rocks or that beach, however many years it's been since you last did your arabesque with a rod and line at the surf's edge. Ghost-like, your DNA holds that place and it holds you.

Sitting in my garden here in Sussex, I remember again that time I buried fishing treasures in the base of the sand dune cliff behind the beach where my father and Pascoe were fishing. I did not know it then but that was the very last time I fished that beach at Swartklip, or Black Rock, on the False Bay Coast of Cape Town. Life whisked me away to other things and to other hobbies, horse riding mainly, and I never returned. No doubt my little hoard lies there still at the base of that sand dune, my little childish pirate treasure, buried all these many, many years as I marched about the world and performed what was required of me. My hoard lay still, anchoring me to the beach, the bay, the views of the mountains, my place of birth, my motherland, marked by a cuttlefish spine and lead sinkers that never went to sea. I am happy that it lies there still. In some strange way it marks my passing, my childhood, who I was then, and I am linked to it as if by a tungsten wire, to that place from which I have been gone so long. You go fishing, but you leave something of yourself be-

A Fisherman in the Saddle

hind, the beach lands you as surely as the fish you landed there. A ghost trace of a treasured time gone by.

Julian's brother Herman after a night's catch of kabeljou at the mouth of the Breede River at Cape Infanta.

A Fisherman in the Saddle

Calico Bass

Sometimes, beginnings and endings come upon you unannounced. New Year 2001 was one such; it was a beginning, an important one, the true start of the new millennium and also the end of something for me, something which had always meant a great deal to me.

We had been planning a trip to Florida, to two of the islands on the Gulf of Mexico, Sanibel and Captiva, where you could find winter sunshine and seashells. It was virtually booked when Imogen, our eight-year-old daughter, said that she would like to meet her Californian cousins, whom she had last seen at six months of age, but naturally enough, could not remember. It was a fair request, and California a happy destination. We switched the bookings to Santa Barbara.

I am not the bravest air traveller; aircraft give me the willies. So the flight to LA was an ordeal. But at LAX my brother stood waiting for us and as the kids slept in the back of his truck, we drove through the soft warm night 100 miles north to his home and family in Santa Barbara. His house stands on a cliff with a commanding view south over an island twenty miles offshore and one or two oil derricks on the horizon. It is beautiful and the sunsets spectacular. Outside, parked on a trailer, sat his 18-foot ski-boat *Green-pea*, named for its unusual colour. He had spent the past year telling me of the wonderful catches he'd made from the boat. We'll go fishing, he said.

For eyes used to England's dim winter light, Santa Barbara was a revelation. The place is a nice manageable size with an attractive Spanish feel – the original Spanish monastery, now a museum, still stands. Fronted by a generous bay, the land, heavily treed, rises gently to a line of hills with whitewashed, red-roofed villas. Behind the hills to the east, a line of high barren mountains rears, cutting the coast off from the harsh desert interior. From those mountaintops it must look plush, an oasis by the sea. It is a wealthy town, but not ostentatiously so, though some film stars have made it their home, Michael Douglas and Catherine Zeta Jones are raising a family there, as are Jeff Bridges and his wife.

There is an excellent farmers' market twice a week on Main Street, and the seafront gardens play host to an art market on Saturdays, where you can admire the work from a hired pedal-car, cycling your way round under the palms. There are one or two very expensive low-rise hotels and dozens of great restaurants. There is a lovely marina where fish restaurants serve excellent food at prices that arouse a mix of delight and envy in British visitors. The wooden pier takes motor traffic out beyond the waves to an aquarium, more restaurants with stunning ocean views and wise looking pelicans drying themselves in the sea breeze. The streets are wide and clean, as are the beaches. And yet, yes there is a yet. The price of property means that this is a tough place to survive if you are not earning serious money.

But as a holiday destination, it is hard to fault. We had a great time. For one thing, we ate too much. Pancakes, maple syrup and clotted cream with bacon and eggs for breakfast is delicious, but can become too much of a good thing. We went exploring and liked what we found. There is much to like. The beaches are spectacular, as are the homes nestled in among the hills and by the sea.

One morning my brother Herman and my son, Dominic and I, took the boat out to sea. We did not go far, there was no need, we dropped anchor about a mile offshore, and using fish bait, cast our lines out. The sun was hot, the swell almost non-existent, and we had pelicans in attendance. To

A Fisherman in the Saddle

the east, the land rose up to the blue mountains, and to the west, the island lay quiet on the horizon. It was blissful. And the fish began to bite almost immediately.

The Santa Barbara Channel is a marvellous place. A mix of deep and shallow water means there is a rich diversity of life here. There are no less than twenty-seven whale and dolphin species that live in the channel, including giant blue whales and the humpback whale. California grey whales, once almost extinct, migrate through the channel and the last annual count numbered some 29,000 animals.

In the spring, that great fighter, the Chinook salmon, passes this way. The Santa Barbara Channel is best known in California as the Calico Bass Capital. There are also sand bass, halibut, white sea bass, rockfish, sheephead, red snapper, and ling in great numbers.

Fishing is done with a variety of artificial lures and spinners, as well as bait. In the marina, boats about to exit the harbour tie up at large holding pens, where anchovy and small sardine are kept ready to serve as live bait. We stopped here and watched as the guy in charge scooped up a ladleful of these small silver fish and placed them in a tank on *Greenpea*. All about the holding pen sat large pelicans, keeping an eye on things.

So there we were, minutes later, fishing in perfect conditions with the fish biting and being hauled in. Nothing huge, but a fair size some of them, three pounds and up with one or two bigger fish of other species.

For me, though, something was missing. Some of the fishing fever was gone. It was so lovely there that I did not want to be killing anything. It was sufficient to be out on the sea with my brother and Dominic, who was having great fun. I reeled in and helped him bait up and cast a little, but he hardly needed help. For the first time in my life, I sat there and was happy to be a non-combatant. I had no feeling against the taking of fish, I simply did not want to catch any. And it was a good feeling. There was no Hallelujah chorus, just a quiet feeling that I had done my fishing, and now it was up to others.

Julian Roup

HORSE MEDICINE: PART TWO

To Janice, who rides beside me; and for Dominic and Imogen, who allow us the time.

A Fisherman in the Saddle

The Lake Isle of Innisfree

'I will arise and go now, and go to Innisfree
And a small cabin build there, of clay and wattles made;
Nine bean rows will I have there, a hive for the honey bee,
And live alone in the bee-loud glade.

And I shall have some peace there, for peace comes dropping slow,
Dropping from the veils of morning to where the cricket sings;
There midnight's all a glimmer, and noon a purple glow,
And evening full of linnet's wings.

I will arise and go now, for always night and day
I hear lake water lapping with low sounds by the shore;
While I stand on the roadway, or on the pavements gray,
I hear it in the deep heart's core.

- W. B. Yeats

Julian Roup

A Fisherman in the Saddle

THE DUKE

I was a spoiled brat – no question about it. My father, an industrialist, had his team of German engineers design and build me a cream and red Noddy car, powered at first by a lawnmower engine and then, when this proved too slow, by one from a Vespa motorcycle, which did the trick nicely. I careened around the factory perimeter, very full of myself. What the engineers, one a survivor of Monte Casino, and the other, a teenage glider pilot in the Luftwaffe, must have made of this, I would rather not know. Ten years after surviving the Second World War, these German stalwarts were building toys for a tycoon's son!

I was a rather sickly child prone to chest infections, so my indulgent father bought a plot of ground next door to a medical friend's holiday home at Bloubergstrand on Table Bay. His friend, a doctor, argued that the bracing winds of Blouberg would cure me of my ills. The place was named for the blue mountain across the bay, but in my mind the word *blou* is more closely linked to the never-ending winds that blow there. My father took great pride in the fact that he erected our double storey house, called Just Ashore, in thirty days flat, his crew of builders working virtually night and day to achieve this. The neighbours in this small holiday village were mostly Afrikaans wheat farmers. We were, in those days, a new element in this community.

It was at Blouberg that horses first entered my life in

the form of a bay 12hh pony called Duke. I imagine he had some of the tough Basuto pony strain in him, for he seemed to live on air, and was fairly forward-going for a first pony. I was not one of those children who long for a pony and who lobby hard for one. The idea of riding had never entered my head until I
was presented with Duke one sunny summer Christmas morning. How little we recognise the major signposts in our lives... that pony was to change my life forever.

I was plonked in the saddle, the reins put in my hands, my father explaining how best to hold them, and then led down to Big Beach, where the tide was out and the hard-packed sand stretched for miles, broken here and there with irregular lumps of smooth red rock, the size of small cars. By the time we reached the beach we had attracted quite a crowd, both young and old. To this day, crowds make me uncomfortable.

On the beach I was led up and down, sedately. The slowness of the pace must have irritated some of the watching boys, because suddenly out of the corner of my eye I noticed one run up behind the pony and give it a whack. The pony was electrified and surged out of my father's grasp; I remember the terror of the animal running away with me. I clung on for
what seemed forever and then fell off, hitting my head on one of the rocks. Blackness descended and I was rushed off to hospital. I had been concussed, and also needed some stitches to the wound in my scalp. Why I ever got back on that pony again remains one of the great mysteries of my life. The concussion must have had a more lasting effect than was first feared, because the next day I was once more back on the pony, this unasked for and unexpected gift. Needless to say, the joys of my Noddy car faded.

It would be nice to say that I learned fast, became an expert competitive rider and represented my country at the Olympics. Nothing could have been further from the truth. I learned slowly. I was a cautious child, something of a loner, shy and a bit priggish I suspect. I certainly had little in com-

A Fisherman in the Saddle

mon with the gang of lads who made Big Beach their turf, playing cricket and rugby there between swims in the icy sea. Passing them on the pony, once I was allowed off the lead rein, I would give them a wide berth and trot off into the hazy distance.

Perhaps, had the pony been based at a riding stable, I might have had the example of others and taken part in gymkhanas and then show jumping. But the pony was kept in an old pigsty with a sandy scrub field near our summerhouse at Blouberg, and for the rest of the year he lived, quite comfortably, in an old shipping crate-turned-stable, at my father's factory in Lansdowne. So my riding was always solo, and probably the richer for it. The pony became a means of escape. This was a drug more powerful than heroin, and its effect has me still in its thrall. The pony took me into other worlds.

I recall as though it was yesterday, the first time I cantered – not counting my first wild ride. The feeling of elation, of freedom, of excitement was indescribable. It was like being given wings and the gift of flight. I was hooked for life.

It seems inconceivable now that Duke and I were given our heads and allowed to get on with it. I cannot imagine myself allowing my son or daughter, at the age of six or seven, to jog off into the wild blue yonder. But this is exactly what happened. The miles of beaches between Bloubergstrand and Melkbosstrand, and the wild untouched sand-dune country behind it, became my playground. I would picnic among the marram grasses and the iodine-scented seaweed washed up by the tides. These huge lengths of sea bamboo could be cut into trumpets, which produced a weird lowing sound, rather like that of a cow seeking its calf. We saw crabs and snakes, and once a great golden dune mole that chattered angrily at us, not giving an inch of ground, as we skirted him warily. The mole holes were a real danger in those dunes, one had to be watchful. But careful or not, every now and then the pony would plunge his front feet deep into one of these dangers. Luckily, he never fell or damaged his legs. It taught me to watch the going carefully.

We would canter a curving S along the foam-edged tide as it reached up the beach. Now and then we'd misjudge the strength of a wave and scatter spray behind us as Duke splashed his way through, his speed unchecked. Great, raucous, black-backed gulls would follow us in flight, and we'd scatter the pattering colonies of sanderlings, known as *strandlopers*. Here and there, black cormorants would sit, wings ajar, drying themselves in the sunshine.

The waters of the bay heaved with fish. Evidence of this was everywhere; in the fish remains on the beach, in the great presence of bird life, in the tell-tale swirls and jumps one could see from the back of a pony, as larger fish made forays into the midst of the shoals of *haarders*, a sort of sea mullet that congregated in their millions along this shore. And waiting for them at intervals with brightly painted rowing boats pulled high up the sides of dunes, well out of reach of high tide, were Coloured fishermen watching the sea for signs of fish. When a shoal was spotted, ten men or more would run that heavy clinker-built boat into the waves, and then row gallantly against the surf, casting the net piled in the rear, into a great hungry half-circle. The belly of the net would be 150 or 200 yards out, while men, women and children hauled at either ends on the beach.

I remember the primal excitement of waiting to see the catch. The trapped fish jumping within the floating encircling net, and the huge mass of silver fish, like new-minted coins wriggling and slithering in their thousands as they finally came ashore. Great wicker baskets would be filled to overflowing with this sea-bounty, some being sold on the spot and the rest taken off in old trucks to Cape Town's fish markets, shops and hawkers. It was an enthralling spectacle to be part of.

The wind, too, was a very real presence here. One could walk leant over at a 45-degree angle and not fall, the loose, dry sand hissing like stinging smoke along this beach that would one day become a famous haunt of surfers and windsurfers, with cigarette companies staging international competitions. But in my day, it was deserted but for the fishermen, my pony and me.

Now from 6,000 miles and a lifetime away, I wonder what became of The Duke, for he was an aristocrat among ponies. He carried me through childhood as gently as a nursemaid. Where, I wonder, do his bones lie? If I knew, I'd make a pilgrimage and put flowers on his grave.

Herman (left) with a galjoen and Julian with a Red Roman, caught at Hamerkop.

A Fisherman in the Saddle

Venus on four legs

My father grew up with horses. His father dealt in them; horses, donkeys and mules, supplying the farmers of the Paarl district in the Cape with horsepower. Dad told me of his favourite, Blackie, who would come when called, and Bluebird, a savage racehorse that tried to run his rider's legs off along a barbed wire fence. Behind my grandfather's home in Paarl was a massive stable complex, which gave visiting buyers great choice. Such was the demand generated by my grandfather's eye for horseflesh, that eventually he began importing horses and mules by ship from Argentina.

My father, at 50, had not ridden for many years, but enthused by my own interest, decided once more to buy a riding horse. He put the word out to his old contacts in Paarl and after a few weeks, Venus arrived. A less well-named animal it is hard to imagine. This great, blunt-headed, black-bay gelding might have been a Thor, or a Warrior, or a Thunderhead – a Venus he was not, and perhaps his name rankled, for he had a wicked temper, though it took us a while to find this out.

There were many weeks in which my father could not find the time to exercise his horse and so I took on this task. Venus was a very different ride from my 14.3hh pony, Don Juan, a chunky bay with a decidedly lazy streak, who would always do the minimum, preferring to go around a jump rather than over it, and pulling up puffed after a very short stretch of cantering. Venus had a look of challenge in his eyes, and a great thick neck that he'd set rock hard against you if he so desired. But it was the feeling that one was riding an unexploded bomb that made outings on Venus particularly hair-raising.

Once I put him over a series of jumps at the nearby Cape Hunt and Polo Club grounds and he went at them with a will, really attacking his work. After the last jump he gave a massive buck and a sort of madness took hold of him. He tore round the field seemingly in search of something, his mouth and neck set hard against my ineffectual tugging. He spotted a stand of tall pine trees and made directly for them, tearing in among the trees and trying to scrape my legs against the trunks. When he finally stopped, he was in a white lather and I was very shaken. We made our way back to the stables as though on springs. I spoke soothingly and
patted his streaming neck, very relieved to have got back in one piece. After that I rarely tried more than a simple hack with him.

My father gave up riding shortly after this. Venus had thrown him badly as they were passing a noisy concrete mixer, at a building site near the stables. The fall had both hurt Dad and shaken him badly. He decided that, as the head of a young family, he would give up riding while he was still ahead. I continued to ride the horse from time to time, though warily. He gave off a sense of menace that I had never before come across in a horse, and have never really felt since.

One day, bravado got the better of me and I decided to teach Venus a lesson that he would never forget. My plan was to use the bottomless sand of the Cape Flats to take the edge off him for good. We set off fairly early through the dune country and Venus worked well. He was a short-coupled, cobby type, around 15.3hh, immensely powerful, with great reserves of energy and with that temper to tap into when the going got tough. We got down to the sea at around 11am and the tide was out, not what I'd hoped for. My aim

A Fisherman in the Saddle

had been to gallop him east, towards Swartklip in the heavy sand above the high tide line, until he called pax. But this was not to be. We certainly started off in the heavy going, but he was having none of that. Soon we were flying down the hard-packed, shining, wet sand, going like the clappers. Despite his shape, that horse could really gallop. The speed and the excitement of the ride, and my determination to teach him a lesson then got the better of me. I began to lay into him with my crop in a way that would have had me disbarred by the Jockey Club. It felt then as though this great monster had moved into overdrive as he sank closer to the sand and flew. I was happy enough to sit still and let the miles chew him up. We passed the odd surf angler who shouted and raised his line as we dashed under and onwards. After a mile or two I began to wonder when, if ever, Venus was going to pull up. Shortly after that I decided it was time, as I'd had enough. And it was at that point that this mad horse really went to work. He had completely turned the tables, and I was being taught a lesson I would never forget. I felt that he was capable of anything. I'd not have been surprised had he turned his ugly head round and savaged me at full tilt. But he was going so fast that it felt as though he might over-reach himself and fall, so mad was the careering gait.

Finally, fearing we would arrive in The Strand or Gordon's Bay before long and run down swimmers on a crowded beach, I let go of one rein and with both hands on the left rein leant back in the saddle and hauled for all I was worth. At first there was no change, but then, gradually, his head bent fractionally toward my left knee and he began to veer up the beach towards the deep sand and the dunes beyond. We made a great, tortuous half-circle before he drew up gasping and shaking, the white foam creaming off him as though a wave had washed over him. I was as exhausted as he was. We rode home slowly. It was a long ride. I knew at last, and fully, that I was on the back of something fearful.

The final straw came shortly after this. I had been out on Venus for a brief hack and found that some friends were about to go out for a ride. I said I'd join them and turned

Venus round to follow as they rode out of the stable yard. Venus planted himself squarely at the entrance and turned to stone, refusing to budge. I could feel a great head of steam building in him and remembering what he was capable of, slipped off promptly. Venus allowed me to lead him towards his stable. I felt foolish, and that I had lost face in front of my friends.

Watching this was Bobby Salkinder, perhaps the greatest trick rider South Africa has ever known. He was famous for his ability with horses, and in his younger days had toured the agricultural shows as a kind of circus rider with a wide repertoire of tricks. He could pick things up from the ground at a full gallop, ride back to front, swing up onto a galloping horse, make his horse sit and then lie down like a dog. They could bow and dance. The grand finale of his show always got a great roar from the crowd. He would gallop into the arena with a dozen or more horses in various formations, standing astride the back three, a great fist of reins clenched in each hand. He was quite a guy.

The stable we kept our horses at was his. He was very popular as a teacher and took rides out three, sometimes four times a day, although he was older now and had so many broken bones in his body that he walked awkwardly and suffered brutally with arthritis. But he remained fearless. He'd seen my small defeat with Venus and told me to bring the horse to
him.

Bobby vaulted up into the saddle, lengthened the stirrups and turned the horse toward the entrance. What followed was something that I could not believe, and will doubtless never see again, nor would I wish to. Venus went berserk. Most horses trying to escape the control of their riders will either buck or rear; Venus did neither. Instead he set his mouth and great neck and ran up the side of the yard past the open stable doors of the livery horses, his flank pressed flush to the whitewashed walls, attempting to scrape his rider's leg off. Had Bobby not been a superlative horseman he would doubtless have lost his leg immediately, smashed to bits on the concrete. But he lifted it up out of harm's way over the horse's quarters.

Venus then ran amok. The stable was a series of leafy rectangles, courtyards within courtyards, each entered through a fairly narrow stonebound entrance. The horse careened round this complex, dashing first one flank then another into walls, doors and gateposts, in his attempt to hurt or kill his rider. People, horses, and chickens scattered before them, and all the while Bobby was turning the air blue, cursing the horse.

It finally ended when Venus ran full tilt into the feed-room door, smashing his way through and nearly decapitating Bobby on the lintel. Both emerged from the dark store limping and bloody. The next day the horse was gone. Venus he was not. A Martian? Maybe.

Setting off from the family's fishing shack at Hamerkop. Herman (left) and Julian loaded with tackle.

Parallel Lives

If you walk down the echoing concrete corridors of the South African College School (SACS), my old school in Cape Town, which I attended from age 6 to 16, you will see hundreds of black and white rugby and cricket team photographs, but you will search in vain for my image among them.

At a school where sport was something of a religion, and participation compulsory, I did not play ball. I was what was known as a 'three-five boy' – one who left the hallowed halls at five minutes past three promptly, when the last bell rang, unless I had detention. As the rest of the pupils prepared for battle on the rugby field or cricket pitch, depending on the season, I would be cycling furiously home, hell-bent on escape from school, headed for my pony and later my horse. I lived two separate parallel lives, and there was a price to be paid for my unsociable behaviour.

I took a great deal of stick for not playing rugby or cricket at this sports-mad school where participation was not voluntary, but obligatory. I had not set out to buck the system – it just happened that way, a sin of omission rather than commission. If I had my time over, I like to think I might have behaved differently, but I doubt it. Was it George Eliot who wrote, 'Character is destiny'?

I was not a very robust child. I had a propensity for colds and was fed on malt and cod liver oil and dressed in scratchy red flannel vests. At 15, I had a touch of TB and spent three weeks 'drying out' in the Karoo. Shortly after this, an ENT surgeon removed the top of my septum to allow me to breathe through the endless colds. As a result of all this, I was much coddled by parents who had already lost a child prematurely. Like all children, I was aware of the opportunity this gave me to swing the lead and swing it I did, spending many a day idling in bed when there was nothing really wrong with me.

After a genuine week of illness, when I was about eight years old, I returned to school to find that my classmates had all been initiated into the mysteries of rugby. Not wishing to appear a fool, I cut rugby for a few weeks, my lack of knowledge and my fear of ridicule mounting. And from that small, stupid mistake, a school life formed which was a foretaste of hell, as I hardened in my position of non-participation, and the school got ever more contemptuous in its position.

What my parents thought of all this I do not know, as my mother's family had all been great rugby players. A number of her brothers played for Western Province, and her cousin, the great Boy Louw, was a Springbok who later managed the Springbok team. To their credit, neither of my parents ever referred to this issue.

From a genuine social dilemma for a shy and uptight youngster, my phobia about rugby and cricket evolved until there came a time when I was simply determined to go nowhere near a rugby field. Now, not knowing the rules were no longer the issue, I was simply scared of being left for dead. Sheer funk, in fact. But there was also bloody-mindedness, a determination to resist the authoritarian force that wished to drive me in a direction I had decided I would not go. Of the many favourite family sayings used by my parents, the one that seemed most to apply to me was: *'Liewe bang Jan as dooie Jan!'* ('Rather scared John than dead John!'). It had an aptness that seemed to sum up my position.

I realised early on that the world beyond school was a tough place. I grew up with stories of my Jewish paternal

A Fisherman in the Saddle

grandfather arriving from Lithuania with two pounds in his pocket, one of which he gave to a friend. He was reduced in his early days to virtual beggary and nearly starved. Longing for the taste of pickled herring, but without the money to pay for this delicacy, he asked the fishmonger in Cape Town's market if he might dip his finger in the barrel to get the taste. This he was allowed to do, and the taste of the salt pickle, without the fish, came down the generations as a warning against poverty and want.

His homespun philosophy was that of a man who pulled a cart round the Cape, working as a *smous* or pedlar selling needles and thread, ribbons and thimbles, to farm wives who could not get these necessities in the Cape hinterland. He must have had huge inner resources, for despite the fact that he could not read or write till the day he died, aged 70 – his formidable wife, Esther, my grandmother, performed these functions for him – he nevertheless managed to build up an agricultural merchant business dealing in skins, seed, horses, donkeys and mules. Having come up the hard way, a world away from his birthplace, he would say that to survive in this world, a man needed to stand with his back to a wall with a gun in one hand and a knife in the other.

Eventually he imported animals from the Argentine to meet the burgeoning demand for horsepower. A huge man, he would carry off the ship, across his shoulders, any donkey or mule that proved reluctant to make landfall. He had a legendary and volcanic temper that went hand in hand with a reputation for fair dealing, and he left behind an enviable reputation that my father honoured and which I and my siblings were told was more precious than gold.

The story of my maternal Afrikaans grandfather also held moral lessons. Gently raised amid wealth and plenty on one of the many farms owned by his family in the Paarl valley, his early schooling was provided by a Scottish governess. He started life with every advantage – looks, wealth, reputation – and ended it with none. My mother explained that he had failed as a farmer – '*Hy het agteruit geboer*' ('he farmed backwards') – and took to the bottle. In his last years, his former connections found him a sinecure job, driving the post cart round the area, delivering post and parcels to many of the farms that he had once been master of, and where he now received charity, a chicken here, a pumpkin there, from people who had been his tenants.

My mother, his second youngest daughter, one of eight children, recalls those times, for she would accompany him often. She also remembered the agonising shame of being sent back to the butcher by her mother, who, scrimping and saving, had told her to ask for the *stywe* – the farthing – that she had been short-changed and which she desperately needed. The one side of the family had outworked poverty, while the other side had been forced to embrace it, reluctantly. These were powerful family lessons that seared themselves into my mind. My mother would warn: '*My kind, om te hê, en dan om nie te hê nie, is swaar*' ('My child, to have and then to have not, is very hard'). She would smile, recalling her Pappie as she called him, Andreas Abraham Louw van Kuiperskraal, and tell how even when things were at their worst, he would still brush his eyebrows at night before going to bed. Money, it seems, may go, but habits cling on.

Perhaps as a means to get me interested in exercise, my father bought me that first pony, Duke, when I was around six years old, and built a summer-house at Bloubergstrand to get me away from the wet miasma of Newlands, where we lived beneath the mountain for the rest of the year. Riding was the only sport, apart from fishing, which I stuck with.

I forget the excuses I used to escape the purgatory of school sport. I have so blanked out the ritual humiliation at the start of each rugby or cricket season that for the life of me I cannot recall what I said. To the school's credit, they knew when they saw a no-hoper and they left me alone, except for the twice-yearly spectacle of the rugby and cricket coaches, two of my regular teachers, who made me stand up at my desk and explain once more to them and the class why I would not be joining my classmates on the playing fields.

In my senior years, it became something of a game. To

A Fisherman in the Saddle

my astonishment, my classmates, who might well have bullied me, this wet non-participant, took a strange sort of pride in my ever-growing ability to flannel the sports coaches. There was something in their interest of the hope a cinema audience has that the criminal will get away with the swag. I did, but at a cost.

I learned to clown, to make myself an object of amusement and ridicule before anyone else could. And at five past three each afternoon, I would escape to my parallel world in the sand dunes of the Cape Flats, where I was not a no-hoper, not a three-five-boy, but a cowboy out riding the range, with the look of far horizons in his eyes.

My saviours were my ponies, Duke, then Don Juan, and my first horse, Quest. Those names say a lot about me, for I named all three. I forget their original names, except for Quest, who had lived till then with the ignominy of being called Japie. Bearing in mind my mother's typical Afrikaans dislike of pretension – though, God knows, she had named me Julian – I renamed him Quest. Later I would smile in recognition of that impulse when my mother repeated the Afrikaans line mocking Anglicisation in the words '*Annie wat Anne geword het, gee aan die konfyt what jam geword het*'. ('Annie, who's become Anne, please pass the *konfyt* which has now become jam.').

But Quest was a good name for a horse that took me in search of myself. I was always drawn to the image of the quest, and my life on three continents seems to endorse that view. All this family and school baggage was taken on board by my willing mounts, who carried me into the dunes, the forests and out onto the broad sweep of uncluttered Cape beaches, where everything was simple. We were figures in a landscape, as inconsequential as dung beetles, yet nature embraced us and showed me that there was an alternate reality to that of school.

I acquired a new pony at the age of 13, a cobby bay 14.2 gelding whom I called Don Juan, a complete misnomer if ever there was one. He was rather like me in some ways, happy to oblige as long as nothing too strenuous was expected of him. We got along fine – his low-revving nature just suited my adolescent moods as we mooched the dunes and beaches together, happy among the marram grass and tide-wrack, sheltering now and then out of the wind in depressions amid the tallest dunes.

When we moved back into town after the summer holidays, he was kept at the livery yard of Bobby Salkinder, opposite the Cape Hunt and Polo grounds, a set of cube-like, whitewashed squares within squares, fringed with tall, rustling poplars whose shadows danced across the walls, keeping the stables cool and dark as dusk, an ideal place for a boy to sit in the sawdust and dream of a life with horses.

Names are strange things; they take on a life of their own. My nickname in my last few years at SACS was 'Javelin'. This referred to my skeletal thinness rather than to any sharpness or warlike attributes. I was not offended by the name, as it indicated some form of recognition and affection.

This was in no small way linked to my sister Jay, two years my junior and a pupil at Rustenburg Girls School. Hanging on the wall of her childhood bedroom in our old home is a black and white picture of her looking like a more beautiful version of Françoise Hardy. She has been posed by a cousin of ours, a talented photographer, and is sitting on the edge of a street pavement, her feet in the road. In her hands she clasps a beaded, buttoned grab bag – the kind of thing that came out of some Afghanistan souk, and which were, along with the wool-lined rawhide coats, so much a part of the sixties scene. She looks as if she might be having a break from hitching. The fact is she was breaking the hearts of my classmates from a very early age and was my passport to some sort of social acceptance, if not inclusion.

Despite the family history, the stories of the dire consequences that attend sloth, and the benefits of hard work, I did little work at school. I was a dreamer, my thoughts always outside the classroom playing in another world. Academic meltdown was inevitable. At 13 years old, I failed a standard and had to remain down, repeating a year. This was a huge shock, having this public acknowledgement of failure amid the younger set that came up to join me from the year below. My father broke the news to me as gently as he could, masking his own disappointment. After sitting quite stunned in my bedroom for what seemed like hours, I decided to go for a walk along the beach. As I left the house, my father hurried after me. Taking me by the arm he said: 'Don't do anything stupid, Pooks, everything will work out.' I nodded and walked off. Slowly it came to me what he had meant. Until that moment no thought of self-harm had entered my mind. I was deeply touched by his concern, yet further depressed by the seriousness he obviously attached to my failure.

Another one of my mother's many Afrikaans proverbs, *'Agteros komook in die kraal'* (The last ox will also reach the corral) seemed to offer less hope than usual. As the very last ox in my class, I felt unsure of reaching anywhere, least of all the safety of a kraal. But as usual the outdoor world, the one that seemed to exist parallel but separate from my usual existence, had a calming effect. The sea was just the same, as were the seagulls and the busy little strandlopers. Cormorants still sat on rocks drying their open wings in the sun. My news had changed my world, not theirs. I envied them their freedom from exams, not understanding that in their world, failure meant death. After two more years at SACS I failed once more, my crucial JC year, two years before matriculation. My parents finally realised that drastic action was needed and a new school was found.

For the next two years Mrs Sampson, head of the aptly-named Progress College, held together the tottering pillars of my self-esteem – helped by a team made up largely of women, Mrs Tabik, Mrs Stevens and Mrs Gesofsky. This group specialised in academic salvaging, giving help, encouragement and hope to a strange mix of pupils who had been square pegs in round holes elsewhere. They treated us as adults and worked with us. My fellow pupils were a cross-section of the unusual, the talented, and the bright. There were few dunces among them; these were boys and girls who had simply not thrived on conventional schooling.

Then a strange thing happened. I began to enjoy

school. My English essays for Mrs Tabik were filled with the images and incidents of my life with horses, and miracle of miracles, she liked them. She liked them so much that for the very first time I felt the glow of a teacher's approval and praise, and like a good horse urged on by a kindly rider, I tried harder. My twin lives were no longer in parallel, separate universes, but joined. The mix of horses and writing was a potent medicine and I began to heal.

A Fisherman in the Saddle

IMPATIENT QUEST

I am not the most patient person in the world. If I want something, I usually want it now and I have had to pay a price for this quality, a price I am reminded of every time I walk up any set of stairs. (I have hesitated to write this particular story, for it does me no favours).

When I turned 15 or 16, I felt that I had finally outgrown Don Juan, who at 14.2hh and cobby with it, and laid-back to the point of laziness, was just not cutting the mustard as far as I was concerned. He had been an ideal mount, bought sight unseen for me by my father, who'd put the word out on his Paarl grapevine that something steady was needed. But after a couple of years riding Don, I was now six foot two inches tall and looked ridiculous on this fat bay pony. It was infra-dig to ride out on such a mount when I was surrounded by people riding elegant thoroughbreds.

The stables I was based at in Lansdowne, opposite the Kenilworth racecourse, hard by the Cape Hunt and Polo grounds, housed a wide variety of horses and people. The place was a home from home for the usual gaggle of horse-mad girls whom I eyed with increasing interest. There were also the learners using the riding school ponies, and a group of adults who kept their horses there at livery. The horses were pretty much what you would expect, a mixed bunch of school ponies with the jaundiced dispositions of their breed; polo ponies used for games across the road, riding horses of every description with elegant thoroughbreds, former racehorses, at the top of the pecking order, to my mind at least.

Our most regular ride was around the outside perimeter of the racecourse in deep heavy sand, but there were one or two grassy fields nearby and the huge open area of the Youngsfield airfield used by the South African Airforce as a training base, with old Harvards droning low overhead, as they took off and landed. Occasionally we'd ride down the side of the airfield and come out near the Royal Cape Golf Club, which would lead to a pinewood with jumps over enormous fallen trees.

It is strange, considering just how much time I spent there, that I got to know the place's human denizens but faintly. I knew the stable grooms, Banana and Long-one, amongst others, even less. They lived beyond the muckheap, to one side of the stable yard, cooking sheep heads and offal in three-legged pots over an outside fire. The smells, while they appalled me, drove the pack of English fox hounds wild. The Cape Hunt and Polo Club kept this pack here, just beside the grooms' quarters. A scouty type in old, hairy, ex-army breeches would regularly hack the hounds out on exercise. At the centre of the main square in this stable yard, Charlie, a captured jackal, spent a miserable life behind wire; his urine-soaked bedding provided the ideal scent trail for the hounds when pulled along the wooded paths of the Tokai forest.

It does not say much for me that all of this was of interest to me – but not a great deal of interest. The real action, as far as I was concerned, took place miles away in the dune country beyond the railway bridge and past Zeekoeivlei, where it rolled on down to the sea at Strandfontein and Muizenberg. I was on nodding and chatting terms with all, but I had no one intimate friend. All the action took place in my head and when the pictures in my head matched the outside reality in the dunes, I came fully alive.

One day I plucked up the courage to ask my father if I might get a full-sized horse. My academic performance at school, I knew, did not warrant me asking for favours. But as

A Fisherman in the Saddle

usual he surprised me and said that we'd go and look together. I was beside myself with joy. There was one horse at the stables which had captured my imagination, Brandtvlei, a burly middleweight gun-metal grey thoroughbred, who still ran in races and whom everyone kept well clear of. His evil temper, size and colour lent him a mystique, which appealed greatly to me, though had I been offered a ride on him, I'm pretty sure I would have hesitated. I suppose I had something like his looks in mind, but with a kinder temperament, when one Saturday my father and I finally set off to the Boland in search of a new mount for me.

At the first farm on our list we were shown a small horse, definitely not a pony but not by much. He was a very attractive animal with real quality about him. He must have had a good dash of Arab, was a rich blood bay and tripled like the wind. I had never before felt this gait and I was a bit bewildered by what the horse was up to. He was as different from Brandtvlei as it was possible to be and still be a horse. I decided to pass. I could tell my father was disappointed, as he liked the animal. The trouble was I just could not see myself turning up in the hunting field on this small tripling thing. The fact that he had a big heart and was a brilliant, active ride, counted for little with me. I wanted size above everything, and elegance. This busy little chap was not for me. I probably missed a very good horse with my silly preconceptions. But looking back now I know I made the right decision – I would not have been happy with him for long, with my feet almost dragging on the ground. Having said that, he was just the kind of boerperd, a farm horse, which were made such good use of by the Boers in their two wars against the British, when guts and stamina counted for more – man or horse – than height and elegance. It was horses like this, trained to lie down and be shot over, and then used to scramble over gulleys and down mountainsides, which gave the British cavalry, with their huge, half-starved hunters, such a very hard time.

At the next farm, somewhere near Riviersonderend, we were shown a big Roman-nosed chestnut with a white blaze, four white socks that came up to his knees and the angriest set of eyes I had seen on a horse. This was a very big horse, a 16.2hh middleweight hunter-type with an attitude. He carried his head high and I could see the whites of his eyes. The farmer had been out riding him – doubtless, I thought, to teach him some manners. The farm was barren under an autumn sky, the wheat long harvested and the land ploughed. We stood on a hill under a vast sky and watched this great yellow beast come at us from afar. Up close, he made a big impression of evil temper.

Gingerly, I got on and walked him back down the hill he had just cantered up. He did not like going away from the farm a second time and edged his way down with some head tossing. I trotted him out once we reached the valley floor and his giant strides were so different from Don Juan's that I was thrown around a bit until I found his rhythm. I pushed him into a canter and it was a rocking chair ride, I give him that. He was right back on his hocks, wasting no energy and light on his feet. I began to think he might do, despite his hideous head.

I pulled him up and then carefully turned him for home. He took a good hold and fairly bolted up the hill with me standing in the stirrups, galloping so fast that he seemed to level out against the rising gravel farm road. I just managed to pull him up by the small knot of onlookers. Someone grabbed his bridle and I scrambled off. I said I would like to think about it once we had seen all the horses that day. I looked back at him, his flanks heaving and his eyes rolling in that great blunt, hammer head. He was well made, and quite flash looking, but for that head, and I genuinely wondered if he might not do.

This was another world – a hard, no-nonsense world – so different from our city slicker's world. But there was magic here too. Here were barns full of black Friesians, high-stepping thick-necked show horses in white rawhide halters, taken out once a year to horse shows, perhaps, if the harvest had been good. They stood shoulder to shoulder in the gloom, chained to the fifty-yard long crib, munching hay.

A Fisherman in the Saddle

Harnessed in teams of eight or twelve, they gave splendid shows of pulling power. These teams were the ten-ton trucks of their day, hauling carts and wagons. Then there were the American saddlers, riding horses, the pride and joy of their owners, equine limousines, kept in darkened stables on built-up shoes, ready to be shown off with gingered tails.

We were offered hospitality everywhere, but we were not easy guests, city folks who were so different. Outside the farmhouse stood my father's vast black ministerial-looking Cadillac, with his driver at the wheel. The conversations were stiff and stilted. The next farm we came to had a comfortable feeling, surrounded by orchards and sunk into the land between hills. There was a rustling line of poplars that ran beside a stream, their few remaining yellow leaves rustling in the breeze.

After the obligatory cup of coffee, the farmer shouted for his 'head boy': 'Ballas, gaan saal Japie op!' ('Ballas, go and saddle up Japie'). Ballas, for that was his name or nickname, went running in his blue overalls to do as his master bidding, to saddle up Japie whom we had come to see.

It was not an auspicious start to the relationship with my next horse. Japie had been hard-used for chasing down jackals, this farmer's particular hobby. The horse was not madly prepossessing – a lean dull bay, a 15.3hh beast, with an odd, dished, though mule-like head. His great asset was his stamina, said the farmer, and the fact that he was absolutely straight, a no-nonsense kind of horse. I looked hard at him and tried to like him a bit. He was bigger than Don by 1.5 hands, not a tripler, and apparently not mad, bad or dangerous to know, like the chestnut we had just seen. I rode him down past the poplars along the river after the farmer had shown him off at the walk, trot and canter. He seemed like a horse resigned to his lot, and I felt rather sorry for him.

His paces surprised me. He had a fairly active walk (the best pace bar none in a riding horse), a ground-clearing trot and a balanced canter not unlike that of a polo pony, and, like those overworked misused animals, he tended to carry his head high. In some funny way, we clicked and I felt that he'd do. It was not exactly love, more like a reasonable compromise. I did not want to go home empty-handed and made a choice, not a brilliant choice, but better than having nothing at the end of the day. I chose Japie.

After some more chat and further coffee and koeksisters – a toothachingly sweet Afrikaans confection, a crisp, plaited doughnut soaked in treacle syrup – at the farmhouse there was a deal-making handshake between my father and the farmer, and we were on our way home. A few days later, Japie was delivered to the stables in Lansdowne.

Looking now at the picture of me on Japie shortly after he arrived, I'm horrified by my seat, too far back and legs too far forward, a very secure 'ride-him-cowboy' position that had come as the result of being self-taught. It was not elegant, but it served. And I see that my long legs are finally well clear of the ground. I also see that I have over-bitted him with a Pelham and rein connectors. His mouth is yawning open, not an advert for a good pair of hands. Poor Japie!

The least I could do was rename him, and this I did, calling him Quest, an inappropriate, high-flown romantic name by a hopeless romantic, for a horse that should have stayed Japie. Perhaps subliminally I was acknowledging the fact that he was not my ideal and that the search for perfection was still on.

They say that handsome is as handsome does, and Quest served me handsomely for three years. He was always there – you hardly had to touch his sides and he'd bound away; he was never lame, sick or sorry. He had grit, that horse. His only fault was that after a long ride down to the sea and back, a six-hour undertaking in the summer heat, he would tend to jog. When you are tired, saddle-sore and thirsty and your horse won't walk, it can be more than annoying.

One day, I was riding in a dreamlike state after a long stretch in the heat, with a great thirst, when Quest started to jog again, and try as I might, he would not settle to a walk. Fed up, I did the unforgivable – I yanked at his mouth. We were some way past the cool gum trees, which give an avenue of respite from the sun. We were out in the blinding light

A Fisherman in the Saddle

coming off the last of the dune country on a baking summer's afternoon. And he would not walk. I yanked hard. I had forgotten that I had him in a long, fancy American bit, with S-shaped side bars that gave immense leverage when used harshly, and I was riding in a cheap cowboy saddle with a bare metal saddle horn. Hurt beyond reason by my temper-fuelled yank, Quest went right up on his hind legs, overbalanced backward and fell onto me. It all happened so fast that there was no time to feel fear. The back of the saddle, the cantle, caught my left knee a tremendous blow, and then the impetus of his fall rolled the horse clear of my leg. We were both up on our legs instantly. We were both shaking and I was desperately sorry for what I had done, and very grateful that I had not been impaled by that six-inch-long steel pommel.

With shaking hands, I checked Quest's trembling legs. There seemed to be no damage, and I walked him for a few hundred yards to calm him down and to steady my own nerves. By then I could feel that something was not right with my knee. I remounted carefully and we walked home. There was no jogging now. We got back safely to the stables, and after I saw to him in the sand paddock where he rolled, I watered and fed him. I then went home but was too ashamed to tell anyone what had happened.

But a few weeks later, it was evident that something was seriously up with my left knee. I had trouble straightening it, and to free it felt as if something inside was tearing. Finally, it stuck in the bent position and I could not straighten it at all. I was taken for X-rays and hopped from the car on one leg supported by our driver, Pieter Brill. I had damaged the cartilage and needed an operation immediately to free the knee. I recall falling asleep on the operating table with my left leg still bent, and waking up in recovery with it straight, but in plaster. The knee has given me a certain amount of grief for years, and one day the whole joint might have to be replaced unless new techniques mean that there is some alternative.

Out of this little excitement came a good lesson – control your temper and impatience or it will cost you, especially if you are riding. I cannot say in all honesty that it's a lesson I've learnt definitively, but when I fail on this front once more, I see myself and Quest falling over backwards and his body rolling off my legs, and that wicked metal pommel winking in the sun, having almost kebabbed me.

A Fisherman in the Saddle

CAPE TOWN COWBOYS

Why is it so intoxicating to be part of a group, especially one that shares one's interests and pleasures? Because it confirms one, strengthens one, and increases one's pleasure and interest? Yes to all of that. I certainly found it so when I became a member of the Cape Flats Cowboys in the late 1960s.

The world may have been experiencing social revolution, the Beatles, the Stones and the Beachboys, all changing the perceptions of youth. Not me, I was riding the range with friends old enough to know better, but oh boy, were we having fun! The advent of the Cape Flats Cowboys was that most innocent and wonderful thing, a childhood gang for grownups. Jackie, Lon, Mike, Phil and I were born-again creatures from the world of Zane Grey. I was no longer a geeky, bespectacled, teenager – I was Doc LeRoy, riding the Appalachian Trail to the great distances of the American West. That all this took place at the tip of the African continent, amid the rising tensions of the Apartheid struggle for change, is the more remarkable, for it shows how we create our own landscapes, our own realities.

As the youngest member of this happy band of brothers, this booted, be-jeaned, holstered and horsed group of happy fantasists, I was to experience intensities of pleasure rarely experienced in company, before or since. We had a part-time member called Cheyenne. An enigmatic, dark skinned fellow of indeterminate race, his long black hair and hawk nose made him a dead ringer for an Indian Scout. He played up to this beautifully, riding without a saddle, just a girth and saddle blanket, a great, sheathed knife at his hip, his skewbald horse with feathers in its mane and on its simple bitless bridle. Cheyenne would ride the sand dune ridges to our left or right as we made our way amid the valleys to the sea, scouring the horizon from the high ground for danger.

There was great camaraderie, badinage and joshing. It felt close to how it must have been for real cowboys, or so it felt to me. I was just 18, the rest of the group in their late 20s and early 30s. We entertained ourselves greatly. At weekends, after a long day in the saddle, it was wonderful to sit round a barbecue at the stables and talk, drink beer and plan our next foray into 'sagebrush country'.

At the time, I rode Hombre, a big middleweight, five-gaited grey that I had bought as a stallion and had gelded – known as *Bitterbos* (Bitterbush) by his previous owner. He learned to collect himself well in the heavy going of the sand flats and cantered in a slow easy beat, well back on his hocks. He was a pleasure to own. He had the two added gears of the five-gaited horse and would triple along on hard-going mile on mile. And, of course, he had that big finish, making a great thing of arriving anywhere. Pulling him right back he would go into his rack, all front elevation and flashing feet, which brought the African stablehands running out to see him. They loved the performance as much as I enjoyed providing it.

At one level, in hindsight, it was all rather embarrassing – the Stetsons and cowboy outfits, the western saddles and long-bitted bridles. People seeing this group of misplaced cowboys must have been bemused, but most waved and shouted comments, 'Hiiiyah Silver!' or 'Ride 'em cowboy!' as though we were a circus act. It was a bit cringe-making, but great fun. The trick was to remain in character, as though we truly were a bunch of hard-riding cowpokes dropped down from the sky in Africa. It was easy enough to do. The skin-tight jeans, the denim shirt and jacket, the black, flat-

A Fisherman in the Saddle

brimmed Stetson, the cowboy boots and rowel spurs ... as one put them on, one became Doc Leroy, just as an actor does in preparing for the stage. One or two of the group had gone to the trouble of getting old American Civil War uniforms and forage caps in navy or grey. Taken as a whole, this posse of romantics really did look as though it had ridden out of history through a wormhole.

As it happened, we saw very few people. The action took place in the great privacy of the dunes. This unspoiled wild country, the heat or cold, and the wind, set the scene beautifully. Once in a while we would pass a woodcutter and his horse-drawn cart and we would acknowledge each other as relics of a past time. The whole thing was about improvising a story line with words and actions, set on horseback, while moving through a landscape. The action, up and down dunes, in and around Port Jackson thickets, wading through Zeekoevlei, created romantic images that satisfied the eye. We were approached by an advertising agency wanting to shoot a beer commercial, but nothing came of it.

A magazine carried a few pictures with captions and this brought an invitation to join the annual long-distance ride at Vredenburg, to the coast at Paternoster – a distance of some 20 miles. The event was organised by local farmers for farmers and was a great social event. We accepted with alacrity, setting out to wow the citizenry of Vredenburg with our cowboy style. It was bound to end in tears.

We boxed the horses up to Vredenburg and stood posing for the local newspaper photographer. After a big welcome speech, coffee and koeksisters we mounted our horses and set off, some sixty riders. The idea was to ride the ten miles to the sea at Paternoster, have lunch there and then, after a break, return to Vredenburg. The Commando leader, a big, bearded man,
said that it was not a race but a pleasure ride and there was to be no galloping. All went swimmingly. It was a lovely warm day, not hot, just pleasant, and the countryside was lovely, new to us and as is the way with new places, a great pleasure to ride through. As we rode, we chatted to our new friends.

There was some friendly teasing about our get-up and tack that was taken in good part. Hombre was much admired, especially his triple gait, which was so comfortable to sit, and which smoothed the miles. Lunch was a splendid affair, after the horses were hayed, watered and tethered in the shade of trees. Afrikaans hospitality is legendary, and has been known to kill. There was an ox on a spit, wine of every description and side dishes too numerous to mention. We ate like cowboys and came back for more. And though we all drank moderately, the wine was strong, the sun pleasant and soon we too, like the horses, dozed in the shade.

At three o'clock the call came: 'Opsaal!' – 'Saddle up!' We struggled with our heavy western rigs, which do not buckle up, but cinch tight with knots. There seemed little need to rush and we were among the last to leave the scene of our feasting. Then the gauntlet was flung down. 'Come, cowboys, now let's see if you can ride!' The challenge came from a group of young men who had been foremost among the morning's teasers, and the effect was instant. Heavy with lunch as we were, we nevertheless rose to the taunt and set off after the fast-disappearing group whose horses were kicking up clouds of dust in a fast getaway move.

I wish I could say that we thrashed them. The truth is that we thrashed our horses. They, poor beasts, were at best weekend soldiers, happy to take us out for a few hours on Saturdays and Sundays, not nearly fit enough to take part in a 10-mile race. For that is what it became, despite the repeated bellows of the headman, the Commando leader who shouted imprecations against the history, the breeding and the native wit of the youngsters who now led us a merry dance.

You cannot gallop ten miles. No horse born of a mare can do that. A good fit endurance horse will trot steadily and break into a canter here and there where the going is good. Now and then, depending on terrain, one must walk. Any other approach will at first distress a horse and then kill it. Of course, we knew all this and yet our honour and manliness had been impugned; our very credentials as cowboys hung in the balance. We, and our mounts, had no choice. We set after

A Fisherman in the Saddle

the blighters with a will.

It was a cruel ride. The ground was hard and rocky, our stomachs overfilled, our horses unfit for action. But we gave it our best. Late that afternoon, as the sun was setting over the mountains, we crawled into Vredenburg. Our taunters were standing at the showground entrance, beers in hand and with a lot to say, none of which I am going to repeat here. We said little, packed our exhausted horses in the trucks and set off the hundred miles back to Cape Town.

A week later we received a press cutting from a local newspaper. The headline read: 'Cape Cowboys Too Slow For Vredenburg Redskins!' Strangely enough the whole incident was seldom mentioned after that, but something of the essential élan of the Cowboys of the Cape Flats had been lost and within a few months I found myself riding the trail on my own once more. It's hard being a cowboy. I know that now.

Julian Roup

Patron saints and privates

To this day, I'm not sure who the patron saint was, my horse, Hombre, a big part-bred American Saddler, or Linda Roos, the girl on the Oudtshoorn telephone exchange. Maybe both? Tell me what you think.

Occasionally you meet someone who just likes you for yourself. There is absolutely no hidden agenda, and their friendship is like a gift, something you keep close and hold onto like a good luck amulet, carried next to the heart. One such was Hombre; Linda Roos was another. And like water in the desert, they arrived in the nick of time. The patron saints of soldiers are a breed apart and mine were no exception – except that both were alive, or so I thought at the time. Later, I was not that sure.

My eighteenth birthday brought many things, among them a form from the South African Defence Force. I registered for my National Service reluctantly, but with the happy thought that at least I would be free from school. A few weeks later I packed a bag with specified items and went to join the Army. We met face to face for the first time, in the inner quad of Cape Town Castle. That first meeting did not bode well for the next nine months.

The Permanent Force NCOs looked a bad lot. They

walked with the swagger of bullies, like Shakespearean villains, knowing the eyes of the audience watched their every move. After much shouting and abuse, the hundreds of new recruits were herded onto a train at the nearby station. We were being sent 300 miles north to Oudtshoorn for infantry training.

It was not a happy destination. The previous intake had made national headlines with the death of a recruit in Oudtshoorn the year before. But youthful bravado is strong wine, and as we were all in the same boat, we made the best of it. For many of us, including me, pampered with luxury all our lives, we were uncertain how we would conduct ourselves. We would soon find out. The weeks that followed that February, March and April of 1969, were like living in a pressure cooker as we drilled and sweated through the Cape summer baking down on this semi-desert place between the mountains. The only happy inhabitants were the ostriches which thronged the farms across the region, and the guides who worked in the cool of the Cango Caves. We never got beyond the barbed wire that ringed the Army Camp for three months of basic training. We learned to know the meaning of fear, learned to eat off metal trays called pig pans, used toilets without doors, and watched the red dust from our hair, ears and every other crevice, cascade like blood down our bodies once the shower water struck. Heat was one enemy, the army another.

We'd arrived in Oudtshoorn at the ungodly hour of 5am, roused from our train compartments by shrill whistles and huddled on the platform. We were not a prepossessing sight. Already we looked like victims, refugees from civilian life. The small dusty town lay encircled by mountains – the Outeniquas and the Swartberge – a natural prison. Early morning mist shrouded the valley floor. We were marshalled into trucks and after a short drive, arrived at an army camp with enormous metal hangars, rows and rows of bunkhouses and the vast, silent, red-earth parade ground we would get to know so well. Behind the camp rose a hill, deeply scarred with shooting range butts. This hill was wreathed in a frightening mythology of its own, which in the days ahead would prove all too accurate. Topped by a mushroom-shaped water tower, it would be the Calvary upon which our soft civilian spirit was first broken and then re-shaped into the semblance of an infantry esprit de corps.

Looking back on it all, it seems impossible that Linda lived so close to that horrible place, and that I made my peace with it in the end, realising that in those nine months I had been reborn in some way. A benchmark had been created by which to judge future pain, future suffering. Nothing again would ever seem so terrible, nor would I ever again feel so cut off from the rational world, so enmeshed in a place where terrible things could and did happen.

The first week was not too bad. You had the feeling that the Army was watching and waiting, deciding our strengths and weaknesses, toying with us. We were shown how to clean a bunkhouse to the Army's satisfaction. The pink linoleum floor was polished and boned till it reflected our faces. With inspections due, we took to 'taxis' – strips of cloth on which to glide over the mirror-like floor, instead of clumping about in our boots, which left scuff marks. The boots themselves shone like the sun, all grit painstakingly removed from the thickly scored rubber soles. Beds were made up for inspection, using cardboard between the blankets to get them perfectly flat and square. Two aluminium dixies were used to bang an exact edge on these useless masterpieces that would not have shamed a spirit level. A roomful of recruits gnawing their squared off beds to improve the crease at the edges, took some getting used to. Hysteria was never far away, and there would be wild laughter in the night.

Soon, however, these things seemed insignificant, minor irritations, as full-scale training began. The day started with reveille at 6am. We marched all morning with our FN rifles getting heavier all the time. As temperatures soared, we'd pack it in for lectures on infantry tactics or rifle drill with our 'wives', as we were told to call our rifles. We learned not to call them guns. Those who did were made to hold their penis in one hand and their rifle in the other and repeat:

'This is my rifle. This is my gun. The one is for shooting, the other's for fun.' The word gun disappeared from our vocabulary.

There was no actual physical abuse. No one struck anyone. So the death of the recruit the previous year had not been entirely in vain. Instead, there was the constant threat to run us off our feet, a threat that was more of a promise. Psychological and physical exhaustion took its toll. Punishment PT was one way of keeping you on edge. Manhandling large sections of tree trunk was an effective way of making you pay for trumped-up misdemeanours. For the really obdurate, and they were as rare as chicken's teeth, there was full pack drill at double quick time, and finally there was Detention Barracks. You did not want to go there.

Out on platoon runs, anyone dropping out or collapsing had to be picked up and carried by his comrades. It made for few dropouts. The system was pure stick and no carrot. The idea seemed to be to push us until someone vomited from exhaustion. Sadly, the system was random and instead of slowly building us up to peak fitness, it caused more physical damage than fitness. You were at the mercy of men who had generally failed in civilian life and could not find work in the police force or the railways. After one particular run, I recall sitting on the bunkhouse steps with others, carefully peeling and cutting socks from our bleeding feet.

Strange things began to happen then. We were in the heart of basic training and the heat beat down relentlessly. Some days it was so hot we were ordered back to the bunkhouses and told to keep still. The temperatures soared into the hundreds. As you lay on your bunk, stripped to your underpants, the sweat ran off you in rivulets, staining the blankets right through to the thin black and white coir-stuffed mattresses. At 6pm, as the heat grew less intense, we were lined up and given milk bottles of ice-cold salt water to replace the salt and liquid we had lost. On days when the heat stayed this side of 100, training continued. The heat liquefied the landscape. The solid aridity of the mountain-encircled plain became wavy; it distorted images and distances. As the

A Fisherman in the Saddle

sun reached its peak, the valley floor shimmered and seemed to rise with the scorching thermals. Out on manoeuvres, the few faint sounds came from afar, the bush around you silent, smashed by the weight of the heat. The smell of crushed khaki bush and red dust entered your very pores. Blowing your nose left something that looked like a nosebleed in the handkerchief. It was an animal-like existence.

Running in that heat, our bodies changed shape, getting leaner and harder. Minds dwelled on simple things, the shiny black insects in the bush where you tripped and fell, feeling the trickle of sweat and the determination to survive. The lightness that came with second wind seemed to carry you above the ground, part of the rising heat haze, a regiment running in the sky. We all lost weight and soon I was down to an emaciated 145 lbs, stretched across my six-foot-two frame. Walking at sunset, my shadow looked even more elongated than usual, my neck like that of some North African woman, elegantly abnormal.

At this low point, I heard Linda's voice for the first time. I had been in camp for two months, though it seemed I had been gone forever. One evening I made my weekly telephone call home, to my parents in Cape Town, from the only pay-phone in the camp. Afterwards, I stood leaning against it, looking deep into the night, but seeing the city of my birth. The phone rang unexpectedly, and I answered it. A soft female voice said playfully, 'Don't you say thank you for the long five minutes?' If a spaceship had landed beside me and little green men had invited me in, I could not have been more surprised. I said: 'I beg your pardon?' She explained that she worked on the Oudtshoorn telephone exchange, through whom I booked my reverse-charge calls, and as she worked most Friday nights it was often she who put me through. She said that in this instance, she had just charged a fifteen-minute call as five. When you have been treated with contempt, as the lowest of the low, for an unremitting eight weeks, chased, cursed, driven, and have struggled to keep going, a sudden unexpected kindness like that unmans you. I felt my throat close up. All I managed to say was a fairly strangled thank you.

I had that most wonderful thing, a friend, a friend who had come out of nowhere, but was out there in the dark, night town, beyond the camp fence, living the life of a normal human being. It was like the shock of diving into a pool on a hot day. I felt transformed – as men do by women. The echo of that emotion has stayed with me down the years. It was a gift beyond price. A woman was speaking to me as a human being. I felt ridiculously grateful. We chatted about life in Oudtshoorn and the army camp. She sounded so sane, so beautifully small-town sane and nice. Walking back to the bunkhouse, I got the army into some kind of perspective for the first time. I realised that life was carrying on as normal beyond the perimeter fence and that seemed oddly reassuring.

With basic training drawing to a close, my father, bless him, arranged to send Hombre up to Oudtshoorn, as on Wednesday afternoons and on Saturdays I'd be free to do a sport of my own choice. The local Oudtshoorn traffic policeman who rode both a motorbike and a horse, which he kept at the show grounds, agreed to look after Hombre for a small fee. I was overjoyed.

I will never forget climbing into the saddle for the first time in Oudtshoorn. I was so light and fit there was no effort involved. As I looked between my horse's ears, this horse that had carried me for so many miles into so many landscapes and now stood ready once more, I felt I was home. I was transported as if by magic to the Faraway Tree, to a land where once more I was master of my fate, where I could go where the wind went, fly with the birds and drift with the clouds, where no fence held me back and my hard-done-by feet were no longer needed. I fell forward into my horse's mane and said a prayer to the God who made horses and gave them the grace to allow man on their backs.

And now it was as if the gods wished to repay me for my time of travail, for blessings flowed thick and fast. Linda Roos, that was the name she gave me, phoned often. She must have told the other exchange operators to let her know when I was calling home. She asked me for details of my training schedule and I filled her in on the worst. The very next day as I formed up with the rest of the company for another exercise on the assault course, the camp Tannoy blared. 'Rifleman Roup, report immediately to the Duty Room!' Given permission, I jogged off, wondering what sort of trouble I was in. The sergeant on duty said there was an urgent call from Cape Town for me. Worrying about what it could be, I ran to the call box and picked up the phone.

It was Linda. Laughing gently, she asked if she had chosen a good time to call. I had to admit that her timing was perfect. By the time I got back to the barrack lines they were deserted, and I loitered in the bunkhouse until the shattered company got back. Incredible as it seemed, though the army had me in its clutches, Linda was calling the shots. I never cut socks off blood-caked feet again.

The truly strange thing about all this is that I never met Linda. The moment I had weekend leave I suggested a meeting, but she was always tied up, she said. I wanted to repay her in some small way for the many favours she continued to do me. I was intrigued by her audacity and naturally wanted to meet her. Without doubt, I was more than a little in love with her. She would tease me, saying she had seen me riding the day before, had in fact passed me in her car, and described Hombre minutely. But she would never agree to see me. Instead, she made jokes and said I wouldn't like her if I saw her. But she continued to phone at key moments.

If I was out at the far shooting range with a six-mile run back to camp ahead of me, even there she managed to reach me. A plume of dust out over the valley floor would turn out to be a jeep on its way to pick me up for an urgent family call in camp. What she said or how she convinced them of her urgent priority over my training I never found out. She would just chuckle when I asked her.

It would be nice to say that when my training was completed, I managed to find her and thank her. In fact, just before we were demobbed, I made my way to the local telephone exchange building and asked at reception if I might

speak to Linda Roos. I was told to wait and, after some time, the receptionist told me, apologetically, that no one of that name worked
there. I knew then that Linda wanted our contact to remain as it was, through the warm intimate medium of the telephone, no more. So I left it. I packed Hombre up and boxed him back to Cape Town.

In the months and years that followed, she would still occasionally phone. I would come home from a date, be falling asleep, and the phone would ring. It was Linda out there in the middle of the night, working her shift. Finally, the calls stopped. Patron saints and privates, it seems, are not intended to meet in this world.

Hombre is long gone. His bones lie at peace and his spirit moves in meadows of some horse heaven, where the blistering heat of Oudtshoorn is no more. About Linda I am less sure. Linda, if you live, may all the blessings of the world be yours – for you were my bridge over troubled water.

A Fisherman in the Saddle

CAPE HUNT AND POLO

I was shocked to discover when I arrived in England in 1980 that I was a South African. That may seem a little obtuse, to live to the age of 30 and not be aware of your own nationality. But there it is. If you grew up in the Cape as I did, it was an easy enough thing to do, surrounded by tales of trout and salmon fishing in Ireland, by dog-eared copies of *Horse & Hound* mailed from England in the tack room, spending time in the company of Biggles, Nevil Shute, James Bond and finally, Jane Austen, while lying on Clifton and Llandudno beaches. It was possible, even with an Afrikaans mother, and a mad-keen rugby-playing brother, to think of oneself as something different from those around you. God knows what I thought I was. Perhaps my identity problem has something to do with my Jewish father – trying to finesse synagogue on Saturday morning and Dutch Reformed Church on Sunday was perhaps just too much for my mind, and a sort of alternate reality, a quite separate identity, was needed to make sense of it all. The melting pot can be a hot and sticky place.

Horses became my nation, my identity and my friends, and horses took me ever deeper into England, even though I lived in South Africa. They took me show jumping at Hickstead, where one day as a reporter on a provincial paper in Sussex, I would write up the shows myself. They took me cub hunting, even as I jogged my pony on Cape beaches. They took me point-to-pointing in Sussex as I groomed my pony in

Lansdowne. They led me to Rupert Brooke, to Sassoon, to *The Irish R.M.* by E. Somerville, to Surtees' world of Jorrocks and Sponge, to a country I had never seen but which I had lived in for so long, albeit in my head.

Horses then took me across the road to the polo grounds in Cape Town and then into Tokai, Vergelegen, Noordhoek, and Philippi, drag hunting with the Cape Hunt and Polo Club. What a very strange world that was. I began as an acolyte of Jimmy and Janet Burns, building jumps in Philippi for the Hunt, using clumps of reeds and Port Jackson branches to knit an obstacle worthy of a thoroughbred at full tilt in the deep sand.

At around the age of 14, I suppose, I made it to my first hunt. Togged up in boots, breeches, white shirt and tie topped off with a tweed jacket and a black crash cap, I appeared at my first hunt breakfast in Tokai, among the pink coats and vermilion complexions, of real *rooinekke* (Englishmen) and would-be *rooinekke*, myself among them. In later years I would hear the expression *soutpiel* or *soutie* and discover its meaning, to my great amusement, during my National Service in Oudtshoorn. It was explained in graphic detail as a man whose allegiance to England was such that with one leg in the old country and the other at the Cape, his wedding tackle hung suspended in the salty sea, hence *soutie*. I suppose in a way I was in *Soutie*-Apprentice mode, standing uncertainly at the hunt breakfast clutching a sausage roll and a glass of squash.

It's hard looking back now to assess the level of pretentiousness, but provincial echoes of a metropolitan ideal usually fall short. I'm sure this was the case in Cape Town, but I was not then in a position to judge. Now that I am, I know that there is just as much social climbing, pretension and bull in an English hunt, as there ever was at the Cape. But I was sufficiently overawed to put my fairly well-developed bullshit detector to one side, trying not to disgrace myself, and at the same time trying to enjoy the occasion for what it was: at one level, an early
morning picnic in ridiculous clothes, and at another, a mad

A Fisherman in the Saddle

fun scramble and gallop along the sandy paths and mountain tracks of Tokai.

There was no fox to hunt, but poor Charlie, that pitiful, flea-ridden jackal, kept captive at the livery yard where I stabled, served instead, or at least his bedding did. Attached to a rope which was held by a mounted huntsman, the hounds and the field went after Charlie's pyjamas and blankets, hell for leather, hunting horn sounding away to echo off the cliffs above us. The only real danger was to the curs, the name for non-hounds, out walking with their owners. Once I saw a sausage dog dispatched (if that's the word for what actually happened), before my eyes and those of its distressed and horrified elderly owner.

Occasionally, there were accidents. Galloping among pine trees can present problems – runaway horses have been known to ditch riders head-first into trunks, or crush arms against branches. There were, too, those large, fixed jumps at the bottom of the hill, the start or the finish of most hunts. I was quietly glad that my horse, which had the same set of self-preserving instincts as its master, did a quick side-step at the gallop, neatly avoiding these obstacles for others, braver than us.

There were some mad horses, too. These were usually picked out for you by their owners festooning their tails with bright red ribbon, denoting a confirmed kicker, but there was no way of knowing whether a horse was fond of human flesh till you rode alongside to find out the hard way for yourself, or pulled up at a check to find that your horse had said something inexcusable to your neighbour's horse, just as you were passing on the last long haul, and now the two wished to have it out, never mind the apologies and curses of their riders.

I once bought a horse in the hunting field, a big-striding 16hh chestnut, a former showjumper, who made quick work of the hunt obstacles and had sufficient thoroughbred pace to make him a nuisance to the Hunt Master, whom you overtook at your peril. With Xanthus, as I named him for his flaming red coat, social ignominy was always an issue, as he liked to take a hold, galloping hard to stay in touch with the hounds and the hunt servants. A horse that had started his working life on the racecourse, he did not disgrace himself at the Cape Hunt Races at Kenilworth, but he could be a bit of a liability once the pace picked up in the hunting field. I recall my shouting the obligatory, 'coming past' as once more we dashed by another rider, whose own horse would rise to the challenge, and suddenly you'd be racing on gravel paths, hedged in by firs with a serious drop down the mountain if you misjudged the corners. Life with Xanthus could be exciting. He was also known to give the odd kick and wore the necessary red badge of shame to warn others.

One day after a particularly good run, where I had managed to control his runaway tendencies and was well pleased with myself, with life, and with him, I found myself standing behind him to undo the ribbon still adorning the top of his tail. The thought struck me vaguely that this might not be the brightest thing to do, just seconds before Xanthus struck me not vaguely at all. My left knee reminds me of this even now, as I climb the stairs.

But at the end of the day, these outings with the Cape Hunt were great fun. They took you to new riding country, where you felt even more privileged than you already were. I recall a perfect crisp autumn day, hunting the edges of the great Vergelegen wine estate in the shadows of the Hottentots Holland Mountains; a day pounding up and down monstrous sand-dunes hell for leather in Philippi; and the sheer exhilaration of galloping an eager thoroughbred in fast company, both human and horsey, up the length of Noordhoek Beach. The fast coiling and uncoiling of massive muscles that sent sand flying into your face and mouth till you managed to pull past and gallop on and on and on.

Then the red and black jackets and the shining coats of the horses, the eager faces of friends, the high-held tails of the hounds, did not seem ridiculous or comic opera-ish. They looked grand, a romantic sight to warm the cockles of your heart, a glad and proud participant. I never did get into polo, though I was happy to watch horsemen better and bolder than myself do the business. It was hunting that got me up at

A Fisherman in the Saddle

the crack of dawn to lever myself into the necessary kit and put horses into plaits, boxing up and trucking to wherever the hunt was to be that day.

Back at my childhood home in Cape Town, there is a faded black and white press photograph from the Cape Times on my mother's dressing table. I am standing there at a hunt breakfast, a glass of champagne in one hand, my horse's reins in the other. Opposite me there is a gorgeous girl, who never did become mine, though we galloped thigh to thigh through many a mile of forest, jumped alongside each other and pulled up laughing and thrilled with life. She was, in the end, as unattainable as an English fox in Cape Town.

Mind you, the Cape Hunt seldom caught its quarry either, and in this, it and I were well matched. Better than I knew at the time.

Julian Roup

Spider trap

Horses can make you crazy, and the more lovely the horse, the crazier you can be. This is something I discovered the hard way. I learned that sometimes what seems an obvious and a shrewd decision at the time can turn out to be a near-disaster.

It was 1976 and the oil crisis in South Africa was in full swing. There was real fear that the petrol pumps would run dry and cars would be off the road indefinitely. I determined to stay mobile and bought a spider trap. I had an American Saddler, with the rather odd name of Cameo's Crystal, who I was sure would make a fine job of pulling a light cart, and I was right. He took to it beautifully. This was a great satisfaction, because I had made a big mistake when buying him. Like a Cameo, he was a dramatic colour, a deep chestnut with a flaxen mane and tail, what they call a sorrel in the US. His romantic looks blinded me to an extent and I did not look closely enough at his feet. When I had bought him and trucked him into Cape Town from up country I discovered to my horror that instead of a 16hh horse I had something much smaller, once the leather pads and built up shoes had been removed from his feet. The poor horse had virtually to learn how to walk in a new way. So I was delighted that while I no longer had a romantic riding horse, I did have a very handy and elegant carthorse.

This opened up a whole new experience for me. I had

never been in, or driven, a horse and cart before, and now I had this smart sorrel gelding and his very elegant attachment – a light, four-wheeled buggy painted black – in which to go exploring the quieter roads of Constantia in Cape Town, where I was currently stabling. I had to get to grips with all sorts of new problems that came with controlling a horse from behind. I learned to keep a sharp eye out for anything that might spook him, buses and large trucks particularly. Now, also, one had to be aware of the width of the spider, judging entrances and exits nicely. And there was the need to allow for sufficient room going around corners. It was all very different and novel. But the pleasure of being hauled along by a game horse on smooth rubber tyres, which were not much larger than bicycle wheels, was wonderful. The fact that the rig drew admiring glances everywhere, did not hurt either.

We tooled around Constantia, the lovely Surrey-like suburb of Cape Town, which shelters behind Table Mountain's more famous face. Here, amid mountain and sea, there are some of the country's oldest wine estates – Groot Constantia, Klein Constantia, Uitsig, Buitenverwachting and Alphen, where one day I would be married amid the venerable oaks in the open air. For a driver of a horse and buggy, this was a charming place to learn the ropes. I had Cameo's Crystal stabled up near the switchback road to Constantia Nek. The restaurant here was a favourite place for a night out, with its views across the twinkling lights of the southern suburbs and the Hottentots Holland mountain range in the distance. The stables belonged to a couple whose home was a showstopper. Built in a hollow square on the side of a hill, it overlooked the tops of pines, its central, glassed-in atrium given over to a range of gorgeous exotic birds. They were friendly people, and they made Cameo and me most welcome. The problem was the incredibly steep drive to their stable yard and its lack of space. There was no way to get the spider up there easily, nor was there enough space to park it.

But help was at hand. A young woman with masses of dark auburn hair, piercing blue eyes and skin the colour of clotted cream, also rode from this stable. She exuded charis-

A Fisherman in the Saddle

ma and had so much confidence in her looks that she could ignore them totally. It made for a tantalising and refreshing mix. To my amazement she offered to provide room for the spider trap at her cottage. I thanked her profusely. Shortly afterwards I drove up to her home. She walked me around the garden, checked the width of her drive, the double garage, and I realised that there was plenty of space for the trap. The cottage was very simple, green and white, amid lawns with a dark pinewood to one side. Table Mountain loomed before you across the treetops, which bent softly in the breeze.

We sat and talked for a while and seemed to find a great deal in common, horses, art, music and travel. My chemistry seemed to be rearranging itself. It was a little like getting drunk. I recall a moment in which it seemed the world had stopped. I felt the proteas on the mountainside nod and the business of the city stand still for a moment. It was all heady stuff. Perhaps sadly, it went no further than that. That afternoon I towed the buggy up to her cottage behind my car and parked it there under a tarpaulin. I was a regular visitor after that and always got a warm welcome. I would ride Cameo up to her cottage and harness him in the cart. Now and then I would pass her on horseback or in the trap and we'd smile and wave. After a few months I heard that she was getting married.

When she moved away the cottage became available. Its stunning setting had greatly impressed me; I loved the peace, the views and the sound of the pines whispering in the breeze. I decided to move in myself and it was one of the best decisions I ever made. Now I began to use the spider more actively. But there was one great problem that I had not foreseen when I hatched my brilliant plan to beat the fuel crisis – the danger of a slow-moving horse and cart on the switchback road up through Constantia to Constantia Nek and along Rhodes Drive to Bishopscourt.

We would be tooling along at a sedate trot of about 10mph when a car travelling at 50mph would come careering around the corner behind us, almost crashing into the back of the cart before managing to stop with a fearful screaming of brakes. We had a number of very close shaves. My nerves and those of Cameo were increasingly on edge. I decided that discretion, in this instance, was the better part of valour, and moved the horse and cart to Philippi where the roads were straighter and quieter.

Things went well for a while, but the lure of an admiring crowd got the better of me in the end. Not satisfied with the admiring glances of the odd motorist or pedestrian, I decided to drive Cameo to a livery yard a few miles away where I had friends. All went well until with great show we swept into the fairly confined yard and I had to do a very tight turn. The horse obeyed instantly, almost doubling back on himself, and in doing so, the right front wheel of the cart was forced under the body, buckling almost double. It was a very long and embarrassing moment. My showy arrival had rapidly moved from the sublime to the ridiculous. It is amazing how much passes through your mind at a time like that. I thought of a great many things, but the one I acted on was to get rid of the spider. I would take the worst of the petrol crisis in my stride; it seemed so much the safer bet.

Cameo's Crystal and that lovely trap are entwined in my mind. And when I think of them, I recall my disappointment after buying the horse, finding that instead of an upstanding Saddler I had something rather smaller. All he was really good for in the end was to pull a trap, and even that had proved to be a dubious pleasure. I was glad to get out of what had increasingly become a real spider trap.

A Fisherman in the Saddle

DOCTOR HORSE

My horse was gone, but I could still feel him moving beneath me, despite the fact that I was crammed into an uncomfortable wooden seat in a lecture theatre at Rhodes University in South Africa. It was 1977 and I was at Rhodes to study journalism as a launch pad – some would say ejector seat – for taking the gap to Europe. I was sick of the country's politics, sick of my part in it as a privileged onlooker, sick of army camps with possibly worse to follow. Apartheid was in its endgame, but I did not know that then. It seemed as if that evil regime would hang on and on and on. I did not intend having any part of that. Europe beckoned as much as South Africa repelled me.

Don't get me wrong. I love South Africa, how can one not? Visitors who spend a week there come away bewitched. I'd spent 30 years there and my family has been there for centuries – the first members of the Louw family, my mother's people, arrived in 1653, a year after the first white settlers landed, and my father's family reached the Cape in 1880. They had used their time wisely and we enjoyed an enviable lifestyle. But at our gates sat mute witnesses to millions who did not live as we did, and finally, for me, that proved intolerable. But as I shifted restlessly in that university seat, listening to an explanation of matrilineal descent in my Anthropology course, my mind turned as always to horses. How would I survive three years at university without a horse? Impossible.

I had sold my last horse, Xanthus, just before starting university, and I was feeling the loss keenly.

Years later, sitting in my Sussex garden, I tried to explain to yet another couple of South African would-be émigrés what it felt like to leave the mother country. I'd been in England ten years by then and the longing for home was a constant, gnawing pain. In some ways it reminded me of that first year at Rhodes without a horse. I told our South African friends that if they left, they could expect to feel the loss of their country in the same way that amputees feel the loss of their legs – they know they are gone but still get pains in the missing limbs. Our friends looked shocked. In the end they never did leave. Perhaps I did them a favour.

It did not take me long to find a new horse, even as I studied for my degree. Varsity holidays are long. I found a lovely, lightly built 16.2hh grey thoroughbred gelding, too slow for the racecourse. I went to see two horses at a racehorse trainer's yard and found a temperamental chestnut mare that nearly did for me in the sand paddock, to the delight of the stable hands, and a kindly, gentle grey. So it was an easy decision to pick Mulligan.

He was a joy. His long, raking stride made short work of the deep going on the Cape sandflats. Rather like an Arab, he floated above it all, and up the back of Table Mountain his light, athletic frame would bend to its work like a bow. Back in Grahamstown for my next term, I took satisfaction in knowing that Mulligan was in Cape Town, eating his head off and building up a head of steam for my next holiday. Mulligan did not get capped, but he should receive an academic accolade here, for he played no small part in my peace of mind while I studied. I was no longer horseless.

Horses have helped me survive life, time after time, and far worse ordeals than the pleasant privilege of a three-year university degree. School is a case in point. Academically, I was a disaster. My parents once considered taking my pony, Don Juan, away as an inducement to work. A teacher whose name is engraved on my heart came to the rescue. 'Stroppy' Straus we called him. He was a short, stocky German immigrant, with a shock of flyaway white-blond hair, who took us for gym and also taught Afrikaans. In fact, he was my class teacher and so had first-hand knowledge of my failings as a scholar and a sportsman. Yet he spoke up for me when the solids hit the fan. *'Dankie Meneer, ek waardeur dit nog!'* ('Thank you Sir, I still appreciate it!')

My mother came to see him and raised the issue of the pony sanction. Stroppy was unequivocal. 'Definitely not,' he said. 'His pony is his one great outlet and it is better than having him hang about on street corners!' While I was never one for hanging around street corners, I felt flattered by the tearaway image, which was a million miles from the intense, inverted reality.

Don Juan carried me through the traumas of my 13th or bar mitzvah year. A half-Afrikaans, Christian Jew is a strange animal, and though I am grateful for the fact that I grew up on intimate terms with two of the world's great religions, and two cultures, it cost me dear. Failing my school class that year was not an easy thing for a 13-year-old boy to face, and, but for Don Juan, who knows what might have been? Horses bring healing – they possess a quality of redemption for those who love them. It is in the quiet, the stillness of unregarded actions, such as riding, fishing, cooking or dreaming, that the most precious things occur. And for me, riding is pre-eminent. It is not in the stuff of action or in the glare of publicly observed rituals that the serious occurs. I find life's pearls form slowly from a grain of thought, or simple, thoughtless actions which allow the subconscious or unconscious to rise and form opalescent beauty in the dark sea of the mind. We spend so much time striving, not surprisingly – there are mouths to feed, things to buy, needs to satisfy. Yet the real gold, not the fool's gold, comes not from these things; not in my experience.

A horse and rider is not just a horse and rider, but someone exploring the world in an old, old way, which opens you to the original human hardwiring and connects you to the sublime. What I am trying to say is that what may appear to be an indulgence – time off from the real stuff of life – is in fact the real stuff. It is like a shower in positive ions, a stoking up of the energy fields, the creative forces. One passes small wild animals, birds, the serried ranks of silent trees, fields of green and blonde grasses, the streams, hills and far horizons – all exist, all matter in the great scheme of things. They say to me: 'Look! We live too, without homes, cars, supermarkets, radio, TV, newspapers, without money or fame. We are here too, and we matter.' In fact, they are part of something greater than our human world, they are part of nature, and remind us of our own part there.

This perspective, the long view to the greater picture, brings peace. And it is the horse that has carried you into that state; unwittingly he has served the function of healer – truly, Doctor Horse.

A Fisherman in the Saddle

THE FIRST ENGLISH CHRISTMAS

England was still new to us that first Christmas, and the country itself was like an unwrapped present. The weather, boring wrapping paper, hid a gift of great beauty and immense value, but it took some unwrapping. We had taken the mad gamble of buying horses shortly after we found work as reporters on a local weekly newspaper in Sussex. It was mad because their cost ate significantly into our limited travel allowance from South Africa, and because we were on a 'Job Specific Work Permit' from the Home Office. It was 1980, we had arrived from South Africa on honeymoon and been granted a six-month stay and the right to work. We had found work on the *Mid Sussex Times*, whose editor, Glynn Britton, was prepared to take me on after experiencing Jan's writing talent for a few weeks. He and the National Union of Journalists lobbied on our behalf, and we were given the right to stay, subject to annual review. That meant coming up to scratch in the same job for five years, at which point we would achieve permanent residence. Professionally it was suicide, but that was the cost of our entry ticket to Britain. We paid gladly and have never regretted it.

It was both a low-key and a stressful introduction to a new country, never being sure if one would be sent back to South Africa. The amazing thing was that we had been given the chance at all, and for five years we shared a desk in the newsroom. We covered flower shows and golden wedding anniversaries, parish council meetings and the South of England Agricultural Show. This was our annual highlight, when the whole newsroom decamped to the press office at the Ardingly Showground. There we would interview farmers about their prize-winning sheep, cattle and pigs, and describe the activity of the main ring. I wrote about the charming country ambiance – which, thanks to some uneducated sub-editing appeared under my byline that Friday, as 'A charming country ambulance'.

Reporting a revolution it was not. Both Jan and I had worked as student reporters on *The Cape Times* and *Cape Argus* in Cape Town during university holidays and had got used to the buzz of a city newspaper, one at the forefront of the liberal debate on the future of our country. We had opted to leave all that behind us, feeling irrelevant and pessimistic about South Africa's future under the Nationalist Government which presided over the catastrophe of apartheid.

Now we had to pay the price, and that included writing flower show reports in which getting the commas in the right place was as important as the list of first, second and third. There was the weather too, unremittingly foul and dark, a massive shock after the light and colour of southern Africa. And we were irredeemably foreign. My greatest surprise on getting to England was realising that I was a South African. That may seem unnecessarily crass, but having grown up in an English liberal milieu, I had somehow distanced myself from my South African roots. It would not be overstating the case to say that they kept us sane, when for tuppence, at times, I would have been on the next plane home. It was Jan who kept faith with our new country and gave me the courage to continue. Today I have an English passport thanks to my wife's indomitable spirit.

We had led privileged lives in South Africa, but here we earned less than dustmen and learned to live frugally and eat simply; we found a dozen interesting things to do with minced meat. Everything is relative of course and we were ahead of the game in so many ways. When you have little to spend, it's hard to go horse hunting, and unwise. Oh God, the hell of horse hunting – the great expectations, the excitement, the disappointment, the people and their unsuitable horses! The grandson of a horse dealer, I was wise to the wiles of horse selling, and no innocent myself. George and Kesh emerged from our searches. The one horse good, the other a nightmare. Even the most cautious gambler must eventually throw the dice, and what gambler is truly cautious? We threw the dice – one came good, the other not. The interesting thing about horses is, that like people, you learn more from the bad ones.

George was a bad one. Kesh, or Marrakesh Express, emerged from an advertisement in the horseman's bible, the *Horse & Hound*. We had seen a number of unprepossessing animals and had no great hopes for this latest trip. The seller was patently a horse dealer, not a private individual selling her own horse, not a good sign. She told us which stable to look for, and when we found it could not believe our eyes. Kesh was that lovely rare colour, a true liver chestnut. He had a wide blaze and a lovely head. Short coupled and well made, he stood around 16.2hh. A bit un-giving in the mouth, he nevertheless had a good heart. We did not believe that we could afford him and wondered what the catch was. But he vetted sound and came home with us. Jan had found the first horse she had ever owned. It was the start of a great love affair.

Kesh was so easy he'd carry both of us quite happily around the apple orchards on the farm he was stabled at, and now and then we would double up for a meander in the summer evenings after work. We had found stabling at a farm near our rented cottage, 15 miles north of Brighton and close to that horseman's Mecca, Hickstead. The owner was a large balding man in his sixties, with a robust sense of life about him, confirmed by the stash of *Playboy* magazines we found discretely stacked in the corner of the barn. His home was a sixteenth- century farmhouse near Bolney in West Sussex, mellow, tile-hung, an oak-framed structure with leaded light windows and bags of character. The place stood amid some 30 acres, which he shot over, the land left largely to fend for itself. In effect, he was a hobby farmer, who had kept a few animals and ponies for his now grown-up daughters. The stables we used had not held horses or ponies for the best part of ten years.

After a while I went in search of a horse for myself. I found George, a dark chocolate bay with a mealy mouth. He had a lighter, more thoroughbred frame than Kesh, and moved beautifully. Someone had done a great deal of groundwork with him. He was thin and his coat dull. We were told he had wintered out and was being brought in for sale as his owner had

lost interest. It did not take me long to discover why. George was a napper, that is, a horse that will either refuse to go forward or fly leap unexpectedly away from the direction in which you wish to go. He was incredibly agile in his naughtiness. You would be cantering along collectedly with his delightfully smooth gait and suddenly you would be cantering in the exact opposite direction. A circus horse had nothing on him. He definitely had a sense of humour. I was at first greatly depressed by this purchase, but persevered and slowly George began to settle to his work. I think he had been over-jumped and had become soured. When he discovered that his new job was simply hacking, he began to relax. His rider, however, could not do the same, for every now and then the old box of tricks would be opened and we would provide onlookers with a spectacle.

We were invited to spend Christmas with the farm owner and his family. We accepted his kind offer with gratitude; we would not, after all, be spending our first Christmas in England on our own. We kept a sharp eye on the Christmas turkey hanging in the apple orchard, high enough to be out of the reach of foxes. The weather was sufficiently cold to keep it from going off, though after ten days we did begin to wonder.

Christmas in that lovely old farmhouse was magical. The company was extremely pleasant and the well-hung tur-

A Fisherman in the Saddle

key, delicious. Toward the end of the meal the family disappeared en masse into the kitchen to bring in the dessert. Jan and I chatted on our own for some minutes. We were not a little surprised to find that our host had tape-recorded our conversation while everyone else was out of the room. Thank heavens neither of us had said anything critical of our hosts. We found this strange behaviour.

After lunch, we sat round the TV to hear the Queen's speech. Later, some new guests arrived for tea and one asked me how I would feel if the Queen turned up unexpectedly. Despite the fact that I had Republican views, I said I would welcome her, and attempt to make her comfortable.

The guest had a hissy fit. 'You make the Queen comfortable? Do you realise that you do not address the Queen until she addresses you?'

I said that was the first I had heard of it. The guest left my side with a 'Humph!' All in all, it was a Christmas rather like the curate's egg – good in parts.

Inevitably, our thoughts were with our families in Cape Town, where the sun baked down and Christmas was so different, occurring in the very heart of the summer. That evening we tucked our horses up in deep straw, gave them an extra ration of oats and bulging hay nets. It was a freezing cold, clear night and we were now in England. We had horses and each other. It was enough.

A Fisherman in the Saddle

MAX WITH THE NAUGHTY EYE

How do you find a horse of good character and impeccable manners? That is the question facing most people who go in search of a riding horse. And there is no easy answer. Those who use horses for competition of one kind or another are bothered less by this issue. That is why some of the most vicious, mentally unstable, and downright bad horses are found racing and show jumping. When people breed for speed, jumping or any other narrowly focused set of requirements, all other useful aspects of an animal's breeding seems to go by the board. And when big money is involved, you're off to hell in a hand basket. To be fair to the horses, not all start out this way, the character weaknesses are not always bred in, but are produced by vicious, mentally unstable and downright bad owners!

At the end of the day, horse hunting is a lottery. It's no game for the faint of heart or those of unflinching faith in humankind. Here it's a case of every man for himself, and the devil take the hindmost. Horses are regularly dosed with drugs to keep them calm or medicated to disguise any trace of lameness. The things that can be wrong with a horse are legion. They can have difficulty seeing, have painful aching backs, semi-crippled feet, breathing difficulties, holes in the heart or arrhythmic heartbeats. They can be subject to colic, a potentially fatal condition. They can be windsuckers or crib-biters, two vices brought on by stable boredom, vices which make them just about worthless to someone seeking a sound horse. There are the stable walkers, who will walk round and round and bloody round, like a blindfolded donkey raising water in Egypt. Then there are a whole bunch of biters and kickers and rearers and buckers – horses you would not want for yourself or have any child of yours go near. There are those who flatly refuse to even leave the stable yard, known as nappers. And there are those who have phobias about tractors, buses, motorcycles or traffic generally.

So when you go in search of that industry yardstick – the bombproof family horse – with three good paces, who will hack out alone or in company, will happily do a course of jumps, go hunting or showing or show jumping or simply hack out; a horse that you can leave for three weeks in the field and then saddle up, knowing you can safely go for a ride, you do understand that you are asking a lot.

And then, of course, you are also dealing with people. Not only are horses not perfect, but people, you may have noticed, come with their own problems and expectations. Few go in search of an ugly horse, a nondescript horse, or a funny-looking horse. Horses are about dreams and beauty. They are about escape from the mundane. They carry our dreams on their backs like a second rider doubling up. So God help you if you are going in search of a horse and would like something half-nice looking, sound in wind and limb, with no bad stable manners, happy to do as it's told, and comfortable with it. You're asking a lot, let's face it.

There are many ways to go on your quest. They include horse dealers (good, bad and indifferent); private sales from people more or less trustworthy (usually less) and there is the breeding option, making your own as it were, and this is no quick way to find a good horse, believe me. There are horses advertised in the local press, the *Friday Ad*, the *Horse & Hound*, and there are horses that come with recommendations from a friend – as good a way as any to lose a friend and frighten yourself silly.

A Fisherman in the Saddle

Most people try all these avenues all at once. They put out the word on the grapevine that they are in search of a horse, they scour the local press and they are on hand at the local newsagents at 6am on Thursday mornings when the *Horse & Hound* is delivered. They even go and see horse dealers, suspicious, cautious and nervy as a horse that has been beaten about the head once too often. The excitement and the heartache then begin.

Price, it must be said, is no guarantee of anything. This is not a world in which a brand new Bentley is available to those who can afford the best. The best has to be made by you spending long hours in the saddle, or you have to become accommodated to the best that someone else has made. There are million-pound horses out there designed to turn your life into a living hell, and there are cut-price versions that will, as readily, do the same.

So, now it's time to be brave and put your small bit of hard-won experience to the test. You begin by eliminating all dealers at the outset. Any horse being sold by a dealer, you may fairly assume, is one that its owner could not sell or would not sell in good conscience. This is not always true and exceptions to this rule do exist – one man's meat is after all another man's poison. But for the sake of time and effort, you decide dealers are out.

So you look in *Horse & Hound*, reading with as much interest as if it were the Holy Grail (and of course, in a way, it is) and see the following advertisement:

> HANDSOME IRISH GELDING: 16.2hh chestnut, 6yrs, good all-rounder (by King of Diamonds) has seen hounds, good to hack, shoe, clip and box. Bombproof. No vices. £2 500. Open to vet. First to see will buy. Same home three years. Horsham, West Sussex.

There is a telephone number attached and perhaps a mobile number as well. Horse people do not spend much time near a landline. Being a private ad, there may be a request that you ring after work or there may even be a work telephone number. Because the horse is based just 15 miles from you, your interest is greater than if it was in Yorkshire or Scotland. This closeness also means that if you really like the horse, your own vet can be brought in to do the vetting. You will then have all his or her great experience to rely on. Your vet is not infallible, but it's better than having to rely on a strange vet. Possibly, if you are stupid – and I've been stupid in my time – you will agree to a vet recommended by the seller, if the horse is miles from home. You make the call. You are asked what you are looking for. You tell them you seek a hack, a friend, a paragon, a good-looking paragon if possible, and kind into the bargain. That is lucky they say, for that by some strange and happy fate is exactly what they have for sale. A character reference then follows that would do a High Court judge proud.

You move into prosecution mode. Why are they selling the horse? Where did it come from? Has it ever been ill? Does it truly have no vices? Just how laid back is it really? Can anyone ride it? How green is it? How well schooled? These and a hundred other questions are put. Most are answered smoothly and with great good humour. Sometimes though the person at the other end is moronic, monosyllabic and just plain useless. Don't be put off – the horse may be great.

You get the address, agree on a time, and drive to see the horse. The girl, it's always a girl, or her mother, shows you into the house. You are sat down with a cup of tea and a sheaf of photos of the said horse winning everything short of the Derby. He looks nice. The lady is nice. Even the tea's not bad. You begin to be interested. You are now at the stage that doctors call 'prepped for the operation'.

You are almost reluctantly walked outside, as though the seller regrets that the moment of truth is now upon them. They know, for they have been this way themselves, many times, that now their flesh and blood horse, with all his well disguised imperfections, will have to meet up with the horse of your dreams, and chances are the two will not match.

You walk out to a small but immaculate stable yard, so much nicer than your own. Everything is ship-shape and

A Fisherman in the Saddle

speaks of competent horse management. Taking a deep breath, you look into the half-dark stable and there, standing belly deep in fragrant gold straw, is a very nice middleweight dark chestnut, with a white blaze down his face and a very naughty white eye. He gleams with care and attention. He's beautifully groomed and his stable is perfection. You look at him and he looks at you. Keeping all emotion out of your voice you say: 'Hmm, nice horse.'

The seller smiles fondly. 'He is nice, isn't he?'

You ask once more: 'Tell me again why you are selling him?' and she replies with tones of deep regret and sadness in her voice that 'Jocasta starts university in September you see, and well, we are over-stocked as it is.'

Despite yourself, you want to believe her.

You walk into the box and the horse stands calmly, showing no inclination to charge you, bite you or kick you. The memory of one recent horse is much in your mind. The seller had barely managed to open the stable door a fraction when the horse whirled round and with both legs gave the door a double whammy! (At moments like that the level of mutual embarrassment is such that no one remembers afterwards quite how you extricated yourself, or how the seller managed to find the will to keep living. But they do).

This though, seems a very nice horse. He 'fills the eye', as horse people say. He has a great depth of girth – good heart and lung room – a nice length of rein – a good length of neck – his head is noble and he is close-coupled – not long in the back with the weakness that brings. This is not a gift horse, so you carefully pry open his mouth. His tushes are out but not overly so, he is indeed six-ish. (The tushes are incisor-shaped teeth at the side of the mouth, just behind the front teeth. When the tushes are fully developed, a horse is considered mature i.e. seven or over) He still does not bite. The white eye regards you with something like amusement. You ignore that ill omen and look elsewhere. He has four good legs, no lumps or bumps that you can feel. He stands square, not over or back of the knee. From the back he looks right too. You take the plunge.

'Yes, not bad. Would you put a saddle on for me?'

Now you watch with particular care. Will they want you away while this is done? Or are they happy to do it as you stand there? Or do they seem to wish you'd rather do it for them? In this instance, they are happy to do it and WhiteEye stands steady as a rock. He's a good-un – or they've got the drug dose just right. As the saddling takes place, you look at the white eye closely, and think of all the horses you've known with a white eye – almost invariably a sign of naughtiness or shiftiness. This white-eyed chap seems calm, as do his owner and her mother.

You mount the horse and ride out to a sand paddock. The horse feels cool – he does not feel as if he has been lunged (exercised) in the ring just before your arrival. He enters the ménage willingly and walks on a treat. He has a lovely active walk and trot even in the paddock, and his transitions from one pace to the next are smooth as silk. A lot of work has gone into this horse. He carries himself in a nice outline, keeping his head down and working well from behind. To achieve this you need hardly use the aids, he seems to come into your hands so easily, and his canter is like a rocking horse. It's time for the next stop. You ask if you may put him over a small jump; he addresses it directly, without hotting up; and lifts off like an old hand with perfect striding and no following buck.

'I'd like to take him out of the yard if I may?' you hear yourself saying. His 18-year-old owner saddles up her mother's horse and off you go. There is no attempt at napping (refusing) as you leave the yard. At this point you think back to your purchase of Mulligan in Cape Town all those years ago, when you visited the racing stable at Milnerton and all the grooms came running to see the fun when you rode his stable mate in the sand paddock. One groom with less of a sense of humour than his mates, running in after the horse had had her fun, and before you were killed. And how easy it was to decide on the sensible grey than on the scatty chestnut mare. But here all seems at peace, young White-Eye is keeping a trick up his girth if he has one.

A Fisherman in the Saddle

You find yourself on a sandy heath and the girl asks if you'd like to give the horse a run. You collect him and he most willingly picks up into a fast canter and in strides you are galloping, your guide keeping discreetly behind you. The horse for all his substance covers the ground with ease, eating up the distance to a line of trees fast approaching. And then it comes; he gives an almighty buck, just once, going full tilt. You smile; it's just joie de vivre. You really like this horse. He pulls up readily and you know the die is cast, the rest just business.

And what about the white eye? Well, OK, he does have a sense of humour, but then so do you. Doubtless the two of you will rub along well enough. Driving home, you think of names. He is presently called Jonjo, after the fabled Irish jump jockey Jonjo O'Neill. It's not much of a name for a horse like this, you think. Maximillian sounds more like it, Max for short, Max with the naughty eye. It's bad luck to change a horse's name, but that's tough.

A week later, the vet confirms your feeling. 'Nice stamp of horse,' he says, and you are pleased. You have found a horse, despite the odds. And now you will avoid the shame of being described, though never named, as a 'timewaster' in the next week's edition of *Horse & Hound*. This is a seller's ploy when a rejected horse is once more for sale and the excuse is 'timewasters', that most lame (though occasionally true) statement which tries and always fails to explain a non-sale.

In the years ahead you will discover that Max does indeed have a sense of humour, but that, happily, you laugh at the same things.

Julian Roup

A Fisherman in the Saddle

THE REARER

Fear does funny things to you. Jan and I spent the summer of 1987 being excessively polite to each other. 'Why don't you go for a ride?' I'd say, and she'd counter: 'I'm fine. Why don't you go for a ride?' We'd be sitting out on the lawn in the Sussex sunshine, not wishing to go riding, and the reason? Fear – fear of Obi.

We were sharing this horse called Obi, as in Obi Wan Kanobe of *Star Wars* fame, and the Force was definitely with him, rather than with us. We were both decidedly nervous of Obi, who should have been named Obiah, the Jamaican voodoo god. He was a scary horse.

We'd changed our lives once again, selling a London flat, which we'd used during the week so that Jan could get home to bed fast from her Financial Times shifts, which ended at 2am. Then at the weekends, we'd drive back to the cottage in Sussex. The sale of the flat funded an extension to the cottage, and now back in Sussex, we were once more in the market for a horse to share. We went horse hunting. What is it that happens to your brain when you go in search of horseflesh? A kind of frenzy or madness descends. Well, it does on us. Doubtless there are cool, calm, calculating horse buyers, but we are not of that calibre. Your biorhythms start to cha cha when normally they'd be doing nothing more violent than a waltz, let's say.

We started buying *Horse & Hound* again. We did look

at the 'horses-for-loan' ads, but a loaned horse, however nice, is not your horse, whichever way you look at it. We set out with high hopes and returned home despondent. We found lovely horses which once vetted, turned out to have heart murmurs or were touched in the wind; we rode horses that went berserk when you got onto them, the seller saying, 'Funny, he's never done that before!' Oh yeah? And there were those that simply would not be got out of a trot and the seller would ask, 'Been riding long?'

There were sweet horses, too plain to suit. There is a special place in hell for people who insist on handsome horses. This fault is inherited from my mother, who never rode a horse in her life, but, commenting on girls in general, was known to say in Afrikaans: 'You want something for the eye as well!' A love of beauty is a great failing. But my brother and I were as one with her on that, and this approach has also affected my view of horses. Ugly, badly put together, long-backed, short-necked, horrible pasterns, bad feet, small eyes, goose rumps, other people could maybe put up with this, not me. Beauty is all. And as we know, beauty comes at a price.

Whatever happened to 'handsome is as handsome does', an excellent approach to buying horses? It does not even get to first base with me. And the buyer of beautiful horses finds out the hard way that, like some beautiful women, beautiful horses can be a wilful lot.

We found Obi in a yard that was selling him on for someone else, the classic case for walking away, but he was a well-made bay warmblood, a handsome Hanoverian. He looked regal in his box, a very powerfully made middleweight with a strong head. I decided to give him a try.

As we rode out of the yard, he gave a massive shy. No big deal I thought, but it should have rung warning bells. A few hundred yards further down the road, he fly-leapt sideways as a car passed us. I ignored it. He was pumped up, had a tremendously powerful stride, was balanced and collected, enabling him to move rapidly, anywhere he chose. In horse language it is called 'impulsion'. Obi had wonderful impulsion, and on an impulse, I bought him.

The second mistake I made in his purchase was not to be there for the vetting. It is just asking for trouble. But sometimes work commitments preclude private pleasure. The vet, an old friend, who knew his horses and moreover, knew me, said in his understated English way that the horse was physically sound but that there had been some 'airs above the ground' at the vetting. It is a little understood phenomenon, but no less true for that – horse buying induces blindness and deafness. Be warned. I ignored this telling remark. It was to haunt me for the next five years.

A few days after the vetting, Obi arrived all gussied up and looking the business. Before taking final delivery of him, I had agreed with the sellers that I would give him a ride on my own ground, and this I proceeded to do. Any horse will be nervous in new country and Obi was no exception. Not that he was nervous, he just seemed super-alert and he moved as though on turbo-charged springs. I took him down to a ten-acre field behind the cottage and let him have a run up it. Some middleweight horses can make heavy weather of hills, not this chap. He flattened that hill as though he was at Epsom. No problem. I bid the sellers goodbye and boxed this new find.

Irony of ironies, Jan, then a financial journalist for *The Guardian*, wrote a feature article about the perils of horse hunting, ending with the purchase of this perfect horse. The story read well and the pictures did both Jan and the horse proud. But you know what they say about pride...

When I went to saddle Obi for the first time, I noticed that he had a small infection on his back, just where the saddle would sit. Riding was out. I called the vet and he diagnosed it as nothing serious, gave us some cream and said no riding for a week or three. Lack of exercise is not good for a horse; it is the cause of most problems with horses, overfeeding and under-exercising. After a three-week break, Obi's back was fine and he felt rocket-propelled, despite lunge work in the paddock and a spell out at grass.

It did not begin well. The first person to ride him was

Jan. She had a weekday off, so she saddled him up for a ride in the woods. He refused to leave the yard, rearing up high, again and again. She unsaddled him and put him away.

'How's the new horse going?' asked Richard Wilkinson, our friend and horse-whisperer who stabled with us, seeing her heading for the tack room with the saddle. He looked closer and realised she was in tears. 'Give me the saddle,' he said, taking it off her. 'I'm never getting on him again!' Jan said.

Richard won out. He saddled Obi, gave Jan a leg-up, and walked behind her along the bridlepath through the woods. Obi went up immediately and did so again every few yards. Watching him closely, Richard told Jan to relax. The horse was not spooked or nervous, he said. He knew exactly what he was about and was in no danger of falling over backwards as a frightened horse might. He was perfectly balanced; just deliberately freaking her out.

Thanks to Richard, Jan kept her nerve and went on riding, and I rode Obi too, although through that long first summer with him, we were very polite, always offering each other first refusal.

For my first ride, I took him quietly round the pine plantation and up into the forest, giving him as little reason as possible to say 'Whoopee, let's go!' which was the wish that every fibre of his being was communicating to me. As we stood by the only road one has to cross on the way home, there was a fair bit of traffic and the waiting proved to be too much for him. He reared. Now, when a horse rears, it comes as a shock. It is as though a car you were driving decided to leap forward at a red traffic light, in other words, do things which it is not meant to do, with possibly fatal consequences.

And there's rearing and there's rearing. Quite a few horses I have known would get 'light in front' from time to time; it's no big deal and indicates spirit more than anything else. Some horses will do a half-rear if excited. Obi was not one to settle for half measures – he reared to his full height and stood there pawing the air. In this situation one's greatest fear is that the horse will lose its balance and fall backwards, crushing the rider. You need to be careful not to precipitate this with a yank in the horse's mouth, which is quite often what happens as you start to slip out the saddle backward and grasp hard on the reins to stop yourself falling. On this occasion, I managed to ride it out, and we eventually crossed the road without further incident.

At the bottom of the hill is a stream, which divides in two, and there are two bridges. Here we had more rearing of the same circus-like quality, right up but perfectly balanced. Obi knew just what he was about, and was an old, practised hand at this stunt. I relaxed slightly, feeling that he was too damn clever to allow himself to fall backwards. But one could not be sure. And one has to adjust to having your heart in your mouth. It is not a happy thing, riding a rearer.

The strange thing was that the probable reason for his rearing, the massive amount of over-schooling that had soured him, had also turned him into a magnificent ride when he was not up on two legs. He was so collected and sure-footed that on the trappy, rutted forest you could quite confidently canter him downhill and he would take his own line with never a foot out of place, cat-like. It felt like driving a formula one car that had a mind of its own.

There are as many so-called cures for rearing, as there are horses that rear. Two old favourites are to crack an egg on the horse's head as he comes up, or alternatively do the same with a plastic bag of warm water. The idea is that the horse will think he has bashed his head on something and that the liquid pouring down his head is his own blood. The thinking is that this should inhibit any future desire to rear. The problem with this approach is that it could have exactly the opposite effect, with the rearing horse becoming frenzied and truly dangerous. We stuck to prayer, shouting and sitting tight.

It all came to a head one day as I was riding home. We were almost at the stable when I decided to enter a nearby field for a last walk to cool the horse down. As we turned to enter the field gate, Obi went right up once more. Something snapped inside me and I lost my temper. I was carrying a heavy, old ivory-handled hunting crop at the time and I was so angry that I forgot to be scared. I whacked him a good one. To my amazement, Obi came down on all fours promptly and set off at a gallop into the field, which had been deep ploughed that week. Feeling that this was do or die, I set to with a will and we tore round that field until Obi was well and truly blown and my lovely old crop was snapped in two. It was a lesson he never forgot.

He was not too bad after that, he would not again do his full circus rear, though he still got light up front if kept waiting to cross the road on the way home. But for the 'rear-McCoy', the true sky-climb was history. Control had been established. And as is the way so often, he became a happier horse, as we became happier riders.

Writing this, I can look up and see a picture of myself on Obi hanging on my office wall. Unusually, it is a black and white picture taken in high summer. We stand amid the huge roundels of straw, which look like fat hairy grindstones on end. That means it is August. Obi has his eye on the photographer. I am watching Obi. In front of us the home valley falls away and then rises to woods and coppices, and the network of fields at the valley head. It is a peaceful picture that belies the struggle and toil it took to achieve that moment of calm.

Above it hangs the picture that accompanied Jan's *Guardian* article. She is standing by his stable door facing the camera with Obi's head on her shoulder. Both look so happy and pleased with life. The caption says: Safe at last: Janice Warman with her new horse'. What no one reading the article could have known at the time, including us, was that the picture heralded a point on the way, not the end of the search. You can't believe everything you read in the papers.

MALARKEY

Never was a horse so misnamed. Malarkey would indicate a somewhat unreliable character, always up to mischief. Poor Malarkey, nothing could be further from the truth. Once I got to know him well, I called him our 'Sunday-go-to-Meeting' horse, for his gentle, effortless, rolling canter. You pointed Malarkey in the direction you wanted to go, told him the pace and that was it, he'd do the rest like an automatic car. One did not have to work at it, keep him collected, or be watching out for shies. This was a horse that ran on rails!

Malarkey was a rangy 16.2hh chestnut gelding we bought for Jan after our return from London. Obi's rearing had brought her close to losing her nerve and understandably, she wanted a horse of her own again. So once more we set off horse hunting, and like everything about Malarkey, this proved easy. He was right on our doorstep, a few miles up the road into Kent, according to the advert in *Horse & Hound*.

We were not much taken with his owner, one of those forthright, formidable English women of indeterminate age, who said she had bought 'Jack' for her husband to hunt, but that he had lost interest. She seemed so much the dealer, who made much of the fact that she had sold a horse to Captain Mark Phillips, the former husband of Princess Anne, and a leading cross-country rider and course-builder. It did not seem a great recommendation to us.

This time we were looking for something 100 per cent straight – the kind of honesty you seek in a child's pony. Jan's confidence needed some serious repair work, and both of us were determined to make this the criterion for our search. We liked Jack instantly. He was a tall upstanding character, whom we first saw tied up in a narrow stall. I'd say his breeding was seven-eighths thoroughbred, but the smidgen of Irish ancestry gave him additional substance, though he was far from fleshy. He had a long, straight, elegant head with a white blaze and the kindest eye. He had a quietness about him – a peaceable air that boded well.

With a minimum of fuss, his present owner slapped a saddle on him and cantered him around a field on her farm, popping him effortlessly over a deep drainage ditch, which was about eight feet across. We were suitably impressed. Both of us rode him and he came to hand easily and seemed a very uncomplicated ride.

Sometimes you strike it lucky like that. He was absolutely genuine and a complete gent. The vet had nothing to say against him either. The only thing we did not like was his uninspired name. We toyed with calling him Sailor Jack, but for reasons that escape me now, settled on Malarkey. It was a fun name and its owner gave Jan a lot of fun and many years of pleasure. Malarkey was the ultimate confidence-giver, a genuine good 'un.

Funny how little I find to say about him. Goodness is like that. Evil is always more interesting. On the day he arrived he gave me two small stabs of concern. He arrived all gussied up in a smart blue rug, with bandaged tail and feet, looking like a big business-like steeple-chaser. And for a moment or two, I wondered if we'd got it right.

On his first ride out on the great open spaces of Ashdown Forest, Jan on Malarkey and me on Obi, we came across one of the very rare cross-country rides on the forest. Horses were cantering all over the place. A horse meeting new country for the first time is always a bit spooky, especially with a strange rider on his back, and Malarkey did some interesting ducking and diving as horses galloped out of woods and burst round corners. But he didn't take off, as many might have. And it was the first and last time he put a foot wrong.

The thing about Malarkey that stays with me was how relaxing he was to ride. He was so responsive to the rein and the leg, that the gentlest contact would have him collected. He'd canter out of a walk or a dead stop for that matter, rather like a polo pony. And he had a lovely, gentle, ground-eating trot. He was that rare thing, 'Anyone's ride' – a true family horse. In an age when transport was by horse only, he would have been a great asset to any family. Doubtless he would have worked in harness as well, though we never had reason to try him in a cart.

While I have mixed feelings about thoroughbreds, there is no getting away from the fact that they are superb athletes, and Malarkey's thoroughbred ancestry helped to make him what he was, a great riding horse. He carried himself and his rider effortlessly over the trappy rutted forest trails. He neither pulled nor had to be harried along, but moved well within himself, collected but moving freely forward. A nice horse, a damn nice horse, and one that I think I only truly appreciated in retrospect.

We sold Malarkey and Obi when we decided to try our luck in America in 1992, and the woman who bought him got a gem. I hope she appreciated him. If ever a horse could be said to be a Christian, Jack Malarkey was that horse.

Julian Roup

HORSELESS IN IDAHO

There comes a time in every horseman's life when land hunger sets in. The desire for lebensraum came upon me in 1991, as the British economy was in freefall and I was sick to death of commuting four hours a day to London from Sussex – two hours each way if everything went according to plan, and British Rail, London Underground or the IRA did not have different ideas.

Dr Johnson wrote that when you are tired of London, you are tired of life. If that is correct, I was ready for death. London had never excited me. I hated the crowds, the ugly back-to-back buildings, and the cheek-by-jowl living. I loathed the pollution and felt each day that I was being swallowed up by a monster as I emerged from my Tunbridge Wells train at Charing Cross or the Gatwick Express at Victoria. Walking in step with all those millions of commuters through the station concourses and down into the guts of London, I felt at times close to despair.

I enjoyed my work, but its setting and the agonies of commuting were too much. I remember standing one snowy December day on the platform at Tunbridge and thinking that it was all madness. Getting on the overcrowded train, I found once more that there were no spare seats and despite my vastly expensive season ticket, I had to stand in the guard's van with dozens of other disgruntled passengers.

When the tube doors slid open and the London Underground mantra of 'Mind the Gap!' was broadcast – warning of the distance between platform and tube door – I did mind and felt that the gap between my ambitions and my reality was stretched to breaking point. I decided to take the gap and escape. The problem was, knowing how.

Who was it said, cometh the hour cometh the man? My brother appeared like the good fairy, on cue. Herman brought news of cheap land and the good life in Idaho. He had left South Africa for the United States at roughly the same time as Jan and I had left for England. For years, Herman and Teri had lived and worked in Los Angeles. We had visited them there and enjoyed a wonderful holiday driving up Big Sur into the giant redwood country. But it would be a cold day in hell before I exchanged the horrors of London for those of LA.

Now he told me he'd found a large slice of Heaven called the Idaho Panhandle. This was the thin northern stretch of Idaho that finally touches the Canadian border, about 300 miles inland from Seattle. He had moved to a place called Cœur d'Alène in the foothills of the Rockies, and he said it was as beautiful in its own way as Cape Town. The city of our birth was the cross we carried; it was so perfect in so many ways that it was hard to replicate. Herman felt I should take a good look at Idaho. And he said, singing a siren song – land and homes were dirt cheap in comparison to South-East England. Small 10- and 20-acre plots with a four-bedroomed home were to be had for less than $100,000. We booked a holiday immediately. We flew into Seattle and stayed a weekend with Tony Giffard, a former Professor of ours who had headed the Journalism Department at Rhodes University in South Africa, our alma mater. He was now teaching at Washington University and he told us we were mad. Settle in Seattle he said, not the boondocks of Idaho. Deaf to his pleas and sick of city life, I dragged Jan off to seek escape forever in the woods, lakes and mountains of Idaho. It was Idaho-Ho we were bound.

I should have heard the mad laughter in that line then. We took a small plane and flew east into the rising sun, the

Rockies on the horizon. We had a wonderful holiday. We caught up on all the family news that two brothers had lost out on for years, we went fishing and boating and we looked at property. We looked at the views, though that is a poor way of describing it; we drank them in, drenching our city-blasted souls with Idaho eye-candy. My God, the space! The mountains, the ski resorts, the forests, the rivers, the salmon, the bald-headed eagles feeding on the salmon. The $40-dollar licences that entitled you to hunt bear, if you so desired. The food. Those breakfasts are with me still.

We stood one day before the club house at Hayden Lake Golf Course and looked up the length of this peaceful lake, fringed with evergreen forest and backed up by the ragged mountains encircling it. With my brother beside me, and my wife at my shoulder, I felt that I looked at the Promised Land and that anything was possible. I was hooked.

For years we had dreamed of land of our own, a place to breed horses, a place of peace and privacy where a man and a woman could walk on acres they owned themselves, independent, self-sufficient, a refuge with horses. Perhaps here at last was a place where such a dream might become reality. For years Jan had dreamed of mustangs and Wyoming; Idaho was near enough to the dream.

At this point my brother urged caution. 'Come again a few times before you make any final decisions, come in winter, in spring, in the fall, and then decide.' But he'd put a match to tinder and I wasn't waiting for anything. The thought of joining the daily queue in and out of London was more than I could bear now that I had these lakes and mountains in my mind's eye. We went back to Sussex and started the ball rolling that would take us to America.

This was no easy thing and it took much longer than expected. By the time we flew into Spokane Airport to begin the next great adventure of our lives we had two children, Dominic, aged two and Imogen, a babe in arms. I remember the view through the cockpit window as the inter-leading door flapped open on our approach to Spokane. I had a child in one arm and the other bracing myself against the seat across the narrow aisle as we touched down. Jan was holding Imogen. I was responsible for a lot of people now: was I being responsible?

The warm welcome from our Idaho family set our minds at rest. We found a cottage to rent on Hayden Lake, on the shore opposite my brother's home, and settled in. It was September and the trees were turning red, yellow and gold. It was all absolutely breath-taking and far, far away from grimy London.

We bought two second-hand vehicles, a Subaru and a Jeep. All around us, horses stood in pastures on small ranches, and when you drove into the hills and mountains there were wonderful homes of all kinds and descriptions from massive Montana log houses to small clapboard cabins, with a horse, as like as not, nodding in a paddock or pasture. This was, after all, great horse country. The local Native Americans were famed for their Appaloosa horses. Now, though, they run casinos, a more lucrative trade than horse dealing and stealing.

The first Europeans to cross this wilderness were French-Canadian trappers, and the Clark Expedition had passed this way. In many ways it seemed barely settled. The residents of the Idaho Panhandle were a strange mix of loggers and miners, Californians seeking land, trust fund kids, summer home people, damaged Vietnam veterans seeking sanctuary, anti-government conspiracy theorists and the neo-Nazis. In fact, Hayden Lake was the HQ of this North American neo-Nazi movement. Truly, here was a last frontier. And it was a strange place for liberal South Africans to find themselves.

One man dominated the whole area. Duane Hagadone had carved a hotel and leisure empire out of the place and his modern multi-storey hotel bestrode the lakeshore. His golf club was famous for its floating tees, to which players were ferried by motorboat. The hotel attracted the rich and famous from across America; Condé Nast Traveller rated it highly. This was not what we had come for. We loaded the kids up and went hunting for property in the hills. As always,

A Fisherman in the Saddle

one's dreams are bigger than one's purse and we found that property was not that cheap, especially without any work coming in. But the sun shone, and we kept at it. Cœur d'Alène offered a range of cute shops, a boutique brewery, a little bit of California in food stores and restaurants – even sushi.

The lakes define the place. They are massive. On one, we were told, the 100-mile-long Lake Pende Oreille, the US Navy had tested submarines during the Second World War, secure from Russian spy subs. The smaller lakes are busy with floatplanes landing and taking off, some for Alaska where many people have connections – a wilderness even more remote. Slow-trolling fishermen in boats powered with silent electric engines, criss-cross the waters, fishing for bass, trout and salmon.

Financially, things were tough. Jan found a job as a journalism lecturer at a Washington University but the deal we'd come in on did not provide her with a work permit. I found one or two clients for my writing and marketing services, and when I landed an agreement to represent *The Times* of London in the Pacific Northwest, selling advertising for its Special Reports section, it sounded like salvation. But there was little interest in *The Times* or in London here. I could not blame the local people – I felt the same way. My efforts fell on stony ground.

But the natives were friendly, though I suspect that to them we seemed to have fallen from Mars. Nevertheless, people said, 'You folks are sure welcome. You make a great addition to the community. It's real neat to have you here, real neat.' And then silence. It got colder and began to snow.

With the snow flying, we witnessed the start of the elk-hunting season, when many local families fill up the deep freeze for the winter with this wonderful meat. This is not the time to find yourself in need of professional help of any kind. Plumbers, electricians, dentists, doctors, lawyers – all of them are out there blasting away.

One night returning from a 1am trip for nappies to the supermarket – some stayed open round the clock – I experienced something surreal. I took a wrong turning, an easy thing to do in the dark, with falling snow, in a new place, and drove into a street party. The whole street, every last person, was out in the night, standing in the light cast from open garages, chatting and drinking beer. When I looked into one, I saw a group of men busy skinning and butchering an elk; it was the same in the next garage and the next. It was a butchering party, the men just back from the hunt and everyone was having a ball. London felt a long way away, Cape Town even further.

Then the snow started falling in real seriousness – we were to have 12 feet that winter – and as temperatures dropped to minus 20 and minus 30, the front page of the local paper carried a startling request. It said: 'Please don't shoot the snowplough drivers.' In a place where everyone was armed to the teeth, most people were extremely polite. I wondered why anyone would want to shoot the snowplough drivers, of all people. I was to find out soon enough. With snow falling in such quantities even a four-wheel drive vehicle needs help and I found myself spending hours clearing our steep drive. As luck would have it, you'd just be finishing when a snowplough would come by and shove a four-foot high 'berm' of compacted snow across the front of your drive. No wonder the locals took the odd pot shot at the snow jockeys.

We went horse hunting, for fun, trying to cheer ourselves up and with no intention of buying. Just looking. We found ourselves at no-nonsense auctions in local stockyards. Tough, nondescript little horses, of Mustang blood, needed to survive these killing winters, came up for sale and fetched modest prices. But we did not have the money, the energy or the property to house them. Things were getting serious as only money can make it. And then we met a horse called Elk. He was never ours and we only saw him once, but in my mind Elk became my Idaho horse.

A small rancher who also worked as a horse-packer – someone who arranges guided horseback tours for greenhorns and city slickers – was selling him. The horse was the best elk hunter he'd ever had, he said. I forget why he was selling him. Elk was a dark bay, almost black horse with real class about him. Clint Eastwood would not have looked out of place on his back. He wasn't large by our standards, but nicely made at around 15.2hh. We stroked his glossy neck and whispered sweet nothings to him. We knew he could not be ours, but he made us feel better, just being around him for an hour.

Then we stumbled on Buttercup Farm, with its yellow shutters and horse paddocks. It looked ideal, just a mile or two into the hills from downtown Cœur d'Alène, but it was to prove too expensive, and by now our faith in our ability to make a living in this place had all but gone. We'd not found work or a home of our own and we certainly had not found land that we could afford.

We heard a local expression for the first time. 'You can't eat the view.' Nor could you, beautiful as it was. Many people were drawn to the region by the beauty of the mountains, the lakes, the rivers and the seemingly endless forests. But the turnover in people was huge. Many were called but few survived their first winter. Jobs were scarce.

When you sit by your children's beds, watching them sleep, while the snow falls in a strange land, the trees groaning and cracking with cold, and little money left, you do some hard thinking. You think some more as you walk round the house with a hammer and a torch to knock down the ice hanging from your roof in lengths as long and as thick as a big man's thigh. Loading the Jeep with candles, chocolate, peanut butter and space blankets – your survival kit in a snowdrift – you think some more. Choosing a country and a nationality for your children is a great responsibility, one that most people never have to make, happy with the one they received at birth. Options can be a blessing or a curse.

We went to the movies to see the adaptation of E.M. Forster's *Howards' End*. England looked lush and lovely and familiar – it looked like home. Had we given all that up? There were tears in the dark, and they were not all Jan's. By now there was almost no money; it was a tough Christmas.

The people renting our house in England had not paid for three months, and there was nothing in Idaho coming in. We packed up and returned to England. We left my dream in the Rockies and headed back to a reality we knew, to Sussex and the future.

However, we did not return empty-handed. We came back with a gift that would grow with value over the years – the knowledge that the grass is not truly greener on the other side of the fence.

Brrramble!

Jane Austen wrote, 'It is a truth universally acknowledged, that a single man in possession of a good fortune must be in want of a wife.' Now that could be true or not; it depends. Yet countless people, still, today, take it as an article of faith. In that sense, I suppose, a family of a certain size, and length of years, is in need of a dog. It's nonsense of course, but millions believe it. I did.

Why I believed it I cannot say. Dogs are, after all, the descendants of animals that used to eat us, and were then clever enough to domesticate us to save them the trouble of hunting down a fresh human every day, preferring to capture and train one to feed them regularly and keep them warm. And we call them man's best friend? We are a sad species. If ever there was a case of mass hypnosis, this is it. So I feel that there may be extenuating circumstances to my experience with a dog called Bramble.

I am that most shameful thing – a failed English Setter owner. I don't know why I feel so bad about it, because in fact we are legion. When, finally, in desperation, we asked the English Setter Society to help us rehome Bramble, they assured us that we were in good company – no less than 30 per cent of English Setter owners fail.

The shame comes into it because I'm still not certain who was the stupider, Bramble or me. After all, it is not as though we were not warned.

'Those loopy dogs, they never grow up.'
'By heaven, they take some exercising.'
'They are the most ridiculous breed.'
'An English Setter, are you mad?'
'You're round the twist!'
'They're nutters.'
'What!'

Who goes ahead after advice like that? So you see, perhaps Bramble and I were well matched to begin with. The trouble is they are beautiful, dopey yes, but adorable. And I'd met two English Setters at university. They came with a studious chap who was a regular in the Reserve Library. There they would lie by his feet, looking lovely, absolutely no trouble at all. I should have known better, nothing is that simple.

But I believed I had a secret weapon, a horse called Sebastian and 6,000 acres of Ashdown Forest on which to exercise a dog – surely, if it was big enough for Arab Horse enthusiasts to hold endurance rides, a dog would quickly find he'd met his match on these rolling hills? Ha.

It is a little known fact that when the Lord expelled Adam and Eve from the Garden, he gave them a dog for company, as a gift, intended to scour their souls, a sort of four-legged hair shirt. More than likely, it was the ancestor of the English Setter.

Blithely, we went dog hunting. Oh, what happy days those were! Puppies and dogs are not the same thing; you know this, yet common-sense deserts you on seeing these delightful, wriggling, happy creatures. We visited three breeders. The first had very slight dogs, a sort of 'Setterlite', but I wanted the heavier kind, the bigger, stronger, more robust kind. And the Setter-lites all came in black and white and I wanted the orange and white – Beltane is the name of this colour, as I recall. We saw a second breeder whose whole operation was so unattractive that we barely stayed five minutes. Then we drove up to the Essex coast and met Bramble and his mother. The breeder was charming, as was Ma Bramble, and we were goners – hook, line and sinkered.

Bramble settled in happily with the expected pools of

pee, poo and masses of mashed newspaper. I think it took him the best part of a year to control his bodily functions. Undeterred, Jan took him off to puppy socialisation classes. When we tell people that now they laugh and laugh, an English Setter at puppy socialisation classes, hilarious. Such larks! The other puppies and their owners did not laugh. Bramble had great fun, though. He finally put a young Weimeraner's nose one click too far out of joint, and received a serious nip. The trainer apologised, but suggested that perhaps some more work at home would be a good idea before we once more attempted socialisation.

As if to make amends and humble himself, Bramble developed a taste for his own messes. I've known a few people like that, metaphorically speaking you understand, but never actually going down to lap up the real thing! Bramble had no such inhibitions – he'd scoff the lot. We hurried off to the vet. Was this normal? Not that unusual, we were told. Scold him out of the habit. You could cry.

To be quite fair, Bramble did eat other things too. He'd have his own food, and then proceed to eat the house. Wooden doors, skirting boards, cupboard doors, wine racks, anything remotely chewable. He ate the roses he saw me planting, thinking, I suppose, that if I was burying these things they must be good to eat.

I decided to limit his range, and so limit his eating habits. On sunny days, I tied him to a steel corkscrew designed to plunge deep into the lawn, a fairly massive thing, robustly made – it would have held the Hound of the Baskervilles, no problem. Bramble snapped it within a day. He moved into my office and lay down by my feet, where I could keep an eye on him. For a year we stayed side by side. He bided his time, his soulful eyes rich and old with cunning.

I decided exercise was the answer. I would so exhaust him that he would not have the energy to get up to mischief. I took him with me when biking down the lane to check the horses. He galloped along, a friend to the world. I took him riding with me on one of those expanding leads. Sebastian and Bramble became like Siamese twins, joined together by my arms. Today, they are longer than they used to be.

I took Bramble riding with me, and he loved it. He and Sebastian went well together, keeping out of each other's way. Trouble was, the dog needed to stop regularly to smell things and the running lead would run out and then, at an end suddenly stop, jerking my shoulder badly as the horse continued forward. It never bothered Bramble being jerked like that; his neck seemed to have been made of steel.

Now and then, foolishly, I'd let him off the lead when I could see that we had the forest to ourselves. Invariably someone, or some dog, would then appear and Bramble would be off like a rocket. I would spend considerable amounts of time looking for him and calling him. I discovered that every second dog in England is called Bramble, as Boxers and Labradors and Retrievers appeared out of the undergrowth to look quizzically at me, their owners explaining: 'His name's Bramble, you see.'

However much exercise he'd had, Bramble still got up to his tricks, biting, chewing, nibbling, eating, gobbling, anything and everything. I thought of shock therapy. Sebastian, a rig, had jollied up a local mare no end. Long in the tooth and well past any ideas of procreation, she had welcomed him into her field as a gelding of good repute. To her shocked delight he gave a good account of himself – a bit of work that would not have shamed a stallion. The thought entered my head to leave Bramble and sex-mad Sebastian locked in a stable for a night. But I feared for Sebastian. I foresaw the pile of bones the next morning and Bramble lying there, not pregnant but inflated to the size of a bull, engorged with horse. Bramble continued to steal food from the kitchen surfaces.

But salvation was around the corner. Strolling up the road one evening, I noticed a walker with a smart black Labrador. Spotting us, she called her dog and he whipped round immediately to sit by her side, tight up against her legs. I was impressed. I decided to confide my problems to someone so obviously a superior kind of dog person. I explained about the stealing. No problem, she said. Easy solution. Pepper sand-

A Fisherman in the Saddle

wiches. Leave a well-sprinkled sandwich on the kitchen counter and let nature take its course. It sounded too easy, but it was worth a try. Perhaps my pent-up frustration with Bramble now took hold and I may have overdone things a mite. I made three sandwiches and loaded them liberally with pepper, peri-peri and slices of chilli! Why not make certain, I thought, as I closed him into the kitchen and removed his water bowl. This would be a lesson he would never forget, and life would return to normal. It did, but not in the way I expected.

I tiptoed away knowing that it would be just minutes before Bramble pounced. It took even less time than that. I crept back, ear to the door, listening to sounds of coughing, barfing, hacking and gasping. I looked in on this happy sight and grinned. Bramble did not look a happy chap. Gone was the soulful look, gone the mischief, gone the sly knowingness. His look said: 'Help!' I closed the kitchen door and lightly went on my way, a smile on my lips.

Half an hour later I decided to relent, to return to the kitchen to give him his water bowl, to graciously accept his apologies and promises of being a good boy for the rest of his life. A shock awaited me. He'd scoffed the other two sarnies and lay in his basket, looking pleased with life generally.

I snapped.

We called the English Setter Society and within a short week a charming, childless couple in their late forties arrived with a small pick-up truck and a huge butcher's bone to collect Bramble. They had always had setters, they explained. They loved them. People in their village, when throwing out old sofas, would call them to offer first refusal. Their dogs, on average, they explained, ate a sofa a year. How nice, we said. Bramble disappeared up the road with nary a backward glance. He knew he'd landed with his bum in the butter.

Now and then, out riding on the Forest, I pass the odd English Setter and stop its owner. I explain my status as a failure with their chosen breed. They nod sagely and agree; they're not easy dogs, not easy.

Last year I had a vision. It stunned me. A man was out

walking two English Setters; they looked beautiful against the blooming heather – a picture of England. Seeing me, he called the dogs to him, and they obeyed! I must have looked thunderstruck. I explained. 'Oh,' he said, looking at his watch, it's 7pm now and we've been out since seven this morning. They're quite glad to have a rest now.' Superman, wherever you are, you have a brother in England.

Each Christmas, we get a card from Bramble's new owners. The first one said they had forgotten how much energy a young English Setter has. Each of them had lost a stone. Bramble was in great form. For me these cards are now essential to a happy Christmas. His absence makes my day.

Poor Sebastian, his feet let him down finally. I sometimes wonder if it was not all that extra work, keeping Bramble exercised. I suppose you could say Bramble had him in the end.

TRUTH, MARRIAGE AND HORSES

Should a husband keep secrets from his wife? On balance, it is not a good idea, though there will be occasions that may justify this course of action – in what the American Constitution terms the pursuit of happiness. But, generally, honesty is the best policy in getting on with one's wife. A popular song advises, 'How to handle a woman? Simply love her.' So, if secrets are inimical to love, truth it must be.

My problem with truth, marriage and horses began with a story in a national newspaper about the sale of the Gucci Arab Stud in Horsham, West Sussex. I was sitting in the garden on a lovely summer's day reading the paper. I turned a page and there was a picture of the most magnificent flea-bitten grey Arab stallion. The accompanying story explained that the Gucci Stud was holding a dispersal sale. Strangely, as it happened, our own excellent vet, Chris Ginnett, had been placed in charge of the stud by the RSPCA when they found a number of animals in very poor shape, some having to be destroyed. For a long, a very long moment, I sat in the sunshine wondering seriously about showing my wife the article, for I knew instinctively that if I did, somehow, in some way that I could not fully comprehend, our lives would change. How right I was.

Some years before, Jan had had a lovely grey Arab called Django, named after the jazz violinist Django Rheinhart. He proved to be well named – he threw her a few times, broke her nose, and of course she loved him and turned him into a wonderful ride and a great friend. Now, years later, we had been sharing Sebastian, a 16.3hh bay hunter gelding of mixed parentage, since returning from a year in America, and I knew Jan was longing to get a horse of her own again.

So in fairness, I thought that I had to show her the news story and picture. That afternoon we sat in blistering sunshine, watching one lovely animal after another sold at auction. As anyone who has ever loved horses will know, the experience created an itch that could only be scratched by going in search of an Arab, as those in the Gucci auction were beyond our modest pockets. We criss-crossed the country, driving a total of 3,000 miles, looking at some likely and some very unlikely animals. At the age of 38, and now the mother of two children, Jan was less keen on having her nose broken or revisiting the steeplechase jockey's 'tuck-in-and-roll' skill needed for 'softer landings'. So we looked with care.

Sadly, each animal was less reliable than the last. In one instance, we drove from our home in East Sussex to see an Arab gelding near Liverpool. We had arranged to meet the owner at a horse show. When we got there, she rather shamefacedly said that the animal was not behaving well, and that she feared even to take him off the horsebox!

We got as far as having three Arab horses vetted. The first two failed for a variety of reasons and the third would not even allow the vet into his box. The tough and experienced Yorkshire vet said he had never seen anything so savage in his life.

We came home exhausted and agreed that we would give horse hunting a break. Jan rode Sebastian, took the children riding at a local riding school on Ashdown Forest, and fell in love. She came home and told me that she had found the horse of her dreams while waiting for the children to return from their ride. A woman had ridden into the yard on this lovely grey – would I come and look at him?

A Fisherman in the Saddle

We jumped into the car, Jan not saying very much. Arriving at the stable I saw a monster: a 17hh grey Irish Draught, humping and jumping in a small corral, making the most dreadful faces. It was then that I realised the search for a horse had finally unhinged my wife. She said he was four years old and had just recently been backed, by his owner, Rachel Cox. Obviously Jan had completely lost it!

I shook my head and told her in no uncertain terms that she was crazy! But to no avail...

'It's not an Arab,' I said in desperation. The horse was saddled and on she got. He did not seem too bothered so his owner urged her to take Dexter, as he was called, out onto Ashdown Forest. I said a quick prayer and followed behind. The pair walked, trotted, cantered and then I was ordered aboard. Gingerly I got on, but the beast did not blink an eyelid. In fact, he seemed to be the world's friend. And so he has proved.

He is by Shauna's Diamond, and has his chestnut sire's head – but in grey. It was not long before Jan was using Dexter to lead the kids out on their pony, hacking him all over the Forest and having the time of her life. Knowing Dexter well now, I am not in the least concerned when Jan is out for hours, returning in the dark sometimes, absolutely enthralled with this wonderful animal.

And now, as I look up the garden to that lovely grey head with a pink muzzle, I am astonished at how all of this started. The moral of the story is: Don't ever be tempted to hide anything from your wife – you will be missing out on the best that life has to offer!

Julian Roup

A Fisherman in the Saddle

CHANCE WOULD BE A FINE THING

Goodbyes are never easy, and when they involve the murder of a friend they can be traumatic. For a year, I have put off the hard decision to have my horse put down. Vets advised me five years ago not to touch him because of his extraordinarily flat feet. They said I was buying trouble. But who listens to vets when love strikes?

Sebastian is a bay 16.3hh Irish hunter. He is a funny mix of laziness and explosive energy. For five years, we have had fun criss-crossing the far reaches of Ashdown Forest in East Sussex. His feet were fine and perhaps, stupidly, I crowed a bit. After all I'd been proved right and the vets wrong.

But then suddenly they are right after all, and I am wrong. X-rays show big problems and Sebastian is on double doses of the painkiller Bute, four-point shoeing, built-up shoes and plastic discs. I've tried them all. He still looks uncomfortable and has fallen down with me three times over a six-month period. I have finally accepted the fact that he is not going to get better.

I make that call. What do you say? I explain that I need to have my horse put down. The only questions I'm asked is when and where – and the cost involved, £80. Cheap, really.

On the day appointed for the knackerman to come, I get up early and go down to his field for a last private goodbye. I have nursed him through the winter hoping against hope that spring sun on his back and new grass might bring us a small miracle. It is not to be.

The knackerman comes on time. His truck does not seem large enough for its grim duty, but he is extremely pleasant and something of a diplomat. I bring Sebastian in from his field close to the truck. As he puts his head down for a munch of oats, a shot rings out and Sebastian collapses.

It is a shocking sight. I feel sick, filled with a shocking sense of guilt and betrayal, and trying hard to appear in control of my feelings. Gently, the knackerman tells me to go for a stroll, not wanting me to see the indignity involved in hydraulically dragging my old friend into the truck. The whole thing takes exactly nine minutes from arrival to departure. I cannot believe it.

During the next few weeks, I wonder whether I should buy another horse or whether I should call it a day. I will be 50 next year, and with a young family I wonder sometimes about how responsible I am being. I definitely do not have the bottle I had at 18. When living in South Africa, I rode racing cast-offs – too mad, bad or lazy to race, American Saddlebreds, or Heinz 57s, anything at all in fact. But the habit of a lifetime does not just go away. I think about the best way of replacing Sebastian.

Various thoughts cross my mind. With my fifth decade in sight I do not want anything too sharp. I want sense, comfort and friendship. I recall a trip to the Dublin Horse Show many years ago and the wonderful Irish Draught Horses I'd seen there. And crucially I think of all the pleasure Dexter has given Jan, carrying her in all weathers, be it at dawn, midday, dusk or night, out onto the Forest, unfazed by anything; clever, kind, comfortable. It is an easy decision really.

I watch that famous trainer of steeplechasers – Jenny Pitman – say her goodbyes at the 1999 Grand National where she pays tribute to her horses, shedding a few tears in the process. One thing she says stands out. She describes her

A Fisherman in the Saddle

horses as her friends and her medicine. I know that is what I need – medicine in the shape of a horse.

But first I have to fix up my ageing body. An old cartilage operation on my left knee is causing me problems and I am booked in for an arthroscopy. While waiting for this I spend my time paging through the *Irish Draught Year Book* for 1998 and various newsletters from the Irish Draught Horse Society. It seems a strange thing to be doing while the war in Kosovo fills our minds and TV screens with unimaginable human suffering and inhumanity. Perhaps horse hunting is, after all, the best thing to do.

The day of my operation dawns. I am more than a little nervous, not as blasé about general anaesthetics as I used to be. I am older and wiser. I'm left waiting alone for five hours in my hospital room through the long, long length of a sunny May afternoon. I think to myself that if for some reason I do not survive the anaesthetic I will shortly be galloping Sebastian through the Celestial Meadows. The thought does not comfort me. What will Sebastian say to me?

But I do survive, and soon I am back on the phone horse hunting. I probably speak to half the Irish Draught breeders in Britain, and what nice people they are. Pictures and letters roll in, bringing news of every Irish Draught permutation known to man. But either they are too young, too expensive or not quite what I have in mind. Then, following a tip from a breeder, Caroline Saynor, I call Sue Benson in Yorkshire. She has a three-year-old 16.3hh steel grey gelding who sounds interesting. She promises to send me pictures.

The pictures arrive and though not wonderful – I subsequently tease Sue about her photography – they show a horse of substance with a lovely head and kind eye. Three days after my knee op and still on crutches, hobbling badly, the family and I drive the four hours up to Wakefield, and find what I have been looking for. Really? An unbroken, three-year-old mountain of a horse. As BBC Radio Two's Terry Wogan might say, I'm having a 'senior moment'.

Chancer, for that is his name, stares out at the world from his box behind Sue's house, with peaceful goodwill. He seems quite happy having Sue hug his back leg, and scratch his stomach. The children love him on sight. Turned out in a paddock, he can barely bestir himself to trot, let alone canter, despite Sue's best efforts. He is either drugged to the eyeballs or very laid back. Sue notes my crutches but with the discretion of horse sellers, a quality envied by diplomats, does not comment.

We have one more horse to look at further west, but it's no contest. This one, also grey, has a sad look to him that speaks of tough times. He is six and has been shipped over from Ireland after what looks like a very cruel young life. I harden my heart. That night I call Sue from our hotel to confirm that I'll be taking her horse, if she'll let me have him. I am delighted, and do a small jig, partnered by my crutches. Patently, senile dementia has just set in.

After Chancer's vetting in Yorkshire, I call from home to hear the worst. I need not have worried. He has passed with flying colours and the vet adds: 'He's some horse. Lovely legs. For an animal that size he certainly moves lightly. He'll be able to carry a ton!' Riding at 12 and a half stone, I hope Chancer will never have to prove himself capable of that. But one never knows, it might come in handy some day. After all I hope he'll see me right till my 70th birthday, unless I pop my clogs before then.

One week later, Sue and her husband Peter deliver Chancer to our house in East Sussex. Despite seven hot hours in the trailer, Chancer looks happy as a sandboy and immediately proceeds to make himself at home by rolling in his box. The sides of the wooden stable block shake, dull thunder rolls out over the garden and I hope it will hold up to the onslaughts of this huge young beast.

We are fortunate to our horse-whisperer friend Richard Wilkinson still stabling next door. At any one time, Richard has six youngsters that he is backing or straightening out. His patience is legendary. The horses are never wrong. Whatever they do to him, and they have done enough for a less hardy soul to have given the game up years ago, he soldiers on. Thanks to him many horses are living good, happy lives that might otherwise have ended up in pet food tins. I am more than happy to hand Chancer over to him for backing. Everything goes according to plan with one memorable exception. On the second day of long reining – Chancer, blissfully unaware of any problem – steps onto an adder in some long grass, which not surprisingly writhes madly, causing Richard following behind at the end of the rein, to jump some feet in the air as he passes over it.

After some more long reining, minus snakes, Richard gets onto him in the stable while I hold his head. No big deal! Richard confirms my feelings that in Chancer we have a 'real good 'un', despite the odd hump or small buck. 'He's got a very low pressure point,' he says. This is one laid back horse.

This in itself can cause problems. One morning I walk down to his field to check on him. He is lying down. I decide to walk in a half circle, rather than directly to him, in the hope that he will remain lying down until I get to him. I approach obliquely, he looks at me lazily and I sit down next to him for a chat.

He puts his head down flat on the grass and groans. Suddenly I'm worried. Colic? I stand up. Chancer lies there, his huge belly extended, pressed upwards. I call to him to get up, quite concerned now. I think to myself in panic, 'this has all been going too easily. Now I'm going to have to pay the price.'

I call to him to get up – still no response. I must get him back on his feet. I run to the hedge and pick a huge branch of holly, and run back to the prone horse, whacking him hard with the holly bush. After a while he puts his front legs out and heaves himself up. I'm shaking. He puts his head down and eats grass with not a care in the world. I imagine him thinking: 'What a wally!'

The snake and holly incidents pass, and after a fortnight I hear the words I have been waiting for from Richard: 'Why don't you ride him back to the field?' Dicky knee and all, I'm up there in seconds, proud as punch, riding Chancer down the lane to rejoin his friend Dexter out at grass. He feels immense, with a great swinging walk, and a lovely length of rein. In forty-five years of riding, I have never bought an unbroken horse. I wonder as we walk down the lane about the wisdom of my choice. After all, I might have bought a real pig in a poke. There is no telling really. And it is early days yet.

'He's got a lovely loose back,' says Richard. He explains how often smaller horses tense up their backs and necks at the start of their working lives, feeling the weight of the rider. Quite a number never get beyond that. Once we reach the grass, I push him into a sitting trot, which feels like a Rolls, it is so smooth. This is no pig in a poke.

The weeks that follow draw me ever closer to this wonderful horse. He is kind and intelligent and seems to thrive on human contact. Each evening I bring him in from the field for an hour-long hack through the fields and pine plantations round our house. Richard and I share the riding. He now works him in the paddock twice a week and I enjoy the results, hacking out alone or with Jan on Dexter. Chancer never does anything untoward, other than pretending to stick to the ground like a rooted oak or give a small buck and squeal at the start of a ride, perfectly understandable behaviour in a three-yearold. Once out on a ride, his small pointy ears stay eagerly pricked. His one vice is his desire to eat Sussex, grabbing at every passing bush, but as his breeder, Sue Benson warned me: 'These horses don't eat to live, they live to eat!'

Six weeks after he arrived, Chancer and I venture out alone onto the wide, open spaces of Ashdown Forest – all 6,000 acres of it. I cannot believe my luck. It is now July, high summer, the sky is blue and filled with skylarks, and the purple heather is just starting to bloom, readying itself for its August crescendo.

Chancer's canter is not properly established yet and he is still very much on the forehand, but all the signs are there of a great horse in the making. What a privilege it has been to get to know 'Chancer Snake Dancer'. Would I ever sell him? Chance would be a fine thing!

A Fisherman in the Saddle

LIFE WITH A CHANCER

It is now exactly a year ago that I drove up to Yorkshire to buy an unbroken, grey, three-year-old Irish Draught gelding. Looking back on it, I think I must have been mad. I say mad, because in my 49th year I was really wanting something safe and steady for hacking out on Ashdown Forest, in East Sussex, not an untried, unknown quantity, that I could not even ride yet! Perhaps what drove this strangely uncharacteristic behaviour from someone who had always bought 'made' horses of around seven, was Jan's purchase of Dexter, who despite the fact that he was only four, and only just backed, turned out to be a saint. Quite a lively, fast saint with a sen but a saint nevertheless.

As Shakespeare put it in Macbeth, 'Our doubts are traitors, and make us lose the good we oft might win, by fearing to attempt.' So perhaps I wasn't that mad after all. But when I bought Chancer, I had no clear idea of what I was getting. After a year I have a much clearer picture. Now I know better.

His big, kind eye disguises a very dominant personality. On entering the field, he would share in summer with Dexter, he lost no time in letting the older horse know who was going to be boss. Today they are inseparable, although Dexter remains cautious around Chancer, especially when food is being handed out.

I recall his breeder, Sue Benson, describing Chancer's

sire as 'really full of himself ' and his son has certainly inherited this quality. He is also strangely vocal, perhaps a baby thing that he'll outgrow? He has an impressive vocabulary of squeals, whinnies and neighs. He does not appreciate being left in his box when Dexter goes out for a ride – the only other horse in the yard. In fact, the first time this happened he kicked a massive hole through the side of his wooden stable in a fit of temper. Since then I have strengthened the box and lined it with thick rubber mats, but I still prefer to throw him out into a sand paddock where he can do his nut without destroying his stable.

To watch him in full fret, you'd not be keen to get on his back, believe me! Yet here is the strange thing. Once saddled, he is a different horse, alone or in company. Unlike so many other horses I've had, he does not spend his time actively looking for monsters to shy at. He has turned into a wonderful ride with a free stride and great paces.

It has taken the best part of a year hacking out on Ashdown Forest to really establish his canter. I'm not mad about sand paddocks at the best of times and with a 16.3hh youngster I decided to school him on rides. This has worked well and he seems to enjoy his work. He responds well to leg aids (no spurs needed) and is going nicely on an eggbutt snaffle. After one initial, back-breaking session with the farrier, Chancer is now his favourite client and stands as patiently as an old soldier.

As the Forest has dried out, we have even been exploring the excitements of galloping. While he is not going to break any speed records, it is an impressive gait. Importantly for a riding horse, once out, he does not bother himself with other horses, coming or going, and he's good with gates. Recently I held a gate open for two dizzy thoroughbreds whose riders said suitably complimentary things.

Eating, of course, is a full-time passion. I've been amazed by how little hard food these giants need. After feeding a mix of sugar beet and horse mix with ad lib hay through last winter I quickly found that I wasn't doing myself or the horses any favours. So when they are not working, they just

A Fisherman in the Saddle

get hay (best quality meadow grass) and thrive on it. I read recently that on Irish farms they used to get chopped gorse and cooked turnips. I was not surprised – they really are the ultimate good doers.

The quality that really impresses me most about these horses is their gentleness and intelligence. Having worked a year with a horse that has just been backed, it has been fascinating to see how quiet voice commands do the trick when the horse freezes, having seen some object of terror. Instead of trying to force him past, I have found that just letting him stand, have a look and quietly talking, gets him past it. Such so-called horrors have included narrow bridges, logs, tractors, cattle, dustbins, rivers, and narrow deep-rutted cattle paths. In fact, the latter gave me a fright and a laugh. Chancer is just too broad-chested for some one-foot-wide cattle tracks, so to balance himself he will lift out his near hind leg from the ditch to balance himself, going forward on three legs in the ditch and one outside! I have also watched, fascinated, as he tentatively put a front foot out to feel what looks suspiciously like bog, only proceeding once he's satisfied himself that the going is safe – a strangely comforting thing, as I was on his back at the time.

It has not been all plain sailing. Inevitably, there have been moments when he has felt as though he is going to explode. That is when I start to sing. This is as much to help me keep my nerve as it is intended to calm him down. And thus far, it has worked. But I have had some odd looks from people who suddenly appear out of a wood or around a corner, hearing me sing my limited selection of South African folk songs with *Sarie Marais*, the old Boer War favourite, well to the fore!

It is early days yet and we still have the terrible teens to get through. But so far, so good. A year ago, the local horse whisperer who backed him for me forecast: 'You'll be looking for any excuse to go riding with this chap.' And so I am.

Julian Roup

LIVING WITH DINOSAURS

Nothing is perfect. When the makers of Persian carpets put the finishing touches to their creations, they always include a small fault to remind themselves that only God is perfect. Knowing this of old, I should not have been surprised to find that my 'perfect' four-year-old Irish Draught gelding, Chancer, has a fault. He jumps barbed wire fences – on his own.

Cycling down to his field recently to check on him and his friend Dexter, I was astonished and concerned to find Chancer standing where he had no right to be – outside his field in a grassy lane. This summer, two new horses moved into the field next door and the well-named Chancer had finally decided to pay them a call. Luckily one of the newcomers was a very expensive dressage horse, and the owners had used a belt-and-braces approach to security – ringing their fenced field with an inner line of electric fencing. But for that, who knows how the visit might have gone.

Chancer was none the worse for wear, having jumped his fence cleanly. But Dexter, who had tried to follow by walking through the fence, had not surprisingly hurt himself and had a variety of cuts on his chest and flanks. I put our two into a far field, away from the newcomers, and went to tell my wife about the injuries to her horse.

I will draw a veil over the next hour as we washed Dexter's wounds and found that he was lame as well. The vet was called and tetanus shots were given, as well as Bute. I went to bed a worried man. If a horse can jump a fence once, he can surely do so again. And a four-year-old filled with the joys of youth was quite likely to try again. I did not have long to wait.

Three days passed. I was enjoying a TV programme about dinosaurs after supper when a friend rang our doorbell. She said that our horses had escaped again, this time they had made it into the garden of a neighbour half a mile away. This lady had also been watching the dinosaur programme when she was startled to see two huge grey heads looking in at her from the dusk outside. Luckily she is not fazed by much, likes horses, and did not object to the effect on her garden – which looked, to put it mildly, as though dinosaurs had indeed come to visit. She said she was just glad that they had not fallen into her swimming pool!

Once again, Chancer did not have a scratch, but this time Dexter was more seriously cut up and very lame. I collected the horses and took them home to their stables. Once again, I stood by as Jan, cleaned up her horse, muttering murderous thoughts about Chancer. Having had two bad shocks, I thought the time had come to apply some shocks to Chancer!

Jan delivered a bottle of wine, flowers and a card apologising for the damage to the neighbour's lawn. And some £300 later, our field was rewired and had an inner line of electric fencing for good measure. After a week in stables, I took Chancer down to the field and put him in, with the electric fence on full power, in 'training' mode. Having heard that some horses will jump an electric fence if they have never been shocked by one, I tried to entice him near with his favourite coarse mix.

But Chancer was having none of it. He stood a good 20 feet off, looking for all the world like a ten-year-old boy who has just been told the summer holiday is over and it's back to school tomorrow. Crestfallen is not the word – he was not a happy camper. But hopefully he was now more securely fenced in.

A restored Dexter returned to the field next. At six years old, he had obviously never met with electric fencing before and it took him three painful shocks to realise that this thin white line was a bad thing, worth keeping well clear of.

Next Saturday as I watched the next part of *Walking With Dinosaurs*, I was nervous, hoping that neither I, nor any of our neighbours, would be seeing two Irish dinosaurs peering in at them. Time would tell.

Meanwhile, I am looking forward to seeing what Chancer can do over some jumping poles. And Heaven help him if he stops! Having 'performance-tested' himself and passed with flying colours, he will be going into the sand school this winter for a proper introduction to jumping. The Irish jumping gene is quite obviously itching to get airborne!

Julian Roup

A GOOD NIGHT HORSE

The Westerns I read as a boy, by Zane Grey and others, often referred to a good night horse. This would be a cowboy's first choice for working cattle during the dark hours. It would be a horse that had good night vision, a steady temperament, and crucially, one that took care of itself and its rider.

I wondered if Chancer, at six, would be a good night horse. I waited until we had a full moon before putting the question to the test. The April night was balmy with spring. My wife had taken the children to a concert and I thought it would be the perfect time to head out onto Ashdown Forest. Moonlight and spring have that effect. They make you take chances.

It was 10pm as I swung into the saddle. Chancer and I have got to know each other and the far reaches of the forest – both the open heathery bits and the secrets of Five Hundred Acre Wood, the haunt of Pooh Bear and Christopher Robin. He is fairly sensible, but like any young horse, can be nervy. A squirrel running up a tree, or a dog appearing suddenly out of the undergrowth can be the cause of some excitement.

I have done a fair bit of night riding. Growing up in the Cape in South Africa, I rode those wonderful beaches both by day and by night. With a full moon shining on the sea and the hard-packed sand of low tide, the beach was a magical place, cleared of its busy daytime character of bathers and runners and walkers, with dogs and children and fishermen. At night I had it to myself, just me and my horse. Knowing those beaches like the back of my hand, I had no fear of galloping flat out. After all, it was five miles from the little village where my parents had their holiday home to the next seaside town up the coast. But generally, it was the pleasure of drifting silently through the night, occasionally startling a couple out for romance, which made it so memorable.

I had also ridden the South Downs with Jan when we first arrived in England. The chalk paths up on the Downs reflect moonlight wonderfully. As you ride, you can see the lights of ships moving up the English Channel on one side and the lights of Sussex villages on the other. But the beaches of the Cape and the South Downs are clear open spaces with no vegetation and fairly even surfaces. Ashdown Forest is entirely another matter.

Would Chancer leave home in the dark, I wondered, or would he reach the end of the drive and refuse to go further? I should not have worried. He sauntered out into the night with an eager air. As I rode past our neighbours' homes I wondered what they would think if they heard the clip-clopping going by. The ghost of brandy smugglers who haunted these parts not so long ago? Or a highwayman, abroad by moonlight, taking refuge in the Forest? But nothing and no one stirred as we glided into the shadows beneath the first trees on our path down into the woodland.

We passed through dark, leafy tunnels where the moonlight did not reach. I kept one hand on the reins and one held up to protect my eyes from unseen branches. It was pitch black under the trees and I hoped that Chancer could see better than I could, knowing that there were many boggy bits where he could easily stumble. I felt for my mobile phone, and it was a reassuring lump in the pocket of my Barbour.

We moved steadily downhill and crossed the little stone bridge without mishap, and then began to climb the 'sorting-out-hill', where local riders come to relieve horses of high jinks with a stiff gallop. We went slowly, emerging once more into bright moonlight. There was a sense of deep satisfaction, feeling the horse calm and moving forward readily. He felt happy to be out in the night and so I was happy too. Then we came to the one road we had to cross. I paused deliberately on it, waiting to be caught in a car's headlights, before urging Chancer into the deep cover on the other side. I tried to imagine the driver's thoughts. Chancer's dapple-grey markings and my black outfit must have looked startling on that lonely country road at that time of night. I laughed out loud.

We stopped at the highest point of the Forest to admire the moonlight on that lovely open space, just sixty miles from London. Standing still up there, we watched the winking lights of aircraft headed for Gatwick Airport. Something very old – a man and horse together in the night – and something new in Earth's skies, just overhead. My thoughts moved down the valley, to the grave of six young Second World War airmen and their Wellington Mk II that had crashed, just a few miles short of safety. I shivered inside my warm clothes.

Then about a hundred yards off, I spotted a lone figure, out walking, the only person we passed on our whole midnight march – other than that car driver. He turned a torch on us but said nothing, nor did I. I was enjoying being a ghost far too much. As we turned for home and headed back into pine plantations, we passed a herd of deer in silent possession of a field. They seemed quite unperturbed by us. Their field sloped down to a pond that attracts wildfowl, its surface like mercury.

Suddenly, there came from the depth of the woods the tormented and ancient sound of screaming foxes. It is a dreadful and unnerving noise, but Chancer continued quite happily. His six summers at pasture have inured him to it. But for me, thoughts of the Sussex Panther came creeping. I listened hard. Were those really foxes? I turned around in the saddle to look behind us into the gloom.

My family had beaten me home. The concert had been a great success. So, too, had my ride. A new bond of trust had been formed.

Julian Roup

Meeting and Greeting

To a horseman, there are just three kinds of walkers – those who studiously ignore you, those who smile faintly and stand aside, and those who greet you warmly, stop you, admire your horse and insist on stroking it, engaging you in conversation enthusiastically, like a long lost friend. I prefer this category to the other two. They make me warm to humanity, they make me feel good, and they break up a sometimes-boring ride. There have been times, I must admit, that they were the reason I went riding in the first place. As a child, I was too shy to enjoy such overt displays of warmth. One didn't know what to say. But with the coming of adolescence, it was nice to have one's horse admired, and bask in the glow of approval. There was pride too, of course, always a dangerous quality in a horseman, given that it usually comes before a fall. But proud I was. I can recall collecting my horse into a better outline, or more collected canter, as I saw cameras appear. There must be photos of my horses and me in photo albums all over the world, because I cut my horse-riding teeth in one of the most stunning settings on Earth, the beaches of the Cape. I was often the figure in the foreground, giving perspective to Table Mountain across the Bay. The tourists loved it. And so did I.

Horses were a way to ride into friendship, into company, even into relationships. I owe horses a great deal. I used horses in the same way that a girl will walk a dog, as much for the pleasure of walking the dog, as for the chance of meeting someone who will admire the dog, en route to admiring her. I took girlfriends riding, some of them never having been on a horse before. I knew the horses made me look good. So great was my confidence on horseback, I even packed picnic lunches, knowing that my luck would hold, briefly, even when I got off the horse for a while. And, after a brisk hour's ride, most girls were more than happy to stop – for a break.

But all that is in the past. Today I ride for the peace it induces, for the relationship I renew with my horse, for the solitude and for the silent, secret, sacred places my horse carries me to. Pride, however, remains. Chancer is without doubt the most stunning looking horse I have been privileged to call my own. At three, he was a dark, charcoal grey; now he is wonderfully dappled, like a child's rocking horse. And his huge size magnifies his exceptional colouring. No wonder he arouses such interest from anyone susceptible to things equine.

One day, I was stopped by a mother and two teenage girls who fell into category three. We had a chat about the condition underfoot on the forest as they patted Chancer admiringly. All of this is such un-English behaviour that it surprises. It must be said that category one, the ignorers, and two, the smilers, are far more numerous. There is something about a man on a horse that arouses strong dislike in some people. I have lost track of the numbers of walkers I have greeted cheerily – my unfailing habit – only to get a blank stare, or a total death-ray beam of hostility. I have been cut dead more times than I care to mention. It's definitely an English thing – Cavaliers and Roundheads, the riding classes and the walking classes. The silent hostility is palpable in some.

So the quiet smilers and nodders come as a relief. They are in the majority, I think, and are perhaps the most typically English. One is acknowledged, but distance is maintained.

Then there are the cursed of the earth – dog walkers.

A Fisherman in the Saddle

Yes, dog walkers. There is a bye-law on the forest that states that if you are walking more than one dog, they must be on leads. This ruling is totally ignored by the doggy brigade, some of whom are out there with a pack of up to seven or eight canines. Some horses are more bothered by dogs than others, usually the ones who have been attacked. Jan was out riding Sebastian once when they were attacked by a bull terrier that was jumping for the horse's nose. Had he succeeded, there would doubtless have been a fatality. Luckily Sebastian lashed out with a foreleg and struck the dog, breaking its leg, before anything worse could occur. It took him about a year to recover his nerve near dogs. The dog and its owners probably never recovered theirs.

There are those dog walkers who on seeing you, quickly leash their dogs, as concerned about their pet being kicked as they are about unsettling the horse. I always thank them. But then there are those walkers who are quite happy to see their dogs race up to you barking and dashing around the horse. 'Don't worry, he won't bite. He doesn't mind horses,' they say. Hopefully, dog lovers and horse lovers will be separated in Heaven, though one would wish for a greater and warmer divide.

Through all this, past the patters, the smilers, the haters and the dog walkers, Chancer makes his way, watchful but at peace with himself and the world.

Julian Roup

TIME MACHINE

A few times a week, I travel back in time, hundreds, thousands, even millions of years. It's not difficult. Man's fascination with the concept of time travel and how to achieve it, is focused on the complex science needed to make it possible. It's a pity really, because the freedom to travel back in time is open to all of us, easily and relatively cheaply, by getting on to a horse.

If you have never ridden, this may seem like a far-fetched claim, missing the point of that spinning vortex so beloved of Hollywood, which transports you physically to the time of the dinosaurs. But there is another way to reach back in time, go riding, and you will find what I mean. The first step is the acceptance of danger, something twenty-first century man seems ever less enthusiastic about. Take the risk, get on a horse and you will find that you live more fully, colours will be brighter, food tastes better, life seem filled with great possibilities – and no white powder is involved.

The second step is to learn to ride well enough to go off on your own into deep countryside or wilderness. That is when the real magic begins. This is not something spoken of lightly. It is an unspoken secret all riders share, at least those among us not committed to show jumping, polo, racing, or any of the other competitive pastimes so beloved of riders. These activities limit the horse's time-reach to just a few hundred years. You can experience all the horse sport of the

Middle Ages by getting on a horse. Your understanding of that time will indeed be greatly enhanced by horse games. You can even go jousting not far from where I live in East Sussex.

But for real long-distance time travel, the really serious stuff, you and your horse must travel alone, take the road less travelled, and shun human company. Then something truly magical begins to happen. The horse, being a herd animal, is justifiably nervous to be on its own, some never truly enjoy hacking out on their own, and some, like my own horse, Chancer, even dislike being left on their own at home. Horses feel vulnerable on their own, easy prey for carnivores. This is something that is hardwired into their brains. And we are no different really. Alone, in deep country, up on a horse, which is itself nervous of every shadow, of every rustle in the bushes, the human mind enters that vortex and returns to a primordial time when we were ourselves a regularly hunted menu item for the large cats. It is strangely exhilarating. Your senses sharpen a hundredfold, as do your reactions. You begin to behave like an animal again. All the sophistication of the past million years sloughs off remarkably fast. You begin to think like a horse. You look ahead for situations that you know will heighten his tension, or frighten him. You look because you don't want to fall off and be left totally alone. Your horse is your security blanket and you want to stay on board.

You move rapidly from couch potato to tense, preternatural alertness. The strange thing is that with the chemical changes this brings about in your body, physiologically, a wonderful elation fills you too. Is this a coping mechanism designed to help us handle danger? I think it must be. This is why I warn people that horse riding is more addictive than heroin. You reach a stage where you simply cannot do without a fix, and the thought of golf as an alternative is a fate too horrible to contemplate. Who would swap time travel for a spot at the pub at the 18th hole?

Living where I do on Ashdown Forest in East Sussex, it is relatively easy to jump a few million years in minutes. By avoiding the near reaches with its hikers and dog walkers, and heading for deep forest, one is suddenly alone with the trees, the ferns, the shadows, birdsong, and the sound of the wind. There are pheasant, rabbits, the odd snake, squirrels, foxes, deer and very occasionally, a badger. These are your fellow travellers, and there is a shared camaraderie, for with the exception of the badger, none of them truly flees from you, the horse is your passport into their world. But they too are watchful.

You notice the ground beneath your feet, both good going and the bad that could trip you up. You notice the leaves on the trees and bushes, you are very aware of the time of year, whether it is hungry winter or burgeoning spring, deep, warm summer or crisp, colourful autumn. You notice the places that would provide shelter from rain and wind, the places where one could sleep. You make note of the lie of the land, the tree, rock, hill and river signs that will lead you back home. And all the time you are watching, watching; in front of you your horse's ears, his inbuilt radar, are also tracking every change of light and movement and sound. You look ahead, to either side and behind you too, now and then.

You feel the tension in your horse, everything from the little starts and wholesale leaps from imagined danger. It spooks you; don't be cross, he is simply intent on saving himself – and you into the bargain. His head will be high, his 180-degree vision in each eye scanning a 360-degree radius. Those ears will be working overtime.

And suddenly, you are there. You have travelled back to a time before cars, trains, planes, houses, TV, carpets and microwaves. There are no shopping malls, no roads, and no lights. You and your horse are alone in a deep wood, the very heart of man's darkest fears. It is dusk and the light is going. There are wolves and bears and big cats that haunt this place, at least in your own human primordial memory, just like that of your horse. The small wind is so high that it just brushes the tops of the trees, but in the gloom beneath the leafy canopy, you can hear nothing of its passing. There is silence, or just a thread of birdsong, which stops abruptly. Why? Now you and your horse are one. You are joined together in your fears, your senses, your shared history as someone else's meat. Your shape changes as your body bends to accommodate all six senses. You listen, truly listen and look in a way that will turn aside leaves and branches, and you smell the forest in the musty wetness of its life. And there is joy here, such joy. For you are alive, you know you are alive, because you know too how soon and how quickly you could be dead.

And then you turn for home. Your horse's steps quicken, he and you are headed for safety. But safety does not have that edge. To be safe is not all there is to life. The years roll back and once again you enter the twenty-first century, as a car passes too close. At home you strip your horse of tack, and turn him out in his paddock, your fellow time traveller. You change out of the clothes that have seen another time, and you find a leaf, a physical object that came back with you from the past to the present. Poor leaf.

A Fisherman in the Saddle

MOUSE COUNTRY

Riding on Ashdown Forest provides many pleasures. These include the views your eight-foot-high eyes now see, scenery coming at you without effort, the magic carpet made flesh. Unlike a passenger in a car, you are in and part of the scene, and unlike a car or a motorbike you are not restricted to roads, and all is silent, but for the steady heartbeat of your horse's hooves. There is the pleasure of a horse walking actively beneath you. He swings along, alert and delighted with life, and it takes a hard heart not to be affected by that spirit. There is the feeling of power in a balanced, controlled trot, where the horse moves from behind and you float over the ground. Then there is the best gait of all, the slow collected canter, which to the uninitiated can best be described as the feeling of riding a friendly dolphin as he rises and falls through the water; there is speed, comfort and that rocking, flowing motion. To be on a fit horse with a comfortable stride and a good canter, is to know bliss. In Chancer, I have such a horse.

There is too the pleasure of landscape, and if you are lucky, as I am, to live on Ashdown Forest in East Sussex, you have a varied and interesting riding country. Ashdown is high ground. It is 700 feet above sea level, which provides you with far horizons to the South Downs, the North Downs, and views into Sussex, Surrey and Kent. The land is hilly, providing a series of bowls, amphitheatres, valleys, each with its own focus. On the hilltops stand circles of dark umbrella pines, the symbol of Ashdown, commanding the open heaths.

One such clump of hallmark pines marks the spot where Camelot came to Sussex. Near Highgrove they stand, the place where President John F. Kennedy spent the weekend at Prime Minister Harold Macmillan's home. There are often secret hidden graves within these tree circles; some commemorated with a simple wooden board low in among the undergrowth, or simply with ash to enrich the soil. Perhaps my final resting place one day too?

Ashdown's 6,000 acres boasts open moorland, deep deciduous woods, with pine plantations on its edges and at least three golf courses nearby which act as land bridges to nearby countryside at Forest Row, Crowborough and the East Sussex National Golf Club at Maresfield. Ashdown is the very heart of the Forest of Anderida, so named by the Romans. Today, it still contains in pockets, remnants of that ancient woodland that once divided London from the coast so effectively that a different Saxon dialect was spoken in each place. The Romans, in their brutal and effective way, punched a road through it, linking Londinium with the Sussex coast. Subsequently, kings hunted it, armies marched across it, and gypsies inhabited it, a landscape that Cobbett in his Rural Rides described as: 'A poor, harsh, barren place.' No wonder only gypsies called it home. Its acid soils are no good for agriculture. Its best crop is grass for livestock, for silage or for hay. Yet with the coming of the railways many found it – and found it charming.

Kipling's 'wooded, dim, blue goodness of the Weald,' surrounds it. The views from its highpoints include Hilaire Belloc's 'hump-backed Downs'. Sir Arthur Conan Doyle lived here and walked Ashdown, his 'Scotland in Sussex'. Its brooding setting, and its microclimate of shrouding mist, rain and cloud, provided the inspiration for many of the landscapes in his Sherlock Holmes books. Holmes, of course, was the creature that England would not let die, the country going into black-armband mourning when Holmes was sent to his death over the Reichenbach Falls by Professor Moriarty, until he was somewhat reluctantly revived by the author. Finally, Sherlock was retired to bee-keeping in Sussex. I, and many others, have our thoughts about this, and a retired army colonel who keeps bees nearby is my chief suspect.

And of course, Christopher Robin of A.A. Milne's *Winnie the Pooh* books made it his, and so ours too, the perfect childhood playground. So one comes to it already biased in its favour, and the reality seldom disappoints. It is not grand country; it's not the Rockies, the Pyrenees or the Drakensberg. It is what my sister once called 'Mouse Country.' She got it right. Miss Tiggywinkle would feel at home here. And so do I.

That huge, dim Forest of Anderida is now gone, the oaks providing ships for Nelson, the rest had by charcoal-burners providing fuel to smelt Sussex iron. It can be a lonely, eerie place in winter, so high above sea level and open to the worst storms off the Atlantic, brought in by howling South-Westers that rattle the window of our cottage and lift the occasional tile.

The place names on the Forest show that many have loved this place, with many named after places in A.A. Milne's books. The Garden of Eden, the Enchanted Place, with its rock-centred picnic spot and the inscription in bronze: 'By and by they came to an Enchanted Place'; the Hollow on the Hill, Hundred Acre Wood. There are deep, still hammer ponds, those reminders that this was once England's iron country, and then there are the odd dips and craters made by V1 and V2 rockets, which crossed these skies and happily fell short of London.

Spring, announced by cuckoos and the hammering of woodpeckers in the hurricane-humbled woodland behind our cottage, brings forth bluebells and wood anemones. There is always yellow gorse, and in July, the purple swathes of heather lift the heart. Amid it all, the silver birch fights to reclaim its own, while the bracken rises and falls like a green tide.

Man has been here a long, long, time. His ancient presence is evident in the small fields bound by hedgerows and by the chestnut plantations regularly cropped for posts and staves. There are the old villages, Nutley, Fairwarp, Chelwood Gate, Crowborough, Chuck Hatch and Hartfield. However, there is also change, and new roads that bring walkers and day-trippers to picnic. Not all change is bad. There is a car park that boasts our favourite ice cream van, a regular stop on the way home from school in summer.

There is also a large, and at times noisy, military presence, not as big as when the Forest was home to thousands of Canadian soldiers awaiting D-Day, but enough to make their presence felt. The rider regularly comes across lost soldiers learning navigational skills with their flapping maps.

'Can you tell us the way back to the Crowborough Army Camp?' they ask awkwardly.

It sits across the valley from my home and depending on my mood, I either tell them or I don't. I recall my own national service in South Africa and the only creatures I might have asked directions from – ostriches, puff adders or a foolish tortoise, which ended up in the pot, my own lack of navigational skills and resulting hunger costing him his life.

There are the radio masts on Ashdown, which mark a vast underground warren, a remnant of the Second World War, now owned and occupied by the East Sussex Police Force. What, one wonders, are they doing down there in those mole-like spaces – certainly not catching burglars or muggers.

There are few pubs on the Forest. Our favourite is The Hatch, because of its food, the views from the garden, and for its snug space and warm fires. It's a regular place for lunch on New Year's Day, giving us a happy break from all the Christmas cooking at home. This place was old before Jan van Riebeeck set out from Holland in 1652 with his three small ships to create a vegetable garden at the Cape. Just over the hill from where I sit writing this, is the Horder Centre, an arthritis clinic, where hips and knees are replaced. It sits patiently under its green roof – waiting for me and my grinding, horse-worn joints – one day, perhaps, but not yet.

Ashdown appeals to man's spirit. It must do. The evidence is all around one here. It is of this world and it is not. Here be dragons, witches and Hollywood stars. There are more religions in this place than in Jerusalem. There is Wikka, the first and the oldest, whose time maybe has come once more. There are the Scientologists who attract California believers and film stars to these parts, and the Rosicrucians up the hill. There are modest Church of England parish churches, where vicars hold tenuous sway over diminishing congregations, and there are the worshippers of the Open Air Church of our Lord or is it our Lady? No matter, this deity combines both masculine and feminine; its double nature fits well with the dual nature of this place.

It's a bog in winter and concrete in summer. Oh God, the mud, the mud! Not for nothing were Sussex girls called 'Sally Longshanks' for the long legs they needed to keep from sinking into the bottomless depth of it. Its ability to suck horseshoes off is legendary.

Ashdown is my adopted country. I am not English, nor ever will be. I love the country, but I cannot claim to know it. I know Sussex and I love Ashdown Forest. So this is my place. It is enough. It is the end-point for me in my family's second great trek – first out of Europe – Lithuania, Holland, France and Norway to South Africa – and then back to Europe again. I share it with literary giants, wild animals, mystics, sheep and a few black Welsh cattle. It is home.

And I have a friend that I share it with and who shares my enthusiasm for it, not so much the hills, or the gallops, but the flat grassy bits and the shady woods in summer. Chancer is always happy to go exploring, as long as he also gets a chance to eat, to browse, to absorb all edible stuff – grass, tender leaves and twigs, bracken, bark. No, he's not a fussy eater. Why should he be? His breed's proud boast must be: 'We'll stay fat on nothing.' Three wild geese fly regularly over my home at dawn each morning, heading for our neighbour's pond. They come in low with calls that thrill you to the marrow. They seem to say: 'Get up and see. Get up and live!'

And Ashdown is out there waiting to be discovered, and Chancer is there, waiting to be fed.

Julian Roup

MUCK AND BRASS

When you own two very large horses you can be sure of one thing; you have your own manure factory. We do a lot of mucking out. The old saying: 'Where there's muck there's brass,' based on the belief that there's money to be made from rubbish, has been inverted in the horse world. As I experience it, where there's muck, there's very little brass left!

At 6.30 a.m. on winter mornings, I'm up at the small stable complex behind the house, hard at it. I turn one horse out into the sand paddock and get stuck in. Never having mastered the mysteries of bedding horses on straw, a tricky, difficult material to work with, we bed our horses on wood shavings, which makes life a lot easier.

We're up there again at lunch time to do a second muck-out, top up water and hay nets, and at 6 p.m. muck out again, feed, water and hay nets; and just before going to bed for the night at 11 p.m., it's the same again. We use rubber gardening gloves, a pitchfork, a multi-tined fork, stable broom, two wheelbarrows and a lot of energy.

I'd be lying if I said that I never think of giving it all up. When you've returned from a dinner party, a movie or a restaurant, the last thing on earth you feel like is doing the horses before collapsing into bed. It's death to romance, that's for sure. When it's howling outside with icy winds off the Atlantic and sleet is coming at you horizontally, you really do wonder – why am I doing this? The answer, I suppose, is that it is the habit of a lifetime and the love of horses.

Now and then my son, Dominic, a strapping 13-year-old, who is going to top out at around 6ft 3in, can be persuaded to pitch in. He's usually up for a bit of mucking out or lawn-mowing when he is low on funds, and there is some new, fiendishly clever piece of kit he needs, for his Palm Pilot or his Gameboy. This is Technology Boy. But he likes the outdoors too.

He's an avid watcher of TV survival programmes and he has camps at various spots in the nearby woods. But if the weather is fine, he's most often to be found up his tree house or 'tree platform' that I in my cack-handed way wedged, nailed and tied into the great old yew which stands just to the front and side of our house. It is our nemesis if the wind lifts that extra knot or two in the next storm. Dominic sits up there thinking who-knows-what, keeping a watchful eye on the army camp across the valley. He has thoughts that boy, such thoughts.

At the age of four he stunned me by saying: 'You know Dad, friends are like chocolate for your head.' Dominic, I'm sure, is going far. Aged eight he came up with an economic theory that would have pleased Karl Marx. One day, after trying to explain money to him and his younger sister Imogen, he commented: 'Why doesn't money work like a kettle and water? As the element heats up, the heat eventually spreads to all the water in the kettle, and all the water gets a fair share and eventually it's steaming.' Oh, my child, greater minds than yours and mine have wrestled with that problem in this wicked old world of ours.

But the army interests him. It has guns and tanks and things that go bang. Really, he is the most peaceable soul, but the army has him thinking, I can see it. Over the valley, target practice has started up on their shooting range and his binoculars are trained on the young cadets going through their stuff. He has recently joined the cadet force and has one advantage over most of them: he'll know the Forest like the back of his hand, and won't get lost on manoeuvres. Physically he

A Fisherman in the Saddle

is powerful, and he's proud as punch about getting his second kayaking diploma recently; one more and he'll be able to teach the necessary skills himself. But it's not kayaking he's thinking of up that tree, it's kalashnikovs, rockets, and unarmed combat. I watch the occasional judo class of his at school and he sets to with a will. He's a boy after all.

And like most boys he's not into horses. He likes them, and has ridden a fair bit, but any animal that will deliberately set out to make you eat dirt, is not on his wavelength. A few crashing falls have directed him to water sports; sailing is his great love at present.

His help is appreciated up at the stables, but when you own horses you need a network of support – farrier, vet, muck-removal man, feed merchant, tack shop, hay supplier, and it's handy, when things get tricky, to have a wise friend to turn to who knows more about it all than you. Richard Wilkinson, horse guru, the horse whisperer who backed Chancer for us, and who manages the DIY livery stable next door for our neighbour, is one in a million. A never-ending fund of sound advice and encouragement, he has not chosen an easy road. After school, he worked briefly in the City but found that finance was not his forte and he decided to follow his heart. He has worked in many aspects of the horse industry, transporting racehorses all over the world being just one. But finally, he has found a niche as the last-chance corral for condemned rogues and misfits.

His success rate is almost 100 per cent and a never-ending stream of dicey horses find their way to him. They must be so happy to have found someone who understands them and who is so patient and kind. Not that they show it. Since turning 50 last year, he has had five hard falls, been concussed twice and had a bone in his hand broken. But he always gets up for more. His is both a calling and a passion.

The farrier, Andrew Casserly, is the best in Sussex. But usually the work is done by one of his young apprentices, currently Randall, a chap of few words but great patience and strength. It is a strange calling in this, the twenty-first century, but it's a shrewd choice – they will never be short of work. An oft-quoted fact is that there are more horses in Britain today than when they were the major means of transport. It's a tough life though, bent double in freezing weather or heat wave, liable to receive many a kick or bite. There are perks though; in a sport dominated by young women, a muscled Adonis will find it easy enough to get someone to massage aching muscles.

Chris, our hay man, is a delightful chap who manages a farm about 20 miles north of us. Because we don't have great storage capacity, he will deliver seventy bales every month or six weeks as needed. Once here, he throws and juggles those bales like oranges while I gasp, heave and sweat. I see his little grin when he thinks I'm not looking. The smell of the hay, good sweet meadow grass, is a delight, as is the feeling of a fully stocked barn.

Our neighbour, Frank Alexander, or his son, Chris, remove our muck trailer once a week in winter. This is a great new blessing. For years we used to bag the manure and cart it to their giant muckheap in the boots of our two Saabs, until Chris suggested that I buy an old farm trailer with a hydraulic lift. He or his father collect it with their tractor and return it empty, all in ten minutes. This saves vast amounts of time and endless backache. And let's not forget Jean Alexander's wonderful cooking and hospitality. What neighbours!

Then there is Ron Manser, owner of our summer field, six acres of so-so grass but with a wonderful old barn for shelter from the heat and flies, or from an unseasonable May snowstorm. He is a true Sussex man, born and bred on this old estate and knowing every blade of grass on it. He is an endless fund of stories about the area, and keen to tell as many as possible.

The feed merchant has just gone belly up, which is sad, as it was a good place to catch up on the local horsey gossip. Staffed by cheerful girls, keen riders themselves, it was a repository of useful things besides feed. There were clothes racks where I found most of my outdoors wardrobe, a good selection of tack, as well as dog and cat food. There was also a notice board filled with horses and ponies for sale or loan,

A Fisherman in the Saddle

puppies and kittens of all kinds and offers of help with riding and mucking out. The word on the wind is that it has a new owner and will shortly re-open. I do hope so.

This network keeps Dexter and Chancer in a manner to which they have become accustomed. Doubtless they hope it continues – if hope is an emotion that horses feel. I believe they are worth it, but it certainly takes a lot of brass.

The Irish Draught is today a rare breed. Their numbers were decimated during the First World War, when they were used to haul artillery, and in the economic collapse of the 1920s and '30s, they were shipped out of Ireland in bulk to be enjoyed as steak by the French.

Today, happily, their numbers are recovering. The Metropolitan Police use them, and they do well as helpmates for the UK Police forces in crowd control. Their great temperament and jumping ability are winning them friends in the competitive world of show jumping and dressage. Created as a multi-purpose animal by Irish farmers to take them hunting, pull a plough, or take the family to church in the cart on Sunday, they are useful and adaptable.

I like their steady temperament best. Chancer will actively help me to open and close gates now, pushing them open with his chest and bringing me within easy range of pushing them closed. He will stand idly by, munching, as I break branches overhead in bridle paths that are getting overgrown. He's a sort of horsey Land Rover, I suppose, willing to go anywhere and do just about anything. But they do produce a lot of muck! When April comes and the horses go out to grass for the summer, five months of peace descends. The horses and I make the most of it. Come September, I'll be getting ready to muck my way through another English winter and a mountain of manure.

That's horses – the do-it-yourself way.

Julian Roup

A Fisherman in the Saddle

Open windows

When life scares you badly, a horse will help you, at least as much as the Samaritans. Hell at work, a failing marriage, bereavement, not enough money for the mortgage or the children's school fees, all the things that life sends when it bares its teeth, are helped by horses. How, I cannot fully explain, it's just so.

Writer John Irving gave sage advice about surviving this world in his book, *Hotel New Hampshire*. He wrote, 'Just keep passing the open windows.' Those windows are always there, they beckon and promise release, and sometimes it takes more courage to walk past and live, than to dive out and die. Horses help you move past them more quickly – they have longer strides.

Horses are simply there. They are beautiful and they are kind – usually. They take a great deal of attention and I suppose that helps to move the focus away from one's own troubles. An Englishman once said that the best thing for the inside of a man was the outside of a horse. I could not agree more. Beauty brings healing.

I think that we poison ourselves with information and stimulation. Like too many uppers, they leave us buzzing and nauseous, twanging like a tuning fork. A horse will earth you once more. They will make you stop and stare, take in the view, dream a little, and then magic happens; peace leaks quietly in. They make you whole. We were not meant to live in artificially heated houses, alive with electricity. I find that by stepping out into the night, the dark electrons of nature in the wind and the air and the dark, wash away the detritus of so-called civilised life. One connects immediately to nature and the madness slows, and then stops. It's hardly surprising, we are stardust after all, the scientists confirm it, but we always knew it.

And then there is activity. The shrinks tell you that physical work releases endorphins into the bloodstream – Nature's own feel-good factor kicks in. Working with horses takes a lot of effort, mucking out, grooming, tack cleaning and of course the riding itself. But simply stroking an animal is beneficial. There are schemes here in England which use pets – dogs, cats, rabbits – to help calm and heal patients in hospital. The old and the young benefit especially. The tactile pleasure gained from stroking soft fur does something to us that slows the heartbeat and turns the brain's alpha waves on.

So it is when grooming a horse. Whistling in the age-old way to keep dust from one's mouth, one works down one side and then the other. In the wild, animals groom each other, as much for pleasure as for ridding themselves of ticks and other irritations. There is much to be said for stroking or being stroked. A child who is not hugged grows up damaged.

So horses have always been my medicine. Half an hour with my horse at night, standing at his shoulder, watching over the stable door, the northern constellations wheel across a winter sky, or the moon scudding between clouds, or just the wind, coming from across the world, brings quiet, and peace and joy. Now and then Chancer will rest his head on my shoulder, snuffle into my neck, and I feel touched by blessings.

On summer evenings, I ride my bike the quarter-mile up the lane to his and Dexter's field, quite often startling a fox or deer. It is light here till late in summer and at around 10 p.m. there is a blueness that brings the sky to earth. I walk through the dew-wet grass till I find them, and with a hand on a horse I commune with the dusk. We search for Eden, for Arcadia; it really is not far, it lies within us, but we have to be still and calm and open. That is a journey horses help you make, without even leaving the stable. Who knows? Perhaps that is why great kings and warriors lie buried with their horses, not only as a sign of status, but as a means of transport to another world, to heaven. After all, when the final window beckons, wouldn't it be great to take that leap with a horse beneath you?

Julian Roup

CAST!

Sometimes you have to wonder about a horse's intelligence. Dexter is no fool; he's like a cat for getting out of difficult situations, but once in a while he surprises…

Once he managed to break a length of rail in the sand paddock. He got out promptly and proceeded to get stuck between a barbed wire fence to one side and a vertical fall to the paddock fence on his other, to which he stood parallel, his way ahead blocked by a holly tree. He could not go back either, as at each step the earth crumbled beneath his feet and he risked impaling himself on the paddock fence below. I saw this and ran for an axe to hack the paddock fence down where he stood. But to my amazement, he did a stately *levade*, and with both front feet in the air, turned a cat-like 90 degrees in the air and jumped back down into the paddock. No problem. No, he's not a fool.

He makes the most awful faces over his stable door — which teaches me that one really must not judge a book by its cover. Dexter is a true Christian — he has the kindest nature. But he was badly gelded I believe, the wound turned sceptic and he had to have six months' box rest. So understandably in winter he gets a bit tetchy, stuck in his box when the weather's bad. He certainly teaches visiting children to mind their fingers, as he will have a little nip for fun. So whether it's boredom or spatial deprivation, I'm not sure, but he will have a roll in his 12ft by 12ft box now and then, and has occasionally managed to cast himself. How it's possible for a monster his size, 16 hundredweight, to get stuck anywhere, is beyond me. He is the nearest damn thing to a Sherman tank. But stuck he gets. Which creates a very tricky life-threatening situation for him, for me and for anyone else who gets involved.

Luckily there is a cast of stars next door at the DIY livery yard. They include an Irishman, Dennis, whose surname, to my shame I do not know – which shows how effectively hysteria destroys manners. The Irishman is a man small in stature, but big in heart. He does a nice line in horse talk, and he hasn't only kissed the Blarney Stone, he's smooched the thing. But unlike some, who talk the talk, he can also walk the walk. I won't hear a word said against him. He saved Dexter from a horrible fate once, by pulling his tail – vigorously.

When a horse casts itself, it lies there, its feet up against the side of the box, unable to roll back and get up. It's undignified and dangerous. In this position a horse could easily twist a gut, with possibly fatal consequences. It's all scary stuff – big time. One morning I was tapping away as usual on my Mac when I heard a roll of thunder from the top of the garden. I glanced up but could not see either horse's head, not a good sign. Running up to the stable block, I once again heard the drumming of hooves against the box walls. Instinctively, I knew what I would find, and yes indeed, Dexter lay trapped against the wall dividing his stable from Chancer's. He had to be made to roll back over, or one would have to take an axe to the wooden wall, with all the fright that would entail. Thinking fast, I grabbed a halter and put it on the prone horse, which thrashed about every few seconds, his front feet coming dangerously close to my head. I then yanked as hard as I could on the rope attached to the halter, trying to move him away from the wall. Have you ever tried to pull a tank stuck in a bog? I made as much impression.

I ran to the house, called Jan and explained the situation. She ran next door to get help from Richard. He arrived with Dennis. The Irishman was barely tall enough to look over the stable door but he took charge instantly. Telling us all to stand well clear, he walked into the box, round to the

A Fisherman in the Saddle

back of the horse and gripped his tail. Now if I had not been so panicked I would have laughed, to see this slight man setting out to right half a ton and more of horse. He was in imminent danger of being kicked to death as Dexter struggled and thrashed. Completely unfazed, Dennis took hold of the tail and pulled hard to the side – one movement. Dexter rolled over and got up in one go. 'Weeelll, good boy, old lad,' said Dennis, patting the horse on his way out. 'Good boy, old lad.' And he was gone, brushing aside my astonished thanks.

What is it that they teach them in Ireland? I do not know, but I wish I had it, that Celtic swagger and twinkle. Women, dogs, children and horses, all are in thrall to it. And so am I.

Julian Roup

THE WOMAN-HORSE THING

What is it about women and horses? There is an affinity, some would say a love affair, that goes on between these two. The coarser-minded ascribe sexual motivations, but I know that while that may be part of it – Freud is shouting in my ear, 'What else, dear boy, what else?' – it is far more subtle and complex than that. After all, I met my wife on horseback, though she was 16 at the time and I was 25, and there was certainly no interest from either side then. But I've known a few horsewomen in my time and the horse thing is not about sex. I think the horse empowers women, and at the same time entrances them with its beauty, gentleness and grace, qualities that so appeal to women. Horses in turn respond to a gender which does not try to dominate them, but which creates a partnership of equals. The horse's instinctive intuitiveness echoes that of women, and the two get on like a house on fire.

You can have a relationship with a horse, which you can't with a car, and women are good at the relationship thing. I do wonder about this, though; after all, isn't the horse the quintessential strong, silent type? Perhaps as this breed of men has died out, with the arrival of The New Man, horses have filled that old niche?

Women feel safe on a horse. There are places no

woman would venture on her own without a protective dog for company, but on a horse, a competent rider can outrun trouble. No wonder this partnership flourishes. But it is strange that men are hugely in the minority in a sport that is so physical. Why is that? Boys, it seems, prefer engines, but it wasn't always so, was it? At the end of the day, the love affair between women and horses is their secret and their pleasure and most men can only scratch their heads and wonder.

I have been lucky to love horses, as they brought me into contact with a world of women. To an inarticulate youngster, having horses in common with girls was a great help. And, as confidence grew between boy and girl, the mutual passion for horses allowed one a freedom to enthuse and a means of discovering a world together, slowly, on horseback. Growing up in the Cape, as I've said before, bestows great blessings. This incomparably beautiful piece of earth, an amalgam of mountain and sea, vineyards and white colonial homesteads, a mix of Provence and Africa, must surely be one of the most enchanting places to grow up. For a horse-mad boy, it offered endless vistas, new horizons, new possibilities.

I rode my ponies and then my horses on the beaches, I rode them round the periphery of racecourses – Kenilworth and Milnerton – I rode them up through Cecilia Forest to the top of Table Mountain. Imagine it, a 16-year-old boy halfway up a three-thousand-foot mountain on an eager thoroughbred, looking down on the backs of gliding raptors. It was intoxicating. I galloped up Long Beach behind the Cape Hunt pack, the hound music echoing off mountain cliffs. And my home turf was the Cape Flats – a harsh, rugged sand-dune country that once lay below the sea, now a dry, desiccated place, home to Port Jackson trees, snakes and tortoises, on whose fringes poor farmers scraped a living market gardening. At its one periphery, the sea, with two mountain ranges framing it and to one side, Zeekoeivlei, the lake named after hippopotami, its original inhabitants.

This was my own private landscape, and to this day I dream of its heat shimmer, even as I toss and turn in wintry

A Fisherman in the Saddle

Sussex. I once more see the dunes whose outlines were my signposts, and the indistinct paths made by woodcutters. I would ride alone, always alone, watching the country pass, at one level, and at another, watching myself, and my horse, pass through it – a self-admiring actor/audience of one. The sheer, hellish heat was made manageable by the south east breezes, and by the water I packed in my saddlebags. If the sea was our destination, I would unsaddle and swim the horse, not too deep, for the bay teemed with shark, including Great Whites, for whom we would have made a banquet, a change from seal.

I would return from those rides like some ancient mariner, looking in wonder at the pedestrian, everyday, ordinariness of suburban life that had continued even as I'd crossed my Xanadu.

One day, I crested the great king-dune that ruled the rest. To one side it was being eaten away for building sand, making a great slide for a brave horse and a silly boy. As I sat up there, now 25, at a crossroads in my life, I saw the future. I did not know it, but I saw my wife.

Jan Warman was a 16-year-old girl, riding a polo pony called Plucky; how appropriate that name was, now that I know the girl turned woman. She was a good half-mile off, alone too, in that sea of sand and scrub. She looked up, saw me on the skyline and quite deliberately turned the horse away and cantered off. She made good her escape for two years, until we met again, at university.

Now her horse, Dexter, stands with Chancer, their fortunes linked by a boy who saw a girl in sand dunes, in another country, another continent, another time. Our history leaves a wake as white and turbulent as a ship's. On Sundays, I take our daughter riding at a nearby stable that has good, safe ponies and a gentle patient teacher. I watch Imogen, at 10, falling in love with this special world and find it hard to believe that some boy may be watching, watching, not seeing the future, just a girl mad about ponies, learning the woman-horse thing.

Julian Roup

A COUPLE OF BAD 'UNS

Into every life a little rain must fall and sure enough, Raffles fell into ours. We had sold our horses to pay the deposit on a flat in London, as Jan was working shifts at the *Financial Times* and on the BBC's *Financial World Tonight* and finished too late to get back to Sussex. So we bought a flat in Clapham where we stayed during the week and returned to the cottage in Sussex at weekends, our two Burmese cats making the round trip with us.

Now, after a horseless year, we were horse hunting once more, looking for a sensible animal to share on our Saturdays and Sundays in the country. We did all the usual things one does when horse hunting and drew a blank each time. Then one day, casting caution to the wind, we edged our way nervously into the stable yard of a show rider who dealt in horses on the side. Her reputation preceded her like an unsavoury smell, but when horse fever is upon you it's like a junkie needing a fix, whether the stuff is impure, or the needle dirty, a fix he must have. We got fixed real good.

We were shown into a busy yard, where a bunch of brisk girl grooms fetched and carried, feeding, grooming and exercising horses. We were shown a number of horses, none of which appealed; an old horse seller's trick. People, after all, seldom want the first thing they see. Then finally, with some reluctance, a nice stamp of horse was shown to us, but we were told it might already be sold. Another trick to whet the appetite. We liked what we saw. This was a pitch-black horse of around 16.1hh, a nice size for a horse destined to be shared by two riders – one of 5ft 7in and one of 6ft 2in.

A groom duly trotted the horse around the paddock and then I rode him. He seemed well schooled and comfortable. Jan took him out with the show rider dealer for a ride round the block. She came back having enjoyed the experience. We agreed to have our vet take a look at the horse. But first we asked quite candidly if the horse was absolutely straight, after all, its owner was not selling it. I forget the answer we got, but the dealer stopped one of the grooms and asked her to tell us what a nice horse he was. The girl just smiled, a rather clenched smile, and kept walking. We should have been warned. The show rider assured us that this was a good horse of impeccable behaviour and was only being sold by her as its current owner was going through a messy divorce, was having brain surgery, or was dying of cancer. I forget the so-called reason.

The vet was reluctant even to visit this yard. Its reputation was such, he said, that no good would come of this horse. We asked him to make an exception, just this once. He had been our vet for many years and gave in with good grace.

He could find nothing physically wrong with the horse but could not resist saying to the dealer, 'He's either straight, or you've got the drug dose just right!' smiling broadly as he said this. Raffles, as we called him, came to stay at a livery yard near us, which would care for him while we were in London during the week. He settled in quickly with a minimum of fuss; you got the sense that he was something of an old soldier – even at eight – and could make himself comfortable just about anywhere, having knocked round some.

The grooms at the livery yard promised to keep him exercised and we felt that all might be well. After all, we had a fine-looking horse and besides, had 'rescued' him from the clutches of this infamous dealer. Who knows where he might have ended up, poor thing. Ha!

The week dragged by in London. Finally, we got ourselves and the cats packed up and down to Sussex, stopping in

A Fisherman in the Saddle

at the livery yard en route to the cottage. Raffles was fine; in fact he lay sprawled in his box like an Indian potentate, looking very much at home and at peace with the world. The grooms said he'd been fine and though they had not had much time for him, he'd had a hop and a skip in the paddock each day.

The next day, we came charging down to the yard to try out our new acquisition on Ashdown Forest. To our amazement, he was lying down once again, seemingly happy as a sand boy.

'Well, he's certainly laid back,' I said, and got ready to saddle him for the first time. He stood nicely and I got on board. We walked slowly through the stable yard and along beside the railed grass paddocks towards the gate, through which the miles of open heath land beckoned. We were about 100 yards from the gate when Raffles realised that we were heading out for a ride and he stopped dead, his four feet planted as though in concrete. I urged him on with my voice and squeezed with my thighs, to no effect. I touched him with my blunted spurs and as though by magic he moved, but upwards, not forwards. He stood up on his hind legs as comfortably as though he preferred that stance, walking on two feet rather than four. Eventually he came down. I was a little shocked, to say the least.

Not wanting to give up just like that, I asked Jan and a groom to lead him onto the forest as I urged him forward from the saddle. He moved reluctantly but finally we crossed the road outside the gate and onto our old riding country. As soon as they turned back so did Raffles, who then took a death-defying hold and bolted for his stable, nearly decapitating me, and we rocketed inside.

We'd bought a napper royal. There are a number of options that you can follow in this situation. You can insist the seller takes the horse back and refunds your money, or you can decide that pride requires some stouter effort from you before you give in, or you can check with the vet if there was something wrong with the horse that made him rear. But as we'd just had the horse vetted, we knew that he was not in pain and besides, his relaxed, happy attitude when not being ridden said it all. Raffles was just not particularly into working. We felt sick.

We opted to give it a few more tries on subsequent days. The results were almost identical, although now nothing on this earth would get Raffles to go beyond a certain point in the yard. Any attempts at persuasion in this direction would end with him rearing. We called the show rider. She could not imagine why the horse was behaving in this odd way, she said. It might just be that he required time to settle down. Horses sometimes behaved in this way in new and strange surroundings, she said. It was evident that we would not get far with our show rider dealer. At this point, I bowed out and brought in the heavy cavalry. Jan got on the phone and started pounding away. The upshot was that the horse would be returned but we would only get our money back when the horse had been sold and a 10 per cent fee paid to the dealer. I can recall Jan's reply to this demand: 'Well, if that's the case, you only really need one horse – you can just keep selling it over and over!'

We were unhappy about this deal. We wanted no part of selling this bad horse on. We thought of legal action based on the fact that we had been sold a horse that was patently not as described, and under the Trades Descriptions Act might have found a remedy to our dilemma. But with some knowledge of the legal minefield we'd be stepping into and the emotional cost of this turmoil, we took the easy option and went along with the deal. We did try to insist, though it was wasted breath, that before the horse was put back on the market it should be retrained – straightened out.

When we took the horse back to the dealer's yard, she said she could simply not understand it as the horse had never to her knowledge stood up. She stopped one of her girl grooms and asked her to confirm this bit of flummery. The girl ignored the question and just kept walking. You got the impression that it was bad enough working for a crook, but lying on her behalf was just asking too much.

We bowed to the inevitable. Raffles went, the dealer

got her 10 per cent and we got the balance – and a dollop of wisdom with it. Buyer beware, oh buyer beware! And, oh yes, we never again bought a horse without having a blood test to check for sedatives.

Looking back on this experience we have to smile at the name we gave him – Raffles was after all a very up-market jewel thief – very much like our show rider dealer. We had not previously seen the irony of the name.

One thing is for sure, though, buying a horse is a raffle. You may buy a ticket, but you can never be entirely sure what you are getting – the bottle of plonk or the trip to Florida.

Now and then we see pictures of this lady in *Horse & Hound*, winning at some show or other, and a small shudder runs through us. Her reputation would shrivel a gentler soul, but she soldiers on, happy in the knowledge that there's a fool born every minute.

Julian Roup

A Fisherman in the Saddle

TOTEM ANIMAL

The horse, oddly enough, is not my totem animal; the stag is. Three times in my life, a stag has spoken to me and I have listened in wonder. Horses were always part of the event, but it was the deer that spoke.

You think this strange? Not half as much as I do, and I was there.

The first time it happened, I was 18 and getting ready for Army service in South Africa, in a heightened state of alertness and nervousness. This unusual state of consciousness could account for what followed – possibly. I was concerned about staying in the country or emigrating, to avoid conscription, and I was worried about simply surviving the Army.

One day, as I rode through the dune country behind the False Bay coast of Cape Town, I stopped in a valley. The sun was low and its effect was to illuminate the landscape so that it looked like something out of a medieval painting of Tuscany, simply glowing with relevance. I don't know for how long I sat my horse in that place. I know I felt transfixed, uplifted. Nothing would have surprised me there. It was a place of infinite possibilities, and sure enough, a stag stepped out of the Port Jackson scrub. It saw the horse and me but instead of whirling away, it came towards us and stopped, barely two car-lengths away. It seemed as though nature itself was stretching the possible, to bring me news. The whole thing was charged with meaning. And it seemed to me that the deer spoke, not in words, but symbolically, through its presence there.

As I sat there, transported, I heard the words of the great medieval abbess, Julian of Norwich, my female namesake, run through my mind. 'All shall be well, and all shall be well, and all manner of things shall be well.' Then the stag turned quietly and walked into the bush.

I wept. Not a tear or two, but great ripping gusts of weeping. Something infinite and inexplicable had occurred, I understood not what, but something had shifted within me and I rode home at peace.

The stag's message proved to be true. I still don't know what happened in the Army, but it was all rather surreal. I coped, well. I learned many great and useful lessons. And I found I had a guardian angel called Linda.

The next incident occurred when I was 35 and living in Sussex. I was riding Max, my big Irish middleweight. He could be flighty and I was conscious of his every move as we felt our way through dense fog in Five Hundred Acre Wood, close to my home. It was so thick that you could barely see beyond the horse's ears, so I had him on a tight rein, watching the ground for footing.

Suddenly we emerged into a gap in the fog, the size of a living room. In it stood a milk white stag, calmly looking at us, totally unfazed. My thoughts flashed back 17 years to that illuminated valley and for the second time in my life it seemed as if a stag spoke to me. It was a simple greeting: 'You are welcome here.' Quietly then, and slowly, he turned, looked back over his shoulder at us and was gone. Only then did I feel the horse's nervous quivering beneath me. I murmured a quiet 'thank you' under my breath and turned for home through the mist, which once more enveloped us. England, I felt, had sent an emissary, one that I could understand. For the first time in the five years that I had lived here I felt as if it might, one day, become my home.

I killed a stag last summer, after living here for twenty-one years, and it upset me for weeks. It happened like this. I went as usual, first thing in the morning, to check the horses,

A Fisherman in the Saddle

out for the summer in their field. I was a little concerned, because I had let the battery run down and the pulser was not sending any charge round the line of fencing. It did not overly concern me, as the horses were now so cautious near it, they would not even venture close. My brother-in-law, who was staying with us, walked down the lane with me, accompanied by his black Labrador. It was a perfect summer's morning in which the English countryside had once more come into its own, the hedgerows heavy with growth, the trees, giant green explosions.

I realised instantly that something was wrong when I saw the horses tearing round their field, eyes popping out of their heads, badly spooked. As we got closer, I saw a magnificent stag, his antlers festooned with electric wire, still caught in the fence line. He was leaping six feet into the air, shaking his head madly, even tethered as he was. From where I stood a hundred yards away, I could hear the animal calling in distress, but no words came, just nightmare groans. Tich leaned down and put a lead on his dog. I ran to get wire-cutters from a nearby house, but when I returned the stag lay dead. We cut him free and dragged him clear of the fence line into some bracken, out of the horses' sight, and reconnected the electric fence with wire removed from his still soft, warm, velvet-covered antlers.

The sheer waste of it all sickened me. I felt guilty. I felt that had the electric fence been on, the stag would have given it a wide berth. As it was, he probably grazed too close, was startled, lifted his head suddenly and got entangled. I felt that I would redeem myself in some way if he was not simply left to rot, so once more I ran up to Barry's place. He's the woodcutter who supplies the green oak for many of the beautiful barn-style studios and garages in the area. I told him what had happened and asked if he would like to butcher the carcass for his deep freeze. He said that he and his family were vegetarians, but that he knew a game-butcher who would come fast. If the stag was left unbled, the meat would spoil quickly. The butcher arrived within minutes and very soon that magnificent animal was just meat. The horses stood trembling in the very centre of their field, as far from that damn fence as it was possible to get.

What did it mean? Was the stag meaning to speak? What was his message? Or was his death the message? Now I will never know. Or perhaps life will yet explain.

What do these seemingly unnatural occurrences – when nature breaks its rules and we search for meaning – tell us about ourselves? Perhaps the significance we ascribe to natural phenomena – well documented in every human society – reminds us that we are animals after all. Our survival as a species would have depended on our ability to read nature closely. Anything on which your life depended was bound to have significance, and the wary instincts of that half-upright ape we once were, casts a long shadow.

So next time you pass magpies and start counting – one for luck, two for joy, three for a letter, four for a boy… you are in good company. Your primal grandparents might not have understood the rhyme, but they would have appreciated the reason. Such is the origin of what we consider magical thinking.

Horses bear a heavy burden; they carry us, and the weight of our dreams, and some are passing strange.

RIDING THROUGH THE TREES

Despite the devastating hurricane of 1987, Sussex remains one of the most heavily wooded counties in Britain, with 16 per cent of tree cover. It no longer possesses the pathless tracts of Anderida which swathed this island's south in an Amazon of green trees, just 1,000 years ago, but this forest still exists in pockets, and I am lucky to live by one such pocket, called Five Hundred Acre Wood, inhabited by a bear called Pooh. This is a fact that delights me, confirmed tree-hugger that I am.

Sussex lies between two tidal waves of green grass, halted for now, to the north and south of us – the North Downs and the South Downs – which run east and west across southern England, and, which like two huge incoming waves, create a sheltered space between them. The bit on which we live is almost as high as both waves, so we are not sheltered, but open to blasts off the Atlantic to the south and west, and from the Urals across the flat vastness of Europe's northern plain. But we do have trees, millions of them, in this still half-wild part of Sussex. They include oak, beech, copper beech, chestnut, ash, silver birch, pines and other conifers. Our children were quick to realise that in the midst of these trees they had Pooh for a neighbour, though he always seemed reluctant to show himself and come to play. But the song – The Teddy Bear's Picnic: 'If you go down to the woods today, you're sure of a big surprise' – gave me an idea.

I was riding through the dappled gloom of Five Hundred Acre Wood one day, when I spotted an enormous beech tree that had lost a major lower branch in the last storm. The lost limb had left a cavity in the half-hollowed trunk, perfect for nesting or secreting things. I rode up to it carefully on Sebastian, careful of his flat feet on the exposed tree roots, and peered inside. There in the darkness something silver gleamed. I put out a hand cautiously, standing now in the stirrups and pulled out a sword! It was a child's plastic play sword with a scarlet 'ruby' in the hilt. As I looked at it an idea came to me and I replaced the sword in its hiding place.

Birthdays were never quite the same afterwards. Each child would be walked down into Five Hundred Acre Wood and lifted high on my shoulders to see if Pooh had left them a present in the 'Present Tree', as it came to be called. Invariably he had, and the excitement of a visit to the Present Tree became a family fixture, until, like Father Christmas and the Tooth Fairy, Pooh himself, and the Present Tree, became just one more adult myth.

But the giant beeches retain something magical for the children and for us. They stand there winter and summer, our local sacred grove, an idea as old as man, offering a place of spiritual refuge in times of dire need and a temple set in the natural world to give thanks when times are good. I have stood in Chartres Cathedral and so many others, but for me they are lifeless and spiritless places, gloomy piles of stone hiding their dead beneath the floor. The Forest lives; long live the Forest, is what I say.

The woods in high summer are vast cool spaces amid a burning landscape the colour of the new South African flag. Black tarmac roads, sticky with heat, divide fields of green corn and grazing pasture from fields of yellow rape and those of golden stubble where the hay has been harvested. The pressed rapeseed yields a vegetable oil that will fry the national dish – fish and chips.

Another seasonal feature of the non-wooded landscape

hereabouts are the great gold roundels of hay and straw, awaiting collection by tractors bearing wicked steel spikes like horned red and green beetles. These giant hay and straw 'buttons' will shortly join the other crops in barns, helping to fasten a carbohydrate cardigan about our animals and us, to ward off winter chills, and provide bedding in fragrant smells of summer.

Before our cottage there are four 15-acre fields, which fall gently to a small river on the valley floor, before rising once more, now clothed in trees, to the ridge beyond. The ghosts of apple trees long gone gently haunt the fields on our side of the valley. A neighbour's home, the Clock House, bears mute witness to the long-gone apple fields and cider press in its arched windows, through which wagons once delivered red and green fruit for crushing. Where this land once grew apples pressed for cider, it now carries a new crop, a beautiful suckler beef herd with its cream colossus, a great Charolais bull. Change is all about us. The great hay roundels mark the changing face of agriculture. The high cost of labour means it is no longer financially viable to make small bales, and now horsemen and women will have to learn to deal with these monsters.

But in the woods, peace reigns still, time is halted and a primordial reality can still be found. The landscape is dotted with tree-friends. There is the Present Tree already mentioned. There is the Grandfather Tree, a beech so massive that nothing grows beneath it, its mat of beech nut husks, a place to lie as if within a Bedouin tent, silent but for birdsong and the scamper of squirrels. There is the Lookout Tree, which commands the valley behind us, overlooking what Sir Arthur Conan Doyle dubbed his 'Scotland in Sussex', a heavily wooded valley that is commercially cropped from time to time. There is a tree I call the Candelabra Tree – of a species I do not know – whose branches curve symmetrically upward like a menorah.

Trees call to me, and my inner being pays them attention. Now and then I still climb one. A few summers ago, I walked down the lane to do the evening check on the horses and stood by a chestnut tree. And as I stood there a huge, gold harvest moon sailed above the valley ridge and on the spur of the moment, I decided to climb the tree. It was relatively easy going and I stopped at around 40 feet above the ground. I sat there in a state of bliss, feeling the evening with every sense, watching the breeze play in the leaves and the grasses below heavy with seed. I heard a twig crack somewhere behind me, and turning carefully, saw the owner of the land, Barry, walking in my direction with his Alsatian dog. I have a very good relationship with Barry; he has built a wonderful double swing for the children and whenever we pass, we stop for a chat. He is an enterprising and hardworking man who also loves nature. But I felt rather foolish suddenly; a middle-aged man up a tree is an odd thing if he is not there to cut or trim branches, or to remove a cat. Why this is I don't know, but it's what I felt.

So I had two options; one, to remain quite still and hope that he would not see me, a good chance as the tree was in summer dress and I was well camouflaged; or the second option, to call out a greeting well before he got close. I had seconds to decide and the dog swung the decision. He looked up into the tree, possibly scenting me. I called out, 'Nice evening Barry!'

He stopped and looked about him, not thinking to look skywards. Feeling really foolish now, I yelled again. 'I'm up here in the chestnut tree!'

Rather tactfully, I thought, he replied: 'Oh hello. Is that you up there?'

I told him that I had decided to spare myself the walk all the way to the horses' field and to check them from the vantage of the tree. I'm not sure that he believed me, because I think he too had been stirred by the moon and had decided to take a stroll, and who knows, even climb what I now call the Moon Tree.

Sometimes I think that trees have a sense of humour. When you are 6ft 2in and regularly sit on top of a 16.3hh horse, you stick out like a sore thumb, and the trees tend to play games with you. Branches regularly lift off the faded vel-

A Fisherman in the Saddle

vet cover of my crash cap when I forget to duck or bow down deeply enough over my saddle when passing under trees. I wonder then about the wisdom of riding such a big horse. Something rather more modest, say 15.2hh, would limit this problem by a good six inches.

Chancer, however, is always happy to stop. It means he can indulge in his first, second and third favourite things – eating. I pull the velvet cover back on the cap, and then lengthen that left stirrup leather once more to remount for the return journey to the saddle. The days when I could vault up are long gone, and I need a little extra length of stirrup leather these days.

Back in the saddle, I shorten the leather once more and off we go again, long grasses hanging inelegantly from my horse's busy mouth. If I were more organised, I'd ride with some kind of shortened machete in a scabbard to keep the dappled or dripping woodland tunnels that I ride clear of overhangs. As it is, I constantly grab at branches, snapping them off, limiting the summer explosion of growth and keeping a passage open. Now and then I misjudge and grab something too thick to snap instantly, Chancer keeps going forward, and my shoulder feels dislocated once more. Sometimes I think I am the only person to ride these hidden paths; the only hoof marks I see are Chancer's and the marks of passage, snapped branches, my work alone.

It does not bother me; in fact, I covet the peace to be found here. Now and then we'll pause in some woodland glen, bluebells thick upon the ground in spring, their lovely elusive scent about you, and a single sunbeam, thick with dust motes, spotlights Chancer's ears. One can ask no more. Divinity is at hand. Such are the joys of riding through the trees.

Julian Roup

WET FASHION

What you wear tells a lot about you. I'm one of those who live in jeans and a fleece. Clothes are not a big part of my concerns. I walked past the stable next door with Jan last Saturday evening, on my way to dinner with the Colonel and his wife, Jane, another chance to check out my suspicions about his real identity as Sherlock Holmes the beekeeper. Richard the 'Horse Whisperer' passed by, bringing a gelding in for the night.

'My God, you brush up well! I wouldn't have believed it,' he said, grinning.

I was not sure whether to be flattered or insulted. Do I look such a scruff usually?

The point about all this is that I'm more concerned about what I wear when riding. It's a tricky business getting it right. After all, this is a climate that can and does produce four seasons on any given day of the year. So if you are out riding for any length of time you want to be sure you are well prepared. The weather forecast can be useful at times, and then there are occasions when it's more of a handicap. It sets you up for sunshine and rewards your delighted expectation with a hailstorm.

The careful, cautious, comfort-loving horseman must – even against his slovenly nature – give up some time to contemplating this issue. Headgear is easy, a crash cap. Not ideal in the wet – a Stetson or an Australian bush-hat would do much better in keeping off the rain, but they tend to blow off. And a hard hat has life-saving qualities. So it's a hard hat. Mine is black, originally, now going brown with age and mildew.

I have a good selection of warm winter shirts, a dozen jerseys in various states, from pristine newness through to battle-hardened favourites of different weights and quality. Jeans are easy as they save one from having to change into breeches or jodhpurs, with jeans one can simply ride in what you are already wearing.

Then there are boots, Muckers for winter and leather ankle boots for summer, both carrying blunt dressage spurs, there to keep the engine at the horse's back-end connected to the legs in front, a considerable task with these Irish Draughts who are quite happy to slop along on the forehand, the back trailing free. Not a good idea in the wet, or on any surface really.

Then there are the two key sartorial additions that life and time have brought me to favour – chaps and a waxed Barbour. A transatlantic fusion, you might say. The leather chaps keep your jeans clean and your legs warm and dry. My wife once said something of the view from the rear, which decided me in their favour forever. Her comment is one of the things I remember when I get off my horse to walk by his side on occasions, giving him a breather or to help loosen up stiffened knees. And then there's the Barbour, that most useful of English inventions, a waxed jacket which is both warm, waterproof and which breathes.

Out riding, one passes puffas and windcheaters, the odd hacking jacket, a variety of jerseys, anoraks, and Australian stockman's coats with caped shoulders – very flash. I'm a Barbour man. It is part of my wardrobe and me. No matter that the wax is now patchy in places – the factory will do a re-wax when things get desperate. It's perfect for riding, or almost. When it rains really hard, there is a little spot around the pommel where the jacket rides up – because you've shoved the back over the cantle to avoid sitting in water. This spot coincides with the top of the chaps where denim reap-

A Fisherman in the Saddle

pears, and of course this is fatal. One ends up with wet underwear and worse.

What can one do? My answer is to carry waterproof trousers, rolled and slung across the back of my saddle in winter. They are a great insurance policy against wet willy. The only trouble is they are a major kerfuffle to get into in the pouring rain. Imagine it. One is up on the Forest being torn to pieces by the wind and then it begins to rain. You think, 'Oh hell, it'll pass.' And by the time you've realised that no, it's not going to pass, 'what am I thinking of?', you are already getting damp in this awkward spot. So you turn for home and the horse, being a chancer by name and by nature, thinks – 'thank heavens for that' and gets a mite more active.

Now you think: 'Do I get off and un-sling the waterproof trousers in the wind and the rain while my horse does the foxtrot around me, just missing my toes time and again, or do I wait to get to a more sheltered spot?' The sheltered spot always wins out. And by the time you are there, wetness has set in with a vengeance.

Now the question is: 'Do I still get off and into the waterproofs or just tough it out as we are on the way home – though wetness is going to be terminal by the time I reach sanctuary?' You get off the horse. He, good chap, eats immediately, anything that is going, and you unstrap the trousers from behind the saddle. Now you have to get wet boots, with spurs and leather chaps, into these awkward flapping things, with elasticised tops and bottoms and which the horse does not like anywhere near him. An undignified dance ensues.

You yank and pull and curse and finally get them on. Now you have turned into a gleaming green, shiny wet-look rustling thing, that the horse wants nowhere near him, least of all in the saddle. And your nether regions are cold and wet. This is when thoughts of golf or dog walking enter your mind, and how sensible the French are, to like horse steak. But you have not ridden for years to give up now; a remnant of expertise comes to your aid, as does a polo mint (for Chancer) and some native cunning. You get a foot in the stirrup, swing up and settle into a little swimming pool, custom designed for your bum. One wet bit says hello to another. You squelch home, disgustedly.

A Fisherman in the Saddle

THE ARK

This cottage should really be named Noah's Ark. It sits on a hill, well clear of the flooding that happens down in Uckfield. Last year, Dominic said, after I'd failed to get him and his sister to school because of flooded roads, 'I'm glad we live on a hill.'

But it's not the elevation that justifies the ark appellation, it's the inhabitants – mother and father, son and daughter, couple of cats (Burmese), two King Charles Spaniels and two horses. It may not be enough for an ark, but it is quite a menagerie. And all of this on a third of an acre with an old stone cottage built in 1760, which used to be the stockman's cottage on Home Farm.

It's a tight squeeze at times. But each one has his place. The cats migrate from their basket on top of the deep freeze in the utility room, to a spot between the boiler and the recipe bookshelves in the kitchen each morning, when I come down to make coffee. They will, at intervals during the day, attempt to exit the kitchen and steal into the house, to lie on south-facing windowsills or on sofas.

The dogs sleep in a basket by the back door in the utility room. Poppy is small enough to squeeze through the cat flap, Toby pays the price of an uncontrollable appetite and larger bones, and stays put till I let him out. If the weather is good – on both days a year – they stay out – if wet, on the other 363 days, they come back into the utility room and kitchen till the evening, when they are invited to join the adults for a spot of TV or reading.

The horses are at the top of the garden in their stables. One at a time, they have the dubious pleasure of the paddock, which is open to the four winds and imminent attack from the pride of lions, which they fear, haunt the slowly regrowing wood behind their stables. The children are at school, or in their rooms doing homework, or whatever else it is they do there, or they are in the garden, or up their tree, or in their 'camp' above a long-forgotten Victorian dump in the woods, a source of treasure--trove bottles, sometime still filled with vaguely pharmaceutical-smelling things.

Wherever the children are, the dogs want to be there too. The cats don't give a fig, as long as they can sleep all day on the boiler or do a spot of kitchen-escaping. Honey, though, has taken to terrifying us by tapping on the playroom/TV room window with her claws at night, asking to be let in. It is a sound to freeze the blood. It could, so easily be the clicking of over-long fingernails ...

They are merciless killers, these cats. Ownership of such animals is truly anti-social, their impact on songbirds ugly. They are indiscriminate slaughterers – on summer mornings, the utility room boasts rabbits, voles, moles and birds – but as yet no pheasant, which is a pity. If only cats could be trained! One bold and beautiful cock pheasant that visits our garden is chancing his arm. Or perhaps he's heard from the adders in the brush that these killers are not invincible?

We must make a strange sight as we straggle down the lane to check the horses on a summer evening. Imogen will be out ahead on her bright yellow bicycle with Poppy all around her – risking an imminent collision, yelps and tears. Dominic will be cruising back and forth on his silver scooter, or his skateboard. Toby will be walking sedately between Jan and me until Poppy comes tearing back to inspect and runs full tilt into him. He shrugs her off. What he thinks of her he's not saying. Like all dogs, they are foolish, of course, but sly with it. These dogs belong to anyone; news of canine loyalty has not reached their floppy ears and popping eyes just yet. Two tarts, they're anyone's. They will as soon go off with passing walkers as stay with us. Vigilance must be constant, or they'll be gone.

Bringing up the rear are the two Burmese, Limoux, a deep bitter-chocolate brown, named after the Languedoc town which produces a form of champagne, Blanquette de Limoux, the holiday home of some English cat breeders we once bought another brown Burmese from – Lushka – who lies below one of our windows helping the wisteria gather strength. Honey, a cream Burmese, more the colour of honey, will be following discreetly, slipping in and out of the woods, now on the lane, now in the trees. Both cats will be making their particularly horrible and annoying wail, typical of the breed. We do get some funny looks.

Any car coming down the lane, usually horsey DIY-ers heading for our neighbour's livery yard, has to slow down at least three times as children, dogs and cats are called to the side. The dogs and children usually obey, the cats either don't give a toss and stroll down the centre of the road or slip off into the woods moaning and wailing like banshees.

When the children have friends to stay for a sleepover, the family's traffic on the road increases proportionately, as the obligatory evening horse inspection takes place. It's all rather like a circus on the move, minus elephants. Mind you, when we are walking our Irish Draughts back to their field after a weekend's work, it's the next best thing.

Now and then – about four times in the summer – Michael and Sally Hands who own Warren House, the great, white, castellated property that was once the 'Big House' on Warren Estate, show off their truly stunning garden as part of the National Garden Scheme. Then a never-ending line of the green-fingered edge down our lane, to look lecherously at this perfect spring garden, awash with Rhododendrons and other glories. I covet the one massive Copper Beech which stands sentinel by the house, commanding breath-taking views across a valley to soft, green, woodcovered hills.

The cars bearing these people slow as they pass, the

children, the dogs, the horses, the cats, and us. What do they see? Is it some country idyll they conjure up, as we make our straggly frieze down the lane, like some uncouth group on a Greek vase? Do they, suburbanites mainly, see a paterfamilias, his wife and brood, out with their animals – some latter-day Constable come to life? Ha, not likely! Doubtless they see an indulgent fool on unattractively intimate terms with his bank manager.

The show garden traffic edges past us, nods and smiles, raised hands and greetings. They to their passion, and us pressing onward to the horse field. To reach this field, one enters a gate to a grassy lane, which leads to this hidden pasture. The gate bears a sign that strikes doubt and fear into the largely middle-class walkers who pass this way. In shaky yellow on black it says: 'PRIVAT no entry'. That missing E and the unsymmetrical jumble of upper- and lower-case letters gives them pause, if ever they think, momentarily, of entering this path. Ultimately its effect is greater than that of a Rottweiler. Who was it that said: 'In the beginning was the word'? No one is sure who put up the sign, but it does the job. Our horses – touch wood – graze undisturbed.

With casual confidence we fling open this gate, watched at times by the wary, admiring glances of timid passers-by. We cross this Styx and stroll onward, past derelict tractors engrossed with weeds and grasses, a static conversation that has lasted years, past tumbledown piggeries and rusty, corrugated iron sheds, barely standing. The birds sing and the rabbits scamper, but no humans follow us down this path.

We leave the horses in their field, with its views across country to the distant blue North Downs. They are the true possessors of this place, which remains, happily, PRIVAT, an extension of the crowded Ark up the lane.

A Fisherman in the Saddle

EAT MY DUST!

The horse wrangler cast a dubious eye over the ten of us. 'How many of you folks have ridden before?' he asked. We were a mixed bunch all right, and I could understand his cool, appraising stare.

We stood on the edge of a dude ranch corral, 120 miles north of LA, just 20 miles from my brother's home in Santa Barbara with its breath-taking view over the sea from a commanding cliff-top position. I liked to tease him about this spot. 'If the big quake hits, you and your home are going surfing down there!' It was a joke in bad taste and did not raise a laugh.

Jan, Dominic, Imogen and I had flown out from a wintry Sussex to spend New Year with Herman and Teri and our three nieces, Bailee, Lindsay and Megan. As the millennium year 2000 drew to a close, California was bathed in mellow winter sunshine, shirtsleeve weather. Breakfasting in one of the many harbour-side restaurants on a surfeit of eggs, bacon, pancakes, maple syrup and cream, cinnamon toast, hash browns, orange juice and coffee, was a great way to start the day, and at 8am it was already warm enough for anyone.

We had done all the necessary exploring of the city, the nearby wine country, the lovely, varied coast, the bizarre Danish town inland was a Disneyesque recreation. And now the whole group of us, plus Bailee's current boyfriend, were off for a spot of riding in the hills back of the coast.

We told the cowboy in his jingling spurs and ten-gallon hat that some of us had done some riding and some hardly any. One by one he asked for clarification and that person got the horse deemed the best match. The horses were not, as you would expect, a prepossessing lot. They stood lank and lean, heads down, preserving their energy in the dusty, dungy flyblown paddock. I drew a 15.3hh bay with a jaundiced but resigned look in his eye, and I clambered into the deep American saddle.

We set out with three of the cowboys in attendance, one at the back, one in the lead and one who spurred his horse unnecessarily, racing up and down the line, showing off for the three cousins – at the age of 16 the twins Lindsay and Megan were lovely, and Bailee, at 20, was a complete knockout. That poor horse paid the price. Imogen's day was made when the head honcho invited her to ride in the lead, riding 'point' he called it. She glowed with pride, looking back down the line from her dusty white grey 13hh pony. Her joy was increased liberally when the cowboy instructed her to shout: 'Eat my dust!' which she duly did, grinning madly.

The ride was much as you would expect, we moved slowly along a rocky trail which climbed up the side of a steep ravine, crossing small foot-wide streams that appeared out of the trees to our left. The horses picked their way cautiously over exposed rocks in these little streambeds. Once or twice, we had a trot and as we neared the highpoint we emerged from the trees and saw the sun setting over the Pacific. It was a good moment. The narrow, densely wooded valley below was already veiled in evening light, but up here there was buttercup yellow sunlight smeared liberally over the vast landscape.

I was riding somewhere in the middle of the line and I looked back. My brother and his wife Teri brought up the rear, Jan was behind me, Dominic and the cousins, and the boyfriend were ahead, with Imogen still in the lead, just ahead of our trail supervisor. For a moment my mind's eye halted the action, and we looked like a frieze of settlers, new people in a new land. And of course, we were. Our heritage

A Fisherman in the Saddle

of course was European, but for the adults our start had been Africa, and now here we were in the American West, playing at cowboys, and looking like horse-borne pioneers from another era, when in fact Herman and his family were settlers of today, in California just twenty years.

We had, I thought, come a long way. Our family was now spread across three continents. Our sister, Jay, her husband Guy, and their two children, Nikki and Kirsten, live in Cape Town; we live in Sussex and of course Herman's family live in Santa Barbara. Harold Macmillan's winds of change had blown us into a triangle that was 20,000 miles round all points. It was a fair spread. Getting together was rare, and I wondered when next we'd be part of such a large family group.

Emigration is no easy call. You pay in so many ways. Without doubt one is enriched, but it comes at a price, a price that involves many great and small losses. I looked back at my brother, younger than me by five years. We were joined by so many things, and now here we were two proud Dads with our wives and children. We were having fun, but also making memories that all would share, memories that would bind us that bit more securely as family.

It seemed good to me to have this moment on horseback. It might have come to me at any point in the holiday, but somehow, riding in a strungout line in those dry Californian hills, it seemed so evident. A family, like a string of beads, together for a while and then broken, the beads scattered to the four corners of the world. One has to wonder at the strange forces that work on us to move us about the world in this way.

If riding does one thing, it connects you to a landscape, and on that Californian trail I saw us all, so clearly, on our collective and individual journeys. We are together for so short a time and then we separate and blow like seeds scattered by the winds.

As I rode, deep and comfortable in the saddle, the mobile cowhand who scooted up and down the line pulled in behind me. 'I see you done some ridin',' he said, as I held the horse together, urging it forward into a more active walk.

'I have,' I said, 'but never before in America. Africa and England mainly.'

We chatted for a while and then once more he went to show the girls how it was done. Imogen's small straight-backed figure still led the way, as the pony now cautiously felt its way down the first steep slope on the way home.

That evening we made a barbecue back in Santa Barbara, sipped wine and looked out over the starlit sea. I felt connected to the place for the first time; the magic had been worked through the old familiar sway of a horse carrying me across a small bit of America. It seemed somehow more real, more ordinary, and more wonderful.

Imogen and Dominic came out for a hug and a goodnight kiss. Sitting within my arms, looking at the fire, Imi turned round and said, 'Eat my dust, Dad!' and she slipped off to bed giggling. It came to me then, that of the ten family riders that day and our three cowboys, I was the oldest by far. Doubtless I was already in my children's dust. We had come a long and strange road out of Africa to Europe to America briefly, and then back to Europe. The road ahead would surely be as rocky in places as today's trail, but if we stayed together as a family as long as possible, I felt sure that we would all make it safe, one day, to the great corral in the sky.

Magic hands

At the moment I am walking the legs off Toby and Poppy. The reason for all the walking is the fact that Chancer has hurt his back.

We were out on the Forest for an afternoon ride when he tripped, going from the light into the dark of a stand of pine trees planted on one of the many hills hereabouts. It was one of those horrible falls, which seem to go on forever as the horse fights to regain his balance. In the end, he did manage to save himself. He seemed fine and we carried on with the ride, which, because of the summer heat, was one of those long slow walks, more of a country ramble than anything else.

A few days later, we were crossing a piece of overgrown grassland beside one of the forest tracks when his front feet plunged down into a hidden trench. I stepped off rather smartly, my stirrups virtually level with the ground. To his credit Chancer did not panic – perhaps he was in shock? He just stood there until I urged him out of the hole.

Once again, no damage appeared to have been done, but the next day I could feel that all was not well. His back end seemed to lose power now and then, rather like a clutch slipping in a car, and his back feet seemed to track sideways to his front feet. Back in his stable, I felt along his spine to see if he winced but could detect nothing. A quick scan of my horse books showed that it could be spondylitis, a sprain or torn ligament where the spine joins the pelvis – the scene of so much pain in human backs. I gave the horse the last sachet of Bute to help with the pain and any inflammation and phoned Dennis, the Irishman with the magic hands.

When he arrived, Dennis heard me out and then went to work on the horse. Within a minute he had found the sensitive spot just where my weight would be pressing down in the saddle, and he also found a pulled muscle in Chancer's neck. Out of his small black bag of tricks he pulled a bottle of oil whose active ingredient, he said, originated with one of the cave-dwelling Native American tribes of New Mexico. I did not ask any questions, just watched as he got to work. After vigorously massaging both sides of the spine around the sore place, he placed one hand over the area and with his other made a fist and thumped down onto his flat hand above the sore place. Throughout, Chancer stood stoically.

Dennis then began to manipulate the horse's shoulders, sliding a hand as deep as he could into the crease of skin he made behind the shoulder blade. Chancer bent and swayed a bit but generally behaved impeccably. Then it was back to the spine until he announced it was done, the misalignment he had felt was gone and all was back in its right place. 'Bring him back into work gently but keep him going. If he does not feel right, get back to me,' he said.

For the hour's work he charged me just £20; heaven knows what a vet would have cost me, had I been able to raise one on a Sunday. Dennis was having a busy day; that afternoon he was off to see some horses that needed help at Pevensey Bay on the Sussex Coast near Eastbourne.

After the visit, Chancer seemed much happier in himself, no longer standing dull eyed and staring at nothing. I turned him out into his field and he started to eat heartily. He had lost a shoe, so I had to wait four more days for the farrier before I could ride again. When I did, the horse moved carefully, like someone who has just got up from an illness, but he moved without that horrible disconnectedness, that scary clutch-slipping sensation, the back end breaking away, weakly. After a few days he began moving more freely, the engine at the rear working well. Dennis had done it, again.

A Fisherman in the Saddle

While concerned about Chancer, I found that there were pleasures to be had in walking. The countryside is at its very best. With summer drawing to a close, there are hay bales in the fields – the huge round ones – and here and there a late, second cut of hay lies drying, filling the air with an almost tangible melon-like sweetness. The first leaf-fall lies crisp on the forest paths, and birds sing in the evening. The only one I recognise is the turtledove, a sound from the Cape, which keeps me company as the dogs and I stroll beneath a sun-dappled forest canopy.

Yesterday I walked a circle route from the cottage down to the stream, up the valley and then doubling back round the hill, coming home through the regrowing forest behind the house and across the back garden. The dogs were delighted to be out for this unexpected treat, just after their supper. Poppy, the two-year-old black and white bitch, must do twice the distance that Toby, the brown and white dog, and I do. She runs ahead quartering the ground and then dashes back, making a little lunge at Toby as if to say: 'For God's sake, come on!' But Toby, a four-square seven years old, is happy to dogtrot by my side, panting in the warm evening. I keep a lookout for adders; they have a nasty bite, which if untreated could do for dogs this size. We see none, just squirrels, and rabbits and birds. I listen for badgers and deer, but they are not around, or too well disguised, lying low because of the dogs. The stream gurgles beneath the two Victorian stone bridges, bringing with it a coolness to the valley floor.

Then we start to climb up the hill to the home of our friends, Ed and Susie, who live right in the middle of the woods with a black Labrador bitch called Bear, and two teen-aged sons, Ben and Charlie. Ed, a farmer turned IT guru, works for Coca Cola and drives miles each day, commuting to beyond Heathrow, a roundtrip of 100 miles. When he's at home he works as hard, maintaining the track to their home, which in every downpour threatens to turn into another river. He has a disreputable old tractor with which he carts stone chippings, which keep his road in shape. He is a very handy man and has built the boys a skateboard ramp – a sort of wooden half-circle up whose sides they career. The forest animals must wonder what the hell is going on. Chancer keeps a beady eye and two swivelling ears well pricked as we pass this thing half-hidden in the forest gloom. But today it is silent as the dogs and I walk past.

We turn right off Ed's track into the woods proper. Up the hill, well hidden in its many wooded acres, is the home of a Rosicrucian sect, whose beliefs are a mystery to me. We walk past clay indentations which still hold the last rainwater, and which Poppy delights in walking through, also taking a genteel sip, as if to savour the forest bouquet. Toby's pop-eyes look on disapprovingly and he skirts these puddles adroitly, keeping his feet dry.

We walk downhill, a new pine planting to our left and old pine to our right – one light and sunny, the other dark and gloomy. Now we turn left along the valley bottom again, on an old logging road that runs alongside what was, until a few years ago, a lovely lake. Neglect caused a blockage in the upright concrete drain and one stormy night the lake overflowed, washing away the earthen retaining wall and sending a twenty-foot high wall of water to cause bedlam for hundreds of yards downstream. Nature has put the damage right, but the lake is now a grassy, five-acre hollow through which the small stream meanders. There is talk of new planning permission being sought to turn it into a fishing lake. I would welcome the return of the lake but am less sure about the presence of fishermen in the woods, a place of utter tranquillity and peace. I am one of those horrible Nimbys – not in my back yard, squire!

Unaware of potential future interlopers, the dogs trot on. We follow the stream now for about half a mile and then turn right over another bridge. Just below this point, a mill once stood, famous for grinding the flour that went to make Queen Victoria's wedding cake. Today there is nothing, the stone long gone to build much-needed homes. As we cross the bridge, I look down at the concrete slipway down which Thom, my nephew, once slid, to his mother's horror. He must have ignited a love of rivers here, for he has just returned from a gap-year in Brazil, which included an adventure up the Amazon, which terrified Gail once more. I do not even know the name of this rivulet, which can become a raging torrent – maybe it is tributary of the Ouse. Dear Thom, from the Ouse to the Amazon, what a leap!

Round the corner, we find a forester laying stones into the boggy bit of the gravel road. We nod a greeting and comment jointly on the wet summer that now requires this work. I call the dogs to my side, and for once, both obey me. I am delighted with them, though in truth it is more probable that they are knackered than that they give a fig for my commands.

Now we have some serious climbing to do. The trail rises steeply some four hundred feet, maybe more; it's the last lap. Near the top we find our bee-keeper neighbour, the Colonel, out with his two white Jack Russells, one of whom is completely blind. He is amazed to see me walking and I explain about Chancer's back. The Colonel is recently back from a trip to Russia – Moscow to St Petersburg – and he tells me about two South African ladies who were always the last ones back on the coach. I tell him my mother's expression – *'Die laaste os kom ook in die kraal'* (the last ox also gets into the paddock). He is not impressed. He tells me how these two women asked a brass band outside one of the great museums in St Petersburg to play the South African national anthem and how *Nkosi Sikelel' iAfrika* rang out, followed by *Die Stem*. We wish each other well and go our separate ways. I think of those two women hearing *Die Stem* played in the heart of Russia, once South Africa's worst communist nightmare. How the world changes, how time changes everything. Things happen.

At home I top up the dogs' water, and start to make supper, baked potatoes, chops and a salad. My bloody feet are killing me, but I feel virtuous for the walk, and filled with images of dappled light.

Looking back on this long week, I will admit that walking's not that bad, but I am delighted to have Chancer back, and doubtless Chancer is pleased to have his back back.

A Fisherman in the Saddle

INDIAN SUMMER

The spring and summer of 2002 started off late, wet and miserable. We put the horses out to grass in March but had to bring them in again for the whole of April. And when we did finally throw them out in May they created mini-craters across the soft spongy field, providing great ankle-turning opportunities for us as the ground set hard later in the season. Wishing to limit the damage to the grass, and our ankles, we kept them in one field, closing the gate to the second six-acre field. With less grass than usual and steady work, they remained trim and elegant (if you can ever describe Irish Draughts as elegant) most of the summer. May, June and July were dull and wet a lot of the time – a typical English summer, in fact.

We then had no rain to speak of for months – August was hot and sunny and September equally so. Just before leaving on the first day of September for our summer holiday in Javea, on the Spanish Costa Blanca, Ron Manser, the owner of 'our' second field, said we should turn the horses onto it as he wanted it grazed down short before the winter. The horses were happy to oblige and in the fortnight of our absence got pig fat on a summer's growth of luscious grass and no work. On our return from Spain they were gross.

We are now into the second week of October and the sun is still shining. Yesterday I cut the worm-cast lawn for what must surely be the last time this year – it seems never-ending, this shearing of England's green fleece.

England in this Indian summer garb is my idea of heaven. The first burst of chestnuts and squirrel-shelled beechmast crunch underfoot as I go to check Dexter and Chancer, still eating and eating in their fields. I will have to keep a watch on their 500-gallon water tank, which is fed from the rain-collecting barn roof. For the first time in our experience, the tank looks like running dry.

The great trees are heavy with foliage, silently being transformed into outdoor tapestries of gold and red and beige and brown and russet, amid their remaining bright green leaves. The hedgerows groan with a mix of honeysuckle, rosehips and blackberries. Small children are much in evidence, with dawdling parents picking at the free harvest. 'Look, there are tons here, come on, this hedge is full of 'em,' we hear from the other side of our ten-foot high garden hedge. We sit quietly, not rustling the Sunday papers, listening to the chat.

Ten-year-old Imogen makes a face, hand on hip, stamps her foot, miming irritation, making a point about 'her' blackberries being scrumped. But really, she is as much amused as us. Frankly, we are all blackberried out. This late in the year, she looks carefully at each blackberry, checking for insects and maggots before putting any into her mouth. We have picked the apples in our garden, mainly Coxes, and the Victoria plums which went completely mad this year, but whose fruit was not particularly sweet. We used these in an attempt at jam, which turned out to be rather more like fruit compote, ideal for the school's harvest festival, for which we are told, produce must be home-made, not bought! That'll teach them.

The spiders, those certain signs of coming winter, are out in force, both outside in the grasses where their webs are dew-starred in the mornings, and inside the cottage, where the brighter ones are booking accommodation for a winter with central heating. Last night a spider the size of a puppy danced across the playroom floor as we watched TV.

The flies are getting fat and lazy, which perhaps explains that spider's size. Soon I know the flies will be filling the cracks between my bedroom window and its frame, where they habitually wait out winter. And I know a day will come in spring, when at last the bedroom is warm enough with sunlight to open a window wide and we will once again – having forgotten again – be invaded by hundreds of still half-sleepy flies.

At weekends, between rides and ferrying the children to friends or sailing at Ardingly Reservoir, Jan and I lie in the garden on our steamer chairs, soaking up the sunshine like two run-down batteries being warmed in the oven for one last burst of energy to see us through the winter.

The stables are cleaned out, the cobwebs brushed off the walls and disinfected, the hay for the winter ordered, and a date for worming pencilled in. Jane Downes has given us a time in her busy schedule to come and give the horses their first clip. They will be easy to do this year, their coats fluffy over plump bulging skin. The New Zealand rugs have been cleaned and mended for another year.

And amazingly, the weather continues to be good. There is a sense of being indulged by a harsh parent, one knows it cannot last and the sunshine is the sweeter for that. Each day of sun is a small miracle to hold to one's face and hands and to say thanks for. The rain and the gales, the grey and the dark, the icy cold and the endless nights, they will be here all too soon. This further reprieve after the indulgence of unbroken sun in August and September and almost half October, must be what summers were like in the childhoods of the 1930s – a gilded time. But we do not have the innocence of youth; we know not to take it for granted. It will be a long, long haul till we see its like again.

How many of the old people who now totter down the lane a hundred yards each day from their nursing home, will be here to see another summer? Old bearded dapper Steve, the 'Ship's Master' as we call him, who remains throughout the summer at the helm of 'his' bench at the turn of Fielden and Warren Roads; will he be here next summer? Will I and mine be here? Please God, I hope so.

On TV, the call has already gone out to get flu jabs, and Christmas is being spoken of once more. Another Christmas. On 12 October I return from seeing a client in London and Jan tells me the horses' water tank has run dry, and that they are standing looking at it as though deeply annoyed. We cycle down and yes, there they stand looking at the tank. Dexter comes when called but Chancer is not leaving the tank. After leading Dexter out of the field, Chancer stops dashing round and lets me catch him – neither of them appear dehydrated. We lead them up the lane, aware that if they are really thirsty they might make a run for it as we near the cottage and their stables. There will be no holding either of them in that case and we walk swiftly, holding on tight. But all is well and we get them into the safety of their stables. Chancer immediately empties a bucket of water but Dexter sips gently, not yet thirsty.

Mid October, and we have run out of water in England! It's unheard of. The only thing about the British weather that you can depend on is that it will surprise you. Now we really do need some rain to fill that tank. I aim to paint the stables with a mix of sump oil and creosote before the weather breaks, the wood needs it and the smell and taste will deter the horses' wood-chewing mania. I have already painted the windowsills at the front of the cottage, which takes the full brunt of the winter gales, the peeling paint and greying timber is now a gleaming white, reflecting light into the living room, dining room and playroom.

There is a strange, bittersweet pleasure in preparing for this annual onslaught. For someone who grew up in the sunshine I am not unfamiliar with weather; the Cape of Storms is, after all, no misnomer. But this Sussex winter – a soft southern joke to the Scots – is for me still a thing to be fought with, a thing to plan for, to try to outmanoeuvre. It's a vain hope, but still I try. The horses will give the winter shape and routine. We will be tied into the daily round of mucking out, feeding, watering, grooming and riding. There will be the pressure to do all this in the face of wild weather, to keep them exercised when our every instinct is to huddle by the

A Fisherman in the Saddle

fire, holed up away from the howling monster keening outside. Two days of no exercise and you know that other monsters lurk in the stables, horses that want to run and buck and shy. Horses clipped out for winter don't like the feel of wind-whipped rain and sleet.

All of this runs through my mind as I watch the clear, still, blessed sunsets and sunrises, which will be just memories on the dark mornings and evenings ahead, through watery skies and wind-tormented clouds. The clocks going back in late October will once again be like a death in the family. The sudden shock of pitch-black mornings, a true reflection of my mourning for this summer past, the more lovely and missed for being Indian.

'Indian summer in October.' I will be saying that all winter, I know, and the rider will be – we're paying for it now!

Julian Roup

A Fisherman in the Saddle

DREAM SPACE

As I criss-cross the Forest on Chancer, I'm aware that I ride on the dreams of many. Yeats wrote, 'Tread softly, because you tread on my dreams,' and so it is for us, as we make our way through this enchanted place. All about us, like the scattered, layered leaves of autumn lie the dreams of those who walked and rode here.

This is a place apart. It is a few miles square of dream space, set down in Sussex. To the north is the mad heaving of London, filled with 10 million struggling lives. To the south is bustling Brighton, sedate Eastbourne and drug-crazed Hastings, where life remains a battle. To the west are Gatwick and Heathrow with Slough beyond, where Betjeman's bombs have yet to drop. To the east is open country all the way to Canterbury and its tourist coaches. Above us is the groan of heavily laden planes, their noise like the lions roaring through my childhood.

Amid all this busyness, the Forest is a sanctuary. Here, business has no remit, nor work, nor want. Here there is peace, not a lot, but enough. It is a fragile peace, one easily disturbed, by fire, by rain, by wind, by noise. But for now, it holds the line – for dreams and dreamers. They pass by softly, their thoughts add meaning to these acres, they hang on trees and cover bushes, they settle gently to the ground, covering paths and gorse and bracken, loading all, lightly as snow, with feeling.

I ride among them. What thoughts, what fantasies. Here are trees as well as serried ranks of prayerful thanks. Here are ponds, and thoughts, reflecting God. Here be distant views and yet more distant hopes. Earth, wind and fire, each and every element is here, and so is man, but gentle with it, seeking solace.

I came to this place with little and it has given generously. I have a blood tie to it now. Here it was I first held my son and saw my daughter walk. There is a link of birth and blood now. This is a landscape of dreams fulfilled and, with luck, dreams to be. Ashdown is dream space. The horse knows it well. It's why his ears are pricked and his steps light. He knows that here is both a world and intimations of worlds beyond. I heed him well. Together we dream this place as it dreams us.

A Fisherman in the Saddle

THE LAST RIDE

Horses have been my friends; it's as simple as that. I don't know what their magic is, even after nearly fifty years of studying them, but I will try to explain what I think happens when human meets horse.

You connect with nature in new and exciting ways and there is great therapy in just that. You put yourself at risk, albeit a limited risk, and the exposure to risk is a good thing for humans. You become responsible for a large, needy, vulnerable animal, and that requires you to be disciplined and responsible, and that is good for you, for it takes your thoughts away from yourself to an extent.

In this process, you kick-start a spiritual awaking. It begins in small ways. You get up early and hear the birds, and breathe that air, and see the sunrise, and feel yourself at one with the world. You switch on the feelgood endorphins that vigorous exercise brings and you get fit with all the advantages inherent in that. You fall in love with this creature to a greater or lesser extent, a creature that is like a mute god. You observe the horse's long-suffering nobility and, with luck, something of that rubs off on you. And finally, you make a connection with beauty.

A love of horses is tied up in some way with our love and appreciation of grace and beauty, and the power of beauty. None of this need apply if the horse is simply used as a tool for sporting success, and for some riders, that is all horses are.

These people are the poorer for it. But even the most goal-oriented, success-driven rider will usually admit to an affection for his equine partner. The horse has a humanising effect, strangely enough, on the most hard-bitten of people. Horses, you see, get under your skin.

I tend to warn aspirants, new to horses, that horse riding is more addictive than heroin and can easily become a lifelong habit. The physical pleasures of riding are easily explained – they take you out of yourself and help to build muscle. It gives you a buzz. The spiritual aspect is altogether more difficult. The horse carries you on a journey, the very symbol of spiritual awakening, and as you ride, you find you begin to traverse the earth's power grid – what writer Bruce Chatwin called the Songlines, in his eponymous book.

Now one begins to approach the central mystery of the horse. They have in their power the mystery of healing. It is a well-recorded fact that disabled children benefit enormously from contact with horses. The expansion of the Riding for the Disabled movement stands as testimony to the healing power of horses. In my own life, like 90 per cent of the human population, I have faced fear, sadness, anxiety and depression, and horses have always been my best medicine. Standing beside a horse that has carried you faithfully over many miles is a good place to be; it's good for the soul. As you groom the horse, it stretches and quivers with pleasure, the coat gleams and the muscle tone, both the horse's and yours, improves. His lines and curves, his shape, his soft velvet nose, his gentleness within that powerful, potentially dangerous frame, stills you, calms you.

In the end the horse and its effect on man is inexplicable. After a lifetime of riding, I cannot claim to begin to understand it. It is more complex than I will ever be able to explain. But I do know this, that if we all forswore our cars, and spent more time with horses, the world's doctors, psychiatrists, priests, and pharmacists, would have a lot more time to go riding themselves! Horse medicine can make you whole. Horses can lead us to the mystery of the Other. Horses can take us to the wellsprings of personal strength, courage and

A Fisherman in the Saddle

ultimately to rebirth and renewal. I know – I have been there myself. And they do this without a word. The Bible says that in the beginning was the word. I don't believe that for a moment. I believe that in the beginning was silence and the music of the spheres. Since then there has been a lot of noise – some of it good. But in the end silence will return and with it, celestial music – perhaps.

The horse, as doctor, teaches us the merits of silence, of patience, of perseverance. This is not to say the horse is some perfect being. Horses can be tricky too. The magic happens when man and horse come together in harmony. But then, that's true of so many of the best partnerships, is it not?

Sometimes things are best left unsaid, unexplained, simply enjoyed. The horse is one such. Climb on board and you will feel better. Ride once a day and you'll take on the world! But one day it must end, I know that. There will come a day when riding is part of my past rather than the centre of my present. It will be a sad day. A great pleasure will have gone, and maybe me with it.

One cannot ride for as long as I have ridden – near fifty years – in the Cape, in California, in Sussex, and not think, once in a while – how will it end? When it comes it may be swift, or it may be just that aching bones and arthritis keeps one by the fireside. The trick is to continue for as long as possible, in the same way that a horse kept in work, keeps working. That is my plan. Life may plan differently.

What is certain is that it will end one day, as I know in my heart it must. It may be that It will wait for me by one of the little wooden bridges that cross the forest streams, funnelling riders and walkers across its many web-like paths. I will take It for a walker in hiking boots and anorak. But It will not be a walker. There will be a slip, a fall, a pain and with luck it will all be over. Maybe I will be reunited with all my lovely old friends once more, Duke at their head.

It may not be that quick. It may be a fall and a foot caught in a stirrup, bumping along the side of a terrified horse, dragged back to the stables unrecognisable. I sincerely hope not. It may be that I will have to sell Chancer and see him go away to another place to carry someone else in strange country. That too will be hard.

As I ride my new homeland, my old one is ever before my eyes. That is the bifocal view of exile or emigration. Ashdown is now my Africa. The miles of rusty, winter-dry bracken is the Transvaal, Five Hundred Acre Wood, dense with chestnut, beach and oak is indisputably the Cape; the wild open spaces of brown winter-burned heather and lion-coloured grass, the Karoo; away in the mist, the line of the Downs, the Tygerburg Hills; the sea in the far distance still, still the Atlantic, but north, not south.

As I ride, my two worlds glide together and mix, kaleidoscope-like. I sing Afrikaans lullabies to an Irish horse, in England. And the strange thing is, he understands. He too is an exile, his roots in Ireland, his birthplace Yorkshire. We, all of us, must learn to adapt to new ways and new places; after all, life's only constant is change.

My horses have been my friends, my constant companions, my confidants, my medicine, my means of escape from the pressing needs of the 'real world', so described by those that run it. They would, wouldn't they?

Horses are a quick way through the looking glass to the world behind, beyond, to the Faraway Tree, to magic. They have hugely enriched my life. They have lent me rhythm and rhyme, poetry and song, good health and a better heart rate. They have driven me half crazy, both with joy and fear. They have taught me my limits, oh what a good lesson that! They have shown me the way to the stars. They have taught me humility and kindness, patience and content. They have made me be still, even in motion. The gift of riding is a gift beyond price. I will be sorry when it ends; but if that end is not also my own, what golden seams of memory I will mine. No squirrel seeking his winter hoard will find greater riches. I will remember the horses on quiet nights as the winter land lies stilled, and summer friends long gone. Horses bedded on straw and cats lying quiet on corduroy. Pheasants strutting the lanes away from huntsmen-haunted woods; stored chest-

A Fisherman in the Saddle

nuts and leaves that rustled, fermenting now on forest floors. The sun will be gone and with it work.

The winter land is still. And so am I.

Julian Roup

GLOSSARY

American Saddler – a breed of horse from the USA, which besides the usual gaits of walk, trot and canter, can also pace and rack, two additional paces which are very comfortable for the rider
Appaloosa horses – spotted horses bred by the Native Americans of the North West USA
Bay – a brown horse with a black mane and tail
Warmblood – horse bred for competition, with the substance and size of the cold blood horse (e.g. Suffolk Punch or Shire) and the speed and agility of the hot-blood, the Arab or the Thoroughbred
Backing – breaking a horse in, or training it to be ridden
Bitless bridle – a bridle that has no bit to go into the horse's mouth, but which gives the rider control by exerting pressure on the head
Box stall – an individual stable
Buck – kick up with the hind legs in an attempt to dislodge the rider or simply out of high spirits
Canter – the comfortable, rolling gait between the trot and the gallop
Cantle – the back of the saddle where it sweeps upward to support the rider
Cast – when a horse rolls in the stable and is trapped, tortoise-like, on its back; this can lead to a twisted gut and death
Cobby – stocky; usually denotes the presence of some cold

blood from a draught horse
Crash cap – safety headgear
Crib-biter – a horse that bites its stable door or any other part of its stable, sucking in air through its mouth; considered to be a vice brought about by boredom
Eggbutt snaffle – a jointed bit that's easy on the horse's mouth
Farrier – blacksmith; a specialist in equine hoof care and shoeing
Fly-leap – when a horse suddenly and unexpectedly leaps sideways or forwards
Full fret – when the horse is bothered or concerned and starts to play up
Gallop – the horse's fastest pace
Gelding – male horse that has been castrated
Goose rump – very angular quarters, said by some to be good for jumping
Gorse – spiky, thorny shrub with bright yellow flowers
Gussied up – brushed up and tidy
Hack – a riding horse
High jinks – high spirits, which can mean airs above the ground
Hand – a hand is four inches, i.e. the palm of a man's hand sideways; a hand unit used to measure horses, from the ground to the withers (the top of the shoulder blade, which forms a bony ridge at the base of the neck)
Hocks – the equivalent of the human knee
Hotting up – getting restive and misbehaving
Hump – half buck
Irish Draught Horse – an animal bred for all round use on the farm, to include ploughing, pulling a cart, going hunting or as a riding horse; now a rare breed
Impulsion – the forward energy that makes a horse's gait lively and active
Lather – a muck sweat
Leg aids – the action of the leg against the horse's sides to tell it to move on, or turn left or right
Lunge work – when the rider stands on the ground and works

A Fisherman in the Saddle

the horse in circles with the aid of a lunge rein, getting it to walk, trot and canter

Mucking out – cleaning stables

Napper – a horse that refuses to go forward or will fly-leap unexpectedly in the opposite direction from the one in which you want to go

Over-bitted – when a horse has a bit that is unnecessarily harsh for it

Paddock – corral

Pasterns – a part of the lower leg, between the hoof and the fetlock, which is the equivalent of the human ankle

Pelham – a solid mouthpiece (unlike the jointed snaffle) with sidebars, which allow more control of a horse, and a better balance

Point to point – a cross-country race over obstacles

Pommel – the front of the saddle

Raking – a long, low stride

Rear – when a horse stands up on its hind legs

Riding point – the position a cowboy takes when riding at the head of a herd of steers

Rooinekke – an Afrikaans term for an Englishman meaning 'red neck' due to the susceptibility of the British troops to severe sunburn

Rowel spurs – spurs with ridged wheels

Short-coupled – a horse with a short back, usually a sign of strength

Shy – lunging away from perceived danger

Smous – peddlar; hawker

Stoeps – verandahs

Straightening out – re-schooling or admonishing

Striding – judging the distance to a jump by the rate of your horse's stride or simply the act of moving forward actively

Take his own line – go his own way rather than follow the pack

Tack – saddle and bridle

Touched in the wind – damaged respiratory system

Triple – a comfortable ambling gate, faster than a walk, and in some horses as fast as the trot

Unbroken horse – unbacked, never been ridden
Vetting – when a vet checks out a horse for soundness in wind and limb and to see if he has any vices; a wise thing to do before buying a horse
Windsuckers – horses that suck in air through their mouths while standing in their stables, a vice which usually starts from boredom and which can ultimately affect their health; it certainly impacts on their value

Other titles by BLKDOG Publishing for your consideration:

**Maxwell's Summer
By M. J. Trow**

Peter Maxwell is looking forward to a nice quiet summer, with perhaps a little light gardening if necessary – as long as the plants don't grow over the door and trap them all inside, it won't be necessary. But, as so often in Maxwell's life, Mrs Troubridge happens and a day out for her and her special friend, Mrs Getty, takes Maxwell and Nolan to Haledown House and from there into a web of intrigue and death.

Maxwell's Summer turns out to be nothing like he planned. As resident conversationalist at a stately home, with riding lessons on the side for Nolan and free dinners when she wants them for Jacquie, Mad Max Maxwell could be forgiven for expecting a pretty easy time of it – with a nice fat cheque thrown in. But murders soon cross his path – almost literally – and with his own life in danger, will he even make it to the dreaded A Level Results Day?

**Closing Time
By Various Authors**

They say a stranger is just someone you haven't met yet.

But chance works in mysterious ways.

Several strangers end up at *The Whistler* on Saturday night, a popular pub in London's vibrant and cosmopolitan Soho district.

These strangers will find, when the clock strikes 22:22, that fate and circumstance has linked and intertwined them in ways they could never have imagined.

Welcome to *The Whistler*, we hope you enjoy your stay.

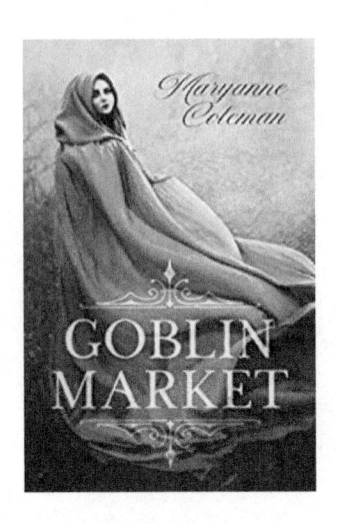

**Goblin Market
By Maryanne Coleman**

Have you ever wondered what happened to the faeries you used to believe in? They lived at the bottom of the garden and left rings in the grass and sparkling glamour in the air to remind you where they were. But that was then – now you might find them in places you might not think to look. They might be stacking shelves, delivering milk or weighing babies at the clinic. Open your eyes and keep your wits about you and you might see them.

But no one is looking any more and that is hard for a Faerie Queen to bear and Titania has had enough. When Titania stamps her foot, everyone in Faerieland jumps; publicity is what they need. Television, magazines. But that sort of thing is much more the remit of the bad boys of the Unseelie Court, the ones who weave a new kind of magic; the World Wide Web. Here is Puck re-learning how to fly; Leanne the agent who really is a vampire; Oberon's Boys playing cards behind the wainscoting; Black Annis, the bag-lady from Hainault, all gathered in a Restoration comedy that is strictly twenty-first century.

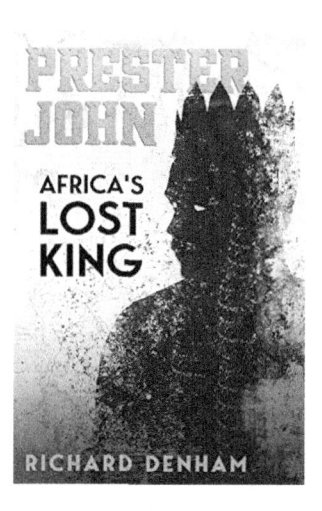

Prester John: Africa's Lost King
By Richard Denham

He sits on his jewelled throne on the Horn of Africa in the maps of the sixteenth century. He can see his whole empire reflected in a mirror outside his palace. He carries three crosses into battle and each cross is guarded by one hundred thousand men. He was with St Thomas in the third century when he set up a Christian church in India. He came like a thunderbolt out of the far East eight centuries later, to rescue the crusaders clinging on to Jerusalem. And he was still there when Portuguese explorers went looking for him in the fifteenth century.

He went by different names. The priest who was also a king was Ong Khan; he was Genghis Khan; he was Lebna Dengel. Above all, he was a Christian king who ruled a vast empire full of magical wonders: men with faces in their chests; men with huge, backward-facing feet; rivers and seas made of sand. His lands lay next to the earthly Paradise which had once been the Garden of Eden. He wrote letters to popes and princes. He promised salvation and hope to generations.

But it was noticeable that as men looked outward, exploring more of the natural world; as science replaced superstition and the age of miracles faded, Prester John was always elsewhere. He was beyond the Mountains of the Moon, at the edge of the earth, near the mouth of Hell.

Was he real? Did he ever exist? This book will take you on a journey of a lifetime, to worlds that might have been, but never were. It will take you, if you are brave enough, into the world of Prester John.

**Fade
By Bethan White**

There is nothing extraordinary about Chris Rowan. Each day he wakes to the same faces, has the same breakfast, the same commute, the same sort of homes he tries to rent out to unsuspecting tenants.

There is nothing extraordinary about Chris Rowan. That is apart from the black dog that haunts his nightmares and an unexpected encounter with a long forgotten demon from his past. A nudge that will send Chris on his own downward spiral, from which there may be no escape.

There is nothing extraordinary about Chris Rowan...

**The Children's Crusade
By M. J. Trow**

In the summer of 1212, 30,000 children from towns and villages all over France and Germany left their homes and families and began a crusade. Their aim; to retake Jerusalem, the holiest city in the world, for God and for Christ. They carried crosses and they believed, because the Bible told them so, that they could cross the sea like Moses. The walls of Jerusalem would fall, like Jericho's did for Joshua.

It was the age of miracles – anything was possible. Kings ignored the Children; so did popes and bishops. The handful of Church chroniclers who wrote about them were usually disparaging. They were delusional, they were inspired not by God, but the Devil. Their crusade was doomed from the start.

None of them reached Outremer, the Holy Land. They turned back, exhausted. Some fell ill on the way; others died. Others still were probably sold into slavery to the Saracens – the very Muslims who had taken Jerusalem in the first place.

We only know of three of them by name – Stephen, Nicholas and Otto. One of them was a shepherd, another a ploughboy, the third a scholar. The oldest was probably fourteen. Today, in a world where nobody believes in miracles, the Children of 1212 have almost been forgotten.

Almost… but not quite…

The poet Robert Browning caught the mood in his haunting poem, *The Pied Piper of Hamelin*, bringing to later readers the sad image of a lost generation, wandering a road to who knew where.

www.blkdogpublishing.com